The
Vocational
Assessor
Handbook

FIFTH EDITION

The Vocational Assessor Handbook
Including a guide to the QCF units for assessment and internal quality assurance (IQA)

Ros Ollin and Jenny Tucker

KoganPage

LONDON PHILADELPHIA NEW DELHI

First published in Great Britain in 1994 as *The NVQ and GNVQ Assessor Handbook*
Second edition 1997
Third edition 2004 as *The NVQ Assessor and Verifier Handbook*
Reprinted 2005, 2006
Fourth edition 2008 as *The NVQ Assessor, Verifier and Candidate Handbook*
Fifth Edition 2012 as *The Vocational Assessor Handbook: Including a guide to the QCF units for assessment and internal quality assurance (IQA)*
Reprinted 2013, 2014 (twice)

2nd Floor, 45 Gee Street	1518 Walnut Street, Suite 1100	4737/23 Ansari Road
London EC1V 3RS	Philadelphia PA 19102	Daryaganj
United Kingdom	USA	New Delhi 110002
www.koganpage.com		India

© Ros Ollin and Jenny Tucker, 1994, 1997, 2004, 2008, 2012

ISBN   978 0 7494 6165 2
E-ISBN   978 0 7494 6166 9

British Library Cataloguing-in-Publication Data

A CIP record for this book is available from the British Library.

Typeset by Graphicraft Ltd, Hong Kong
Print production managed by Jellyfish
Printed and bound by Ashford Colour Press Ltd

CONTENTS

Section two Units for internal quality assurers 189

Unit 4 Understanding the principles and practices of internally assuring the quality of assessment 189

Unit 5 Internally assure the quality of assessment 222

LIST OF FIGURES AND TABLES

Figure

Tables

FOREWORD

It was in 1994 that Alistair Graham, the Chair of the Training and Development Lead Body, wrote the foreword to the first edition of this book – then entitled *The NVQ and GNVQ Assessor Handbook*. At that time I was in the Department of Employment, promoting the benefits of GNVQs as part of my role as what was known as the 'licensed gadfly' in the Education Department, pressing for a greater understanding and awareness of the importance of the vocational. I moved on to the development of modern apprenticeships, in which NVQS played a core role. So the messages and practices in that first book were a great support to the mission in which I was engaged.

In that foreword, Alistair said, 'We owe both authors a debt of gratitude for the plain English guide to the assessment process with excellent examples and case studies. I am sure this book will be the standard guide for many years to come.'

Well, here we are in 2011, and on the fifth edition of the book, and it's still a standard guide – offering practical advice and examples, very much a 'how to' guide – and still in plain English, which is a miracle given the jargon and acronym-ridden world of qualifications in which it lives!

That world of qualifications has rapidly shifted many times over the past 17 years, but the core principles of good assessment and quality assurance remain, underpinning both effective learning and the demonstration of competence. As the Chief Executive of the Learning and Skills Improvement Service (LSIS) I am committed to driving up both standards and quality. Since we in LSIS took on the standards and qualifications function from Lifelong Learning UK earlier this year, including responsibility for the qualifications in that sector (PTLLS, CTLLS and DTLLs), my interest in the effective delivery of assessment has deepened. That is why I am so delighted to have been invited to write the foreword for this book.

Good assessment and quality assurance of assessment is all about people and making a difference to their lives. It is not about ticking boxes and inches-deep portfolios. Improved performance will be achieved if systems are built for the development of people around qualifications in the workplace. And with integration into the day-to-day management of the organization, assessment and related quality assurance become part of core business practices, rather than tiresome and expensive 'add-ons'.

Now more than ever, there is a general recognition that education and training lie at the heart of our economic and social futures. This book will help support effective training through effective assessment and quality assurance, and so help the investment we all make stretch even further and achieve even more in these straitened times.

Rob Wye
Chief Executive
Learning and Skills Improvement Service

PREFACE

We wrote the first edition of this book primarily as a support guide for assessors and internal verifiers who were studying for the new 'D' Unit qualifications produced by the Training and Development Lead Body. We included a significant amount of background knowledge relating to the processes of assessment and quality assurance because we have always thought, and believe this book has consistently demonstrated, that unless understanding of the process of assessment comes first, the quality of that process (and we don't mean signing bits of paper) goes out of the window. We also suggested that the hefty paper-based portfolios and associated administration were detracting from effective and efficient assessment and internal quality assurance.

Well, it feels as if the wheel has turned full circle. The revised qualifications for assessment and quality assurance, based on revised National Occupational Standards and that are part of the new Qualifications and Curriculum Framework (QCF), require candidates to take a unit comprising underpinning knowledge. Better still, the knowledge units can be taken as freestanding awards by anyone interested in the principles and practices of assessment and internal quality assurance.

Substantial reform over the last five years now means that many of the organizations and qualifications that existed in 2007, when the last edition was being prepared, no longer exist, are undergoing review, or have been replaced by different organizations and qualifications. In contrast to 1994, when the first edition was published, NVQs are now being phased out rather than being phased in, and there is as then, a renewed emphasis on apprenticeships. 'A&V' Units (discussed in the third edition) have been superseded by the new QCF units. The unit on assessment developed for teachers, tutors and trainers in the lifelong-learning sector (see Edition 4) has now been revised and is the same as the QCF Unit 'Understanding the principles and practices of assessment' covered in this book. The political reforms we identified from 1981–94 could be listed in one and a half pages. There are another four pages for the next 14 years, and as this book is being revised, we seem to be adding to that list on a weekly basis!

Perhaps the truly significant difference for all those involved in the training, assessment and quality-assurance process, whatever their role, is the very much improved information available whether this is from awarding organizations, regulatory bodies, authors or websites.

ACKNOWLEDGEMENTS

We hadn't anticipated doing a 5th edition, but thanks to Kogan Page for asking us, and to the various professionals who have helped us, particularly Rob Wye (LSIS), Chris Morecroft and Fiona MacMillan (AoC), Jessie Blindell, Kimberley Booth, Linda Gatti and Jane Quibell. It has been a great privilege to have had a book in print for so long. We greatly appreciate the many positive and helpful comments received from practitioners over the years.

Thanks, good luck and best wishes to all our readers, past, present and future.

And speaking of the future, we dedicate this book to our grandchildren, Reuben Henry, Ethan James and Elsie Grace, all of whom arrived during the preparation of the new edition.

Introduction to using this book

This book aims to provide information and advice to anyone wishing to know more about the new qualifications for assessment and the quality assurance of assessment developed for the Qualifications and Curriculum Framework (QCF). We hope that it will also provide a basis for exploring assessment and quality assurance of assessment in general, and give readers a vehicle for examining their current competence and knowledge. It is most relevant to the education system in England and Wales. The book should be of particular use to:

- candidates working towards becoming accredited assessors or internal quality assurers (IQAs) for QCF qualifications;
- candidates for teaching qualifications in the lifelong-learning sector (PTLLS, CTLLS, DTLLS);
- those wishing to gain a deeper understanding of the principles and processes of competence-based assessment practice, including NVQs;
- those working to becoming teachers in the further education and skills sector (FES) or who work in schools, who wish to get greater understanding of vocational assessment;
- teacher trainers of vocational education assessment practice who require a reference book for themselves or their candidates.

Those of you who wish to compare the existing qualifications with previous assessor and verifier awards (D32, D33, D34 and A1, A2, V1) can find these in detail in previous editions of our book.

Note about terminology

This book covers the assessment and quality assurance of QCF vocational and work-based qualifications.

We have had to decide on the terms we will use for roles in order to be consistent throughout the book, but they are not meant to indicate any particular bias. Table 1.1 summarizes different terms commonly used and the terms we will be using in the book.

TABLE 0.1 Roles of those involved in work-based learning, vocational education, training and assessment

Person who:	Work-based learning (inc NVQ)	Vocational education	We will use
Provides the guidance for knowledge and understanding to take place	trainer	teacher, tutor, lecturer	teacher
Gives additional support, particularly with the specialist subject	adviser	learning support staff, mentor	mentor
Is following a programme of learning	trainee	learner, student	learner
Is taking a course or qualification	candidate	student, candidate	candidate, learner-candidate
Makes judgements on what has been achieved/learnt	assessor	teacher, tutor	teacher/assessor
Monitors the quality of judgements	internal verifier	internal moderator	(IV/IQA) internal verifier/internal quality assurer
Trains and supports his or her team of assessors & quality-assurance staff, and probably liaises with the awarding organization re individual qualifications	internal verifier coordinator	internal verifier/ moderator coordinator, team leader	IQAC team leader
Is responsible for the operation of the accredited centre	centre manager	centre manager, programme manager	centre manager
Registers and enters candidates for examinations and qualifications	administrator	examinations officer	examinations officer
Is appointed by the awarding organization to check the quality of the assessment process within a centre	external verifier	external moderator, external examiner	external quality assurer (EQA)

The new QCF qualifications relate to a broad range of contexts in which competence-based training and assessment take place. The terminology used can be confusing because different organizations use different terms for the same role. So someone who helps people to learn vocational skills in a school or college will be called a 'lecturer' or 'teacher', but in the workplace or a training organization would be called a 'trainer'. Added to this, although traditional NVQs are being phased out, terms used in the previous assessor and verifier awards are still being used by some individuals and organizations. In fact 'NVQ' will be retained in the title of many revised qualifications as a brand name, because employers and others have become used to it. Within assessment and quality assurance, the role 'verifier' has been replaced by 'quality assurer'. However currently you will still find reference to verifiers and verification in numerous publications. In this book, we may use the term verifier when we are referring to the checking of quality in particular qualifications without reference to any wider management roles. If we are referring specifically to the coordinating role carried out by those who will hold the Certificate in Internal Quality Assurance we will use the term IQAC.

Jargon and abbreviations

At the back of the book is a list of abbreviations for departments and organizations since 2007 (abbreviations before 2007 are in Appendix 1), and of terms and abbreviations connected with assessment and quality assurance qualifications.

Finding your way around

The book has four parts, each of which is self-contained.

Part One gives a general overview of the development, delivery and regulation of the new Qualifications and Curriculum Framework.

Part Two gives background information, advice and guidance for those intending to become candidates for QCF assessor qualifications.

Part Three is a practical guide to the new QCF units for assessment and quality assurance. These are intended for practitioners of assessment and quality assurance within work-based learning and vocational education and training. In this book we have used the numbering system given to the units in the QCF assessor and quality assurer qualifications. We give detailed guidance to Units 1 to 5. The knowledge unit (Unit 1) 'Understanding principles and practices of assessment' also forms part of PTLLS, CTLLS and DTLLS qualifications.

Awarding organizations are responsible for training and providing the guidance for their external quality-assurance staff, who work to the specifications for Units 5 and 6. We give an outline of these units in the introduction to Part Three.

Part Four contains practical guidance on Unit 8, 'Plan, allocate and monitor work in own area of responsibility', which is for team leaders. In the context of this book, it is for those managing teams of internal verifiers and assessors.

The appendices give essential information that is referred to throughout the book. There is a list of abbreviations and key terms followed by a list of supporting materials and useful websites.

PART ONE
Setting the scene

Introduction

In Part One we cover:

- governmental, economic and educational changes that affect vocational education and work-based training;
- an overview of vocational qualifications, including the QCF;
- the organizations involved in the development, delivery and quality assurance of national standards and vocational qualifications.

In the 4th edition of this book, written during 2007/08, we wrote that: 'The urgency of the need to qualify the workforce must surely drive those in positions of influence towards enabling the early creation of a coherent system with minimum bureaucracy and a comprehensive qualifications framework.' The publication coincided with a change of government. Since then, there have been significant changes to the organizations that develop and accredit qualifications, and to the funding of both deliverers and of learners. The introduction of the Qualification Curriculum Framework (QCF) has meant a radical revision of the structure and content of most vocational qualifications, including those for assessing and quality-assuring those qualifications. Change is still occurring: consultations are underway on developing a single qualification for teacher training and assessment across the whole sector. The system is still complicated and could do with further rationalization, and there will be a further review in 2013.

The following sections give the background to these developments.

01

The drive for a skilled workforce

Education and the skills gap

In 2006 Lord Leitch produced a report titled *Prosperity for All in the Global Economy: World class skills*. The report contained this stark warning about the future of a country lacking in the high level skills to compete in the global market:

> There is a direct correlation between skills, productivity and employment. Unless the UK can build on reforms to schools, colleges and universities and make its skills base one of its strengths, UK businesses will find it increasingly difficult to compete. As a result of low skills, the UK risks increasing inequality, deprivation and child poverty, and risks a generation cut off permanently from labour market opportunity.

In identifying this skills gap Leitch suggested that training an appropriate workforce is of the utmost urgency if the UK is to remain as a key player in the global economy. His report linked skills with qualification levels, with the need for a shift of balance for intermediate qualifications from skills at Level 2 to Level 3 and above. It also identified the pressing need for all adults to have functional skills of literacy and numeracy at Level 2 or above.

The Leitch report has been influential in shaping the direction of government policy, the issues it raised are still current. For example the management journal *Management Today* reported in May 2011 about how the skills gap was affecting employers:

> The UK's higher-level skills gap isn't just a problem that will afflict us in the future: it's hurting the recovery even now, judging by the latest employer skills survey from the CBI. Apparently, nearly half of the companies surveyed are already having problems recruiting people with the necessary qualifications in science, technology, engineering and maths, aka the STEM subjects... the survey also showed an alarming deficit in basic literacy, numeracy and employability.

In addressing the skills gap, all governments have recognized the importance of effective education and training. They have considered the role of work-based learning and of vocational education and training in colleges and training establishments and the relationship between learning in the workplace and in formal education/training contexts. The recent growth in apprenticeships, which combine workplace learning with acquiring more formal qualifications, shows how both contexts are important in contributing to developing a skilled and qualified workforce. This is why both contexts are covered in the units for the QCF assessor qualifications.

A brief history of vocational education and training

Vocational education – concerned with helping learners acquire the skills and knowledge related to the world of work – has a long history in the UK. Craft guilds and apprenticeships started in the Middle Ages where those wishing to work in a skilled trade were apprenticed to a master craftsman for periods of five to nine years before gaining a licence to practise. This system continued until 1814 when compulsory apprenticeship was abolished. In the mid-19th century, as industrialization took hold in Victorian England, workers wishing to improve themselves joined with wealthy well-wishers to provide classes. One example was Wath-upon-Dearne, South Yorkshire, where aspiring learners raised money by public subscription for the Wath Mechanics Institute. In the same town today, learners attend Dearne Valley College built on the site of the former Manvers Main Colliery. Examples like this can be found all over the UK.

Changes to the age at which a child or young person is considered ready for work are a reflection of the economic and social life of a country. The Balfour Education Act of 1902 made state education free for all children. At this time, the school-leaving age had just been raised to 13, although elementary schools did provide for education up to the age of 15 years. The focus was on arithmetic, writing and reading, along with religious education. Schools had long summer holidays, originally to enable children to help with the harvest or piecework. In the first two decades of the 20th century, various groundbreaking approaches to the education of young employees were taken by progressive, liberal-minded employers and education authorities. For example, in 1911 Cadbury's directors agreed to provide a compulsory day-release scheme for their young employees if the local education authority in Birmingham would provide the school. Nearby, classes were also started in the Bourneville Day Continuation School (BDCS), whose function was 'to provide young people with a sound general education which will fit them to meet the demands of life and work in the best possible way'. Recently, in October 2011, the direct descendent of the BDCS, the new Bourneville College was officially opened. In 1918, the compulsory school leaving age was raised to 14 years and the Fisher

Education Act made provision for school leavers between the ages of 14 and 18 to attend Day continuation schools for vocational training.

By 1972 the Raising of the School Leaving Age (ROSLA) Act extended this to 16 years. Over the next 20 years, various government initiatives were introduced to try to counter rising youth unemployment and provide some sort of structured vocational training, but without major success. The Education and Skills Act (2008) attempted to address this problem and now, from 2013, all 16-year-olds will be required to participate in education or training. From 2015 this requirements will be extended to 17-year-olds. The aim of this is to help reduce the growing numbers (18 per cent, around 21m) of 16–24 year olds not in education, employment or training, who are currently known as Neets. At 16, most young people choose to enter a school, college or academy sixth form, a further education college, work-based training or work.

The table in Appendix 1 gives a chronological overview of major changes affecting vocational education and assessment in the last 30 years.

Policy affecting vocational education since 2007: addressing the skills gap

In 2010, the change of government from Labour to a Conservative/Liberal Democrat coalition brought a swift change of education policy. From 2004–07, government policy under the Education secretary Ed Balls was to work to implement the 2004 Tomlinson Report, which recommended closing the divide between academic and vocational education. This division has been an issue that has faced governments for decades. On the one hand successive governments have promoted the idea of academic and vocational qualifications as being equal in value. On the other hand, for some people, academic 'A' levels remain the gold standard for education with vocational qualifications being seen as second best.

However the importance of a well-qualified and skilled workforce to the economy and the future of the country, means that government policy needs to promote good quality vocational education, training and work-based learning.

UK vocational qualifications fall broadly into two types:

- Where candidates have to demonstrate workplace competence to national occupational standards (competent/not yet competent), such as National Vocational Qualifications (NVQs). These were devised in the late 1980s, initially for semi-skilled and skilled but unqualified workers, and have since been taken by millions of adults outside and in the workplace.

- Where there is a more academic approach, placing an emphasis on knowledge and understanding and where work may be graded, for example, on a fail/pass/merit/distinction basis, as in BTEC technical certificates and diplomas.

Addressing the skills gap in compulsory education

Whilst in opposition in 2009, the incoming Secretary of State, Michael Gove, had already clearly set out his expectations that all children should follow an academic curriculum until the age of 16. This was despite the evidence that many non-academic children would benefit from being allowed to make a vocational choice at 14. The Wolf report (March 2010) makes it clear that there needs to be much improved guidance for vocational qualifications offered to those under 16, and that vocational education should take up no more than 20 per cent of the school curriculum. This is currently a subject of heated discussion, as is the introduction of an academic baccalaureate to be taken by all school leavers at the age of 16. The CBI and many employers would prefer an earlier entry at 14 into vocational education and training for those learners who are less academic.

Part of the Secretary of State's argument is that the literacy and numeracy levels of around 20 per cent of school leavers are unacceptable, and that all school leavers need a rounded education, including the classics, if they are to make the most of life opportunities. Pupils will not be able to give up maths or English early, or be encouraged to rely solely on functional skills that are more vocationally orientated. From 2013, most GCSE qualifications will revert to a non-modular (linear) format, with the focus on teaching and examinations rather than coursework assessment, and with a return to an expectation that students' performance in written English will have an effect on their marks. The intention is to produce school leavers who will go on to gain qualifications at Level 3, and thus be able to fill the skills gaps identified at this level by Leitch (2006), particularly in engineering.

Addressing the skills gap in post-compulsory vocational education

Another push to address the skills gap is the drive to improve opportunities for vocational options for young people once they have left school. In November 2011, there were the highest unemployment levels and rates, and lowest employment levels and rates, for 20 years. The decision that from 2013 young people will need to stay in education, or undertake training until they are 17, has raised the debate about the meaning of 'training' and what this can include. This education or training need not be full time and if an employer offers a young person an apprenticeship, this will be

TABLE 1.1 The structure for post-16 vocational education (September 2011)

Age	Provider	Qualification and level	Quality assured by	Regulatory and supporting bodies	Funding
16–18	Sixth form school* Further education college Work-based training	GCSE retakes: Level 2 Apprenticeships: Levels 2 and 3 A levels – Level 3 NVQs** BTEC, C&G and other 'traditional' vocational awards, certificates and diplomas: Level 2/3	Ofqual awarding organizations	DoE SASE QCF ASSC	SFA Employers/DoE YPLA
19+	Further & higher (technical) education college Work-based training University	A levels: Level 3 BTEC, C&G and other 'traditional' vocational awards, certificates and diplomas: Level 2/3 NVQs** Apprenticeships: Level 3/4 Degree 4/5+	Ofqual QAA	DoE QCF SASE ASSC QAA	

* Schools – the independent sector is funded and quality-assured independent of government agencies. Academies and free schools (operational from Sept 2011) are funded by the DoE.

** NVQ levels are based on job role; enrolment to free standing NVQs is due to be phased out by 2013. NVQ will be retained in the title of some QCF-approved qualifications as a brand name.

acceptable. The drive to ensure that school leavers meet appropriate standards in English and maths will continue.

In the higher education sector, it remains to be seen whether the decision to charge much increased fees at English universities will have an even greater detrimental effect on addressing the need for a qualified workforce and employers' need for employees with higher level skills. Signs are that the applications for higher education are falling. The first set of statistics published by the Universities and Colleges Admissions Service (UCAS) on applications to university for September 2012 – when tuition fees rise up to £9,000 a year – show that the number of UK-born applicants plummeted by almost 12 per cent. Whether younger people who would have applied for university are now seeking employment and work-based training instead, or applying for highly practical vocationally related qualifications at colleges or training establishments, remains to be seen.

In 2010 the findings from 23 sector skills assessments identified that the training at the lower end of the occupational spectrum was still not effectively addressed, and that there would be a contraction in admin/clerical and lower-skilled trades and elementary occupations. It was also identified that it was unlikely that training needs, particularly of literacy and numeracy, would be adequately addressed until there are sufficient skilled managers (Goskills, 2010/11).

All of these factors mean that there are considerable challenges for vocational education and the lifelong-learning sector in the coming years.

The lifelong-learning sector (LLS): education and training providers

It is accepted that individuals can continue to learn effectively throughout their lives. Much of this learning is informal, acquired through life experience. There are also many ways that formal learning can be accessed at any age, for personal or professional reasons. Formal learning gained in this way often helps employability.

Education and training providers in the LLS include:

- Further education: a prime provider of vocational courses, full and part time, from entry level to Level 3 and beyond, though most adult learners are studying part time. FE provides much specialist education for those with learning disabilities and difficulties.

- Higher education: full and part-time courses across the curriculum are taken by many adults. Higher education certificates and diplomas, access courses and foundation degrees, as well as the wide range of programmes offered by the Open University in conjunction with the BBC, have greatly expanded the opportunities for adults to develop their vocational skills and knowledge, and consequently to enhance their careers. Most higher education is offered through universities but there has been a considerable growth in higher education being offered in further education colleges (HE in FE).

● Further adult and community education: this sector was originally a vibrant provider of courses aimed at supporting leisure activities and providing short courses that gave learners the courage to move onto qualifications courses. However, the provision has been drastically cut over recent years, with the emphasis now being on short courses leading to qualifications, and literacy and numeracy provision. Courses are funded by the Skills Funding Agency and Young People's Learning Agency; many more private and voluntary organizations and individuals, including the media, contribute to a rich programme nationwide.

● Further offender education: there is a huge push to educate, to at least Level 1, the 80 per cent of offenders who have no qualifications and extremely poor basic skills. Unfortunately, the way that prisoners are regularly moved around the system mitigates against this.

● Workplace learning in both the public and private sectors: employer engagement is being encouraged by the government, which wants all employers to provide training at work for employees with no qualifications, and to encourage all employees to gain an L2 qualification.

● Voluntary sector education: there is a huge voluntary movement in the UK that supports educational and social development, and has become recognized as part of the government's 'Big Society' idea. A 1995 study found that 12 million men and women were involved in voluntary activities in 1.3 million organizations. Voluntary activities usually include some form of learning opportunity. The sector includes formal, non-formal and informal vocational and academic education. Some examples are U3A classes (University of the Third Age), speakers who give talks and provide activities for community groups such as those in care homes, and leisure centres that teach sports to adults.

Overview of vocational qualifications and the QCF

02

A qualification is vocational if its primary purpose is to:

Provide learners with knowledge, skills and/or competence directly relevant to work or employment, either within one or more sectors or for specific occupations; AND/OR provide enhanced labour market opportunities for those currently in work or employment.

(UK Vocational Qualification Reform Programme Board, April 2007)

Recent qualification reform has been a response to the needs of the economy and learners. The reforms are aimed at making it easier for people to build their skills at a pace that suits their circumstances and finances. Employers are now able to decide on a group of units that would benefit their workers, and gain approval from awarding organizations of their choice to become centres running their own work-based qualifications. McDonald's and Network Rail are two examples of employers who have responded to this opportunity. Normally, vocational training up to Level 4 is run in further education colleges and private training organizations (often in conjunction with employers), and Level 4 and above is delivered through higher education institutions (which include FE colleges running higher education programmes).

From 2010 qualifications have been, and continue to be, revised and rationalized into the Qualifications and Credit Framework (QCF).

Qualifications and Credit Framework

The QCF is a system for recognizing skills and qualifications. It does this by crediting qualifications and separate units. Each unit has a credit value. The value specifies the number of credits gained by learners who complete that unit. The flexibility of the system allows learners to gain qualifications at their own pace along routes that suit them best (Ofqual website).

Every qualification in the framework has the same format. Qualifications are made up of varying numbers of units. All units have the same structure. Each unit states the learning outcomes and assessment criteria with which learners will be assessed. One unit represents 10 notional hours of learning – the time the average learner would take to complete. There are eight levels, from Level 1 (entry level) to the hardest, at Level 8. (To compare: GCSEs are at Level 2; A levels are Level 3; a PhD is Level 8).

There are three types of QCF qualification – these are defined by their size:

- Awards (1–12 credits);
- Certificates (13–36 credits);
- Diplomas (37 credits +).

Each qualification title will indicate the level (1–8), the size (eg award) and the content: for example, Level 2 Diploma in Health and Social Care. Note that some qualifications may include some units at different levels.

The units for a qualification are set out in a specification prepared by an awarding organization. Each centre decides how it wishes to teach the content, but must adhere to the assessment requirements laid down by the awarding organization. Internal quality assurers check the centres' assessment processes, and in turn the centres are externally quality assured by the awarding organization.

The Framework is designed with the purpose of making it easier to combine units from different areas together to make coherent qualifications. For example, the Internal Quality Assurer Certificate includes two units approved by the Management Standards Centre. It also provides a way for qualifications gained earlier to be credited against a new qualification, so that learners do not have to repeat content they have already learnt.

Learners with diplomas and certificates awarded before the QCF, who want to use them for recognized prior learning for example, will be able to see their equivalence on the table provided by UCAS.

National Vocational Qualifications and the new QCF

When first introduced in 1994, National Vocational Qualifications (NVQs) were part of the national qualifications framework (NQF). NVQs were intended to be based in the work context and designed for accrediting the skills of working people and providing a system for identifying where skills and knowledge need to be acquired or updated. They took as their starting point the question: 'What skills and knowledge do particular occupational areas need?' NVQs are concerned with measuring, assessing and accrediting whether someone can actually perform competently within that occupational area. NVQs:

- are based on an analysis of work roles in terms of what functions need to be performed;
- are led by employers and industry-specific professional bodies – not by 'education';
- focus on the ability to do the job competently and not on whether someone is as good as or better than someone else;
- define five different levels of competence;
- concentrate on assessment of outcomes.

NVQs will be phased out by 2013, but until then there will still be a significant number of candidates who are in the process of completing their qualification. Employers have become familiar with the competence-based nature of the qualification, and the title is now familiar currency in the workplace, and so many qualifications will retain the title 'NVQ' as a brand, rather than a particular type of competence-based qualification. For example, the HABIA NQF title was 'Level 1 NVQ in Hairdressing and Barbering'; the QCF title will now be 'Level 1 NVQ Certificate in Hairdressing and Barbering'.

NVQs were also offered by education providers such as colleges, where candidates for the qualifications had to find real work experience before they could complete their qualification. NVQs developed a bureaucratic life of their own, and a frequent outcome was the presentation by candidates of huge paper-based portfolios claiming evidence of competence, as opposed to a collection of assessor statements that confirmed competence as assessed by them in the workplace. One consequence was a public perception that the teaching of the required knowledge base for a vocation was neglected. The new QCF awards, certificates and diplomas address this by including compulsory stand-alone knowledge-based units.

National Occupational Standards (NOS)

Occupational standards are drawn up by employers working with sector skills councils and awarding organizations. QCF vocational qualifications are linked closely to NOS, which are revised on a regular basis. The occupational standards on which the Assessor and Internal Quality-assurance qualifications are based were approved by the Learning and Skills Improvement Service (LSIS). These standards also make up qualifications within the NVQ and new QCF learning and development qualifications. They also form the basis of a unit within the PTLLS, CTLLS and DTLLS qualifications for teachers.

Apprenticeships

Traditionally the apprenticeship system has been a means of giving young people a chance to learn skills on the job through working with, and being supervised by, experienced workers. In 1995 the government introduced the Modern Apprenticeship scheme, which was based almost entirely on occupational competence, without a requirement for formal learning. In 2003/04 the apprenticeship scheme introduced the technical certificate, which required theoretical knowledge as well as practical skills, with the implication that off-the-job training was included. In 2008 the National Apprenticeship Service was introduced and given overall responsibility for the scheme. In the last few years, numbers of apprenticeships have grown; according to the NAS website there were 279,700 apprenticeship starts in the 2009/10 academic year in England, compared with 239,900 in 2008/09, with an increasing number of successful completions. In their current form they link work-based learning and formal training, with employers being a part of the process and achievement of QCF qualifications an integral part of the scheme. The recent government strategy document *Skills for Sustainable Growth* (DBIS, 2010) places apprenticeships at the heart of the system for developing and improving work-related skills and knowledge.

Since 2010, funding for apprenticeships has been significantly increased. Figures for 2010/11 indicate there were 442,700 apprenticeship starts. Over 85,000 employers offer apprenticeships in over 200 job roles across a wide range of occupations, but the soaring rate of youth unemployment means that there needs to be steady encouragement for employers to participate in the programme. The Wolf Report recommends offering more apprenticeships to those aged 16–19, as previously they have been concentrated at the over-19 age range. All those taking an apprenticeship have to obtain a good standard of literacy, numeracy and ICT (where the latter is appropriate for the industry) via a range of routes, including Functional Skills (replacing Key Skills).

All apprenticeships, whether L2 Intermediate, L3 Advanced or L4 and above, or Higher, have to meet the Specification of Apprenticeship Standards for England, 2011 (SASE), and be approved by the Secretary of State for Business, Innovation and Skills. This framework sets out the criteria, which include English, Maths, ICT and Personal Learning and Thinking Skills, and identify the Qualifications and Curriculum Framework (QCF) or technical qualifications that each apprentice needs to gain.

Funding for qualifications: learners and candidates

Learners under the age of 19 are funded through the Department of Education (DoE). The Education Maintenance Allowance (EMA) scheme, providing some financial support to young people who stayed on at school or college, closed to new applicants in England on 1 January 2011. Schools, colleges and training providers have bursary funds that students can apply for if they are facing financial hardship.

The Skills Funding Agency (SFA) confirms which qualifications are to be publicly funded in England for those over 19 years of age. Qualifications that have been confirmed for funding are published on the SFA website (**http://qcf.skillsfundingagency.bis.gov.uk/qcf-funding/confirmationfunding/**).

QCF assessment standards for assessors, quality-assurance staff, teachers and trainers: the assessment of vocational and work-based qualifications

In 1994, standards for assessment for vocational assessors and quality-assurance staff were introduced. These were known as the 'D units' and, following revision in 2007, the 'Assessor and Verifier' units were issued. The standards behind the A&V units have now been revised and a new range of qualifications have been developed. These comply with the QCF framework, and are known as 'The QCF Credits for Assessment and Quality Assurance'. Individual awarding organizations can give their qualifications different titles. The 2010 revision:

- Incorporates underpinning knowledge and understanding into the qualification for the first time. These units can be taken by anyone interested, whether or not they are practising assessors or quality assurers.
- Ensures the units meet the requirements both of vocational assessors and of teacher training candidates, as well as of work-based assessors.

QCF assessor qualifications and post-16 teacher training

In the spring of 2007 came the publication and implementation of the new *Professional Standards for Teachers, Tutors and Trainers in the Lifelong Learning Sector*, developed by Lifelong Learning UK (LLUK). For the first time, it became mandatory for all those in the government-funded post-16 field to take an appropriate qualification based on these standards. Existing teacher training qualifications were simplified. The standards are grouped into different units, which form the PTLLS, CTLLS and DTLLS qualifications. True to the transferable spirit of the QCF, the unit 'Understanding principles and practices of assessment' is common across these qualifications and the QCF assessor qualifications.

The structure of teaching roles was also revised, identifying 'associate' teachers, who teach a limited range of subjects or groups, and 'full' teachers, who teach the full range of a subject across a range of levels. The threshold licence to practise (PTLLS), then a certificate at L3/4, is most likely to be taken by associate staff, The diploma at L4/5 is for full-time teachers who may also opt for the DTLLS higher education equivalents – the Certificate in Education/PGCE, at L4/5/6. There is now a requirement for all staff to show they are competent in the core skills of literacy, language, numeracy and ICT. It is expected that existing staff will take some units as CPD.

National standards and qualifications development, delivery and regulation

03

Since 2007, there have been considerable changes to many of the organizations involved. Some changes have been to reduce the numbers of organizations so as to make systems more effective; others have resulted from approaches to bringing key players, such as employers, more closely into decision making. Further reforms are proposed to some of the organizations described below. (See the list of abbreviations at beginning of book, and the glossary at the end.)

The Department for Business, Innovation and Skills (BIS) is responsible for policy related to vocational training and skills. The Department of Education (DoE) is responsible for state-funded schools provision policy.

Standards development

National occupational standards are developed by the standards-setting organizations and the 29 Sector Skills Councils (SSCs: **www.ukstandards.co.uk**). The Learning and Skills Improvement Service (**www.lsis.org.uk**) took over the functions of the former SSC Lifelong Learning UK in 2010, and is responsible for the standards for assessment and quality assurance referred to in this book (also see the Foreword).

Awarding organizations

The Dearing Review of 1996 suggested a rationalization of awarding organizations, since the monitoring of the very large number in existence had become an almost impossible task, and over the past 15 years there has been an attempt to reduce the number. There have been some major mergers, notably with the large public examination bodies. OCR was formed from the merger of Oxford, Cambridge and the Royal Society of Arts examining bodies. In 2002, EDI plc (**www.ediplc.com**) was gradually built up from LCCI, JEB and ASET awarding consortiums, amongst others, to be one of the largest providers of work-based qualifications for industry and commerce in the UK. The number of awarding organizations is still large, at over 100. The Federation of Awarding Bodies is a trade association with over 100 full members and around 20 associate members (see **www.awarding.org**).

The role of an awarding organization is:

- to take responsibility for the quality assurance of its qualifications;
- to deliver and publish qualifications specifications;
- to approve centres to run its qualifications;
- to provide centres with information about qualifications, including training and assessment materials, produce publications, arrange training for programme deliverers and assessors, and provide consultancy;
- to authorize specially adapted assignments or qualifications that a particular centre might wish to use;
- to ensure risk is assessed and managed in the delivery of qualifications;
- to arrange for the marking of examination papers and the checking of coursework marks from centres;
- to award results and grades to candidates;
- to issue certificates to candidates.

Quality assurance for qualifications has, since 2010, been placed firmly with awarding organizations, instead of being shared between a number of regulatory bodies. Awarding organizations recruit, train and appoint external quality-assurance staff (previously and sometimes still referred to as external verifiers and moderators) to do much of this work. They are the link between the awarding organization and the delivery centre.

The Skills Funding Agency (SFA) website (see **www.skillsfundingagency. bis.gov.uk/**) gives details of awarding organizations and the qualifications they offer.

Approved centres

There are thousands of organizations, from large colleges to small training centres, that awarding organizations approve to be centres for offering accredited qualifications. Centres offer advice, guidance and training for particular awards, and register, assess, internally verify and accredit candidates. They are subject to external quality assurance from the awarding organization, and to external auditing from Ofqual (see below). Their main link to the awarding organization is through the designated external quality assurer (EQA). If EQAs find a lack of compliance with quality procedures, they recommend appropriate sanctions to be applied to the centre. Sanctions can range from an action plan to withdrawal of the right to register and certificate candidates, and are lifted once compliance has been restored.

Awarding organizations will supply lists of approved centres.

Regulation of qualifications

There are four independent regulatory authorities for the United Kingdom: the Ofqual (England), DELLS (Wales), CCEA (Northern Ireland) and SQA (Scotland). Ofqual was established in 2007 through the Apprenticeship, Skills, Children and Learning Act. Its function is to approve and regulate awarding organizations through a risk-based regulatory approach to such regulation.

All awarding organizations have to apply for accreditation to offer qualifications from Ofqual. If Ofqual is dissatisfied with the risks posed by an awarding organization, then the accreditation to award qualifications is withdrawn.

Full details can be found at **www.ofqual.gov.uk**. The Quality Assurance Agency performs the regulatory role for higher education (**www.qaa.ac.uk**).

Monitoring of qualifications through inspection

Four previously separate inspectorates are now merged into the Office for Standards in Education, Children's Services and Skills (Ofsted). Ofsted's mission is 'Raising standards, improving lives'. Inspection and regulatory visits are made to awarding organizations and accredited centres who offer approved qualifications to:

- promote service improvement;
- ensure services focus on the interests of their users;
- see that services are efficient and effective and promote value for money.

The findings of the inspection visits to providers are published in reports that can be found on the Ofsted website, along with the inspection toolkit for learning and skills inspection (**www.ofsted.gov.uk**).

PART TWO
Preparing to do the units: being a candidate

Introduction

In Part 2 we work through the experiences you may have if you are a candidate for a QCF qualification, together with some practical hints on how to prepare and make best use of your time. We outline the new qualifications, and explain knowledge and understanding and the practical activities that must be undertaken by candidates for the new qualifications.

In earlier editions of this book, we described in some detail the ways that candidates could present their (assessor/IQA) evidence for assessment. Awarding organizations now give detailed guidance on this subject, and many have developed their own preferred documentation and systems. We have always taken a common-sense approach to the selection and presentation of evidence for assessment. We have favoured a holistic approach, where one activity can provide evidence across a range of criteria within or across units. Holistic approaches to demonstrating competence are encouraged in the new Assessor and IQA awards.

04 Making a good start

There are some learners who enrol onto courses for the joy of learning and have no need for a qualification, and so sometimes opt to do limited assessments, but for the vast majority assessment of their work is a crucial part of their study. We hope this section helps that process. It is also useful to make the most of what you can learn about being an assessor from being a candidate yourself. You can improve your own performance by learning from what others do. By being a candidate you can learn good practice from your assessor (or learn to avoid making the mistakes with your own candidates that your assessor has made with you!).

The candidate as an active participant

The more prepared you are before you start your course, the better you will be able to settle down to the work involved. A day spent 'finding out' before you register for a qualification can save you precious time later. It can feel strange going back to learning as an adult, but we can assure you that you certainly won't be the only one wondering what is going to happen and how you will cope! The more you understand about what might happen, the better you will be placed to ask any necessary questions. Many adults forget most things they have been told in the first couple of sessions because it's all so new, but overall you will probably find you learn more quickly than when you were at school because you have life experience to build upon. Once you are committed to a qualification, then being proactive in setting yourself targets, checking your progress regularly with assessments and meeting deadlines will give you positive feedback and the motivation to finish with a flourish!

Those of you who are confident and well-practised in assessing your vocational or work-based subject may find that a route that takes account of your prior learning (RPL) is more appropriate. This could minimize your attendance at a taught course. You may also find that your centre uses a virtual learning environment (VLE) for teaching and training, which means you can do much of your learning in a place and time to suit yourself.

Starting your course or qualification

05

There are three parts to the introductory phase of starting a course or qualification: pre-course information, guidance and advice; initial assessment; and enrolment and induction.

Pre-course/qualification information, guidance and advice

Your approved centre should be able to provide you with information on your course or qualification and the entry requirements, and also on the assessment scheme, the type of assessments and when they are to be done. You will need details of costs and whether you are exempt or can access funding from elsewhere. You will normally find this information on the centre's website. Many centres have open days or general information sessions. You may need to book an appointment, or there may be a queuing system. It is usually possible to drop in to centres and talk to someone about general issues, though specialist trainers or teachers may not be available. Candidates who are preparing to teach, train or assess other adults should ensure they are qualified (usually to at least L3) and/or well experienced in their specialist subject, such as construction, health and social care or cleaning science, before they plan to take their assessment or teaching/training qualification. However, the QCF assessor and IQA (A/IQA) Units 1 and 4, which are solely related to underpinning knowledge and understanding, can be taken by anyone with an interest and the ability to complete the units. If you are taking Units 2 or 3, you will need at least two candidates to assess, each registered for a QCF qualification.

Candidate-assessors or IQAs who will be assessing or verifying learning and development certificates or diplomas (QCF) or the former NVQ (NQF) version, including those who may be assessing the A/IQA units as part of another vocational NVQ, need to meet the assessment strategy for learning and development developed by LLUK (now subsumed within LSIS). For qualifications including management units (see Unit 4) they need to meet the assessment strategy of the Management Standards Centre, currently overseen by the Council for Administration. This includes competence in the vocational area of learning and development itself, usually taken as holding a teaching or training qualification at L3 or above. These assessment strategies should be found within the qualification specifications.

Initial assessment

Ideally this takes place before you enrol with an approved centre, so candidates can check their suitability for a chosen qualification. Prospective candidates may be asked to complete a self-assessment of current job role against the standards towards which they intend to work. This latter could take the form of a self-assessment checklist or skillscan. This identifies your familiarity with the tasks you need to cover in the units of your proposed qualification, and will help to identify whether you need any further training or experience before undertaking assessment.

Candidates might be asked to take tests to check their functional skills and preferred learning styles. Those who do not have the required levels of literacy, numeracy and/or ICT should be advised at this stage whether they would be better improving these skills before progressing with the course/ qualification or whether there will be sufficient support available for them to progress at the required rate and achieve at the required level. If your proposed qualification involves written work or study at L3 or above and you are a bit 'rusty', a study skills course taken before you start your course might make all the difference to the ease and enjoyment of your studies. If you have specific needs, such as requiring help with physically getting around, having English as a second or foreign language, or needing staff to take account of speech, sight or hearing issues, you can ask the centre to explain what additional resources may be available and consult the access arrangements for each awarding organization.

It is normal for candidates to present much of their written work in word-processed formats, and for course information for candidates to be presented on internal websites. Candidates need to know how they will access the required resources if they do not possess their own computers or internet access, and cannot find the time to use a learning centre.

Enrolment, registration and induction

Enrolment with the approved centre that will support you through your studies usually takes place before registration with the awarding organization that will eventually award you your qualification. Certainly in a college, enrolment and registration involve the completion of several forms and this, together with payment, can take some time. If your fees are being paid for you, perhaps by your employer, the centre will need proof of this when you enrol and/or register. The forms are often quite complicated. This is because much of the information on them is used to provide data to the government. Check the small print – often you have the right to withdraw from a programme within the first couple of weeks of a course if you find it is not what you expected, and get your money back. It should be clear at the outset exactly what procedures are involved in your assessment process, and what associated costs there are, such as for equipment or additional assessment, particularly if there is an hourly, instead of a flat, rate for assessment.

Many courses now involve online enrolments and, in our experience, some of these are more user-friendly than others. One issue that sometimes comes up is that you can't save what you've done and then return to it later, so make sure you give yourself enough space and time and have all the relevant information to hand before you begin the application. Make good use of helplines if you need them and always keep a copy of what you send.

One of the aims of the QCF review of qualifications has been to enable candidates to 'mix and match' units. You may be able to enrol for the single units, or for a combination making up an award, certificate or diploma that can be added to over time. Some awarding organizations ask candidates to register for the qualification within a certain number of weeks of the start date of the programme. Your registration for a qualification may be valid for several years. However, your centre may well expect you to complete within say one year, as their funding to support you through visits and tutorials might be for just one year. You need to be clear on what the financial arrangements would be in the event that you fell behind with your work and had to complete some of your assessments the following year.

At induction, you should find out about the centre and about the resources you are entitled to use and any others you will be expected to provide yourself. For instance, if written documents are available to you online, you may need to purchase paper or photocopying cards if you prefer to read from paper rather than a screen. The requirements of the course and the qualification will be explained, and candidates should receive all accompanying documentation, including details about both the centre and the awarding organization's complaints and appeals systems, and have these explained. It is useful to have the web addresses of your awarding organization and your centre, plus any centre student guidance.

Using a mentor

Candidates are often advised, and sometimes required, to have a mentor. A mentor does not need to be your line manager. Good mentors are frequently specialists in a vocational subject and recognized for their experience and are regarded as role models. If you use a mentor, that person will need to understand the context of your qualification or course and your work, and should be able to point you to useful additional sources of information and advice. Your mentor does not need to be in your organization, and may even have retired, though you need to check that he or she is currently up to date. Normally the relationship is of 'wise and experienced professional' with the 'new or aspiring role holder'. Mentors rarely receive payment for the time they give, so you probably need to negotiate at the start of your qualification what time might be needed and what is reasonable. Mentors should not be involved in your assessment, but they might be prepared to observe you on an informal basis to give you some feedback before a formal assessment. They may need to give their details, including their qualifications and experience, to your centre, and the centre may invite them to briefing sessions and should provide them with documentation about your qualification and its requirements. If your course requires you to have a mentor, it is best to seek one out before you start your course as you will find that you get into the swing of things much more quickly.

Assessment planning

06

The most important thing to remember as a candidate is that you need to know how well you are doing. However, you cannot get any feedback from your assessor on this until you have given him or her something to assess, whether this is a workplace assessment, test answers or a piece of written work. Don't put off doing your assessments because you feel the work isn't as good as you could do, or because you aren't sure what the assessor wants or because you won't be good enough yet (all reasons we have heard from our candidates). Check out with your assessor that you understand what you have to do – if you make some notes that show what you intend, then that will be helpful. If you have to do any written work such as an assignment, have a go at your assignment as a draft, and ask for feedback. Assessors are there to give you constructive feedback and tell you what you have done well and how you can improve where necessary. Assuming you have had the necessary training and practice, it is better to get stuck in and get it 60 per cent right within the due dates (especially if there is an option to rework and improve) than to put off assessment until you feel you are 'ready'. You could get so behind that you never catch up and, worst of all, you are not building the positive feedback relationship between you and your assessor that will help you to progress. There is nothing worse for an assessor than a candidate who does not hand work in on time, as that means the assessor is totally unable to help the learner.

You should not be put in the position of negotiating and agreeing any assessment plan before you are fully familiar with the assessment scheme or process for your awards and for your centre's operation of its qualification. It is always a good idea to have an overview of the assessment requirements before you start, so that you can see how your learning applies not just to your work role but also to the assessments. If you are a candidate for a vocational qualification you are likely to have a number of written assignments given to you at regular intervals throughout your course. If you are not given a schedule, ask your teacher/assessor for the due dates of the assignments and any tests or examinations. Dates for external exams or tests are likely to be on the awarding organization website. You also need the dates you should expect marked work to be returned. Most organizations have a policy on this, commonly a maximum of 15 working days.

This will enable you to plan your life to make sure you leave enough time for studying, writing and arranging work-based visits.

You should always allow leeway for the unexpected to get in the way of your work, as we all know it does sometimes, and you really don't want to spend your holidays doing assignment work. Neither do you want the even worse scenario, where the course has finished, you have no more tutorial time due to you, with the work still not completed. That's bad for both you and your teacher/assessor, and can get expensive, as additional tutor time may have to be paid for separately.

In work-based qualifications, assessment will often be 'continuous'. Your skills for particular tasks will cover a range of outcomes, often across several units, and you will build up a profile of competencies that match the required learning outcomes over a number of observed assessments. There will also be a summative assessment when all your claims to competence are checked through and the complete units are finally signed off.

Candidates assessed in the work environment

In work-based assessment for qualifications such as Units 2 and 3 for the assessor/IQA units or traditional NVQs, your first assessment planning meeting with your assessor should give you an overview of how the assessment for the whole qualification is envisaged and should result in detailed planning for the assessment of at least one complete unit. Experience in the past has shown us that NVQ candidates who plan for their option units first are likely to finish their award most quickly. This is because, as the option units are completed, the candidate will also meet many of the criteria in the mandatory units. It also means that the candidate has longer to develop any new skills needed to complete the options. For each unit, your negotiated plan should cover the methods that will be used to assess your knowledge and competence, what you will need to do or present to demonstrate knowledge and competence, what this will involve who will be involved and the planned timescale.

Being questioned

Irrespective of your position and experience, being questioned by an assessor can be a stressful occasion, if only because you may be highly practised and knowledgeable and will be expecting to be deemed competent!

The assessor may ask you to describe or explain your actions or documents. Don't be afraid of referring to documents you are in the process of completing, or that are stained by coffee rings or have doodles on them if they are key to an assessor's understanding. They are checking your workplace competence, which includes using and referring to live, working materials, not whether you can photocopy clean, original documents to show them at a later date. Often the focus will be on exploring how much knowledge is covered by the activities the assessor has seen you carry out in workplace practice, or asking you what other learning outcomes you think are met by some of your evidence. The assessor should, following good assessment practice, have a pre-prepared list of questions, from which an appropriate selection is made, and should record your answers. (See Unit 1 for help on devising questions to check underpinning knowledge and understanding.) Table 2.1 gives a sample list of questions that could be used by an assessor or IQA assessing natural performance.

Some questions might be of the 'closed' variety, particularly if the assessor is checking fact: for example, 'What was the tolerance on that measurement?' Others are likely to probe processes, such as 'How did you help the teacher to plan that work?' or 'What is the basis on which you have drawn up your sampling plan?' You might be asked such questions immediately after assessment of your performance, or in a summative assessment check if assessors are unclear as to whether what they have observed meets the range of criteria they had down to observe from the assessment plan.

If you have had the opportunity to work through similar lists of questions beforehand (for assessment techniques and for underpinning knowledge and understanding), you could include your notes as supplementary evidence, as that may avoid unnecessary oral questioning. On the other hand, you may prefer to prepare the answers mentally and answer oral questions rather than put a lot down in writing. The assessor will also be determining the authenticity of your evidence – this is particularly important where candidates have been working as part of a team and where there may be some 'common' evidence. If this is the case, it is really important that candidates are clear about why the evidence demonstrates their own competence, rather than that of a team or of another team member.

You should of course receive constructive feedback after any assessment. Most assessors will give this verbally, but usually there will be an additional written report confirming how the assessor is convinced you have met the identified outcomes, or detailing where competence has not been fully shown.

Assessments can vary considerably in time. The variation may be due to the amount of evidence presented, the nature of the evidence (eg an assessor may choose to look at the whole of a video recording in addition to other performance evidence), the overall grasp of the assessment process shown by the candidate and the candidate's ability to respond concisely to the details needed. New assessors frequently take longer to complete the assessment process, owing to a variety of factors, not least of which can be the lack of coordinated planning of assessment opportunities in the workplace and the impulse to encourage candidates to include additional material unnecessarily 'to be on the safe side'.

TABLE 2.1 Sample questions for use with observations in the workplace

1. How has this assessment been agreed with your candidate?

2. What determined the physical arrangements, eg where you stood, when you asked questions?

3. What did you do to encourage the candidate to select and present relevant evidence?

4. How did you decide/construct the questions you asked orally? Are the questions written down?

5. What is your definition of a 'leading question'? How can you avoid asking them?

6. Why did you ask the number of questions that you did?

7. How are you sure that you can infer competent performance in other situations where the task/activity might occur?

8. In what ways can you involve candidates in their own assessments? How effective was the candidate's performance in this case? How might it be improved?

9. What rules do you follow when giving feedback?

10. How do you encourage individuals to ask questions as a natural part of the feedback and evaluation process?

11. What makes this assessment fair, reliable, valid and sufficient?

12. Did this candidate have any special needs for which you had to cater? What special needs might candidates have and how would you accommodate these?

13. Are there any aspects of my assessment of you about which you are unclear or that you wish to discuss further?

Receiving feedback

It sounds rather simplistic to say that candidates who incorporate advice from feedback into their practice, and reflect on how this is changing the way they work, tend to move forward in leaps and bounds. It is very important to listen to or read carefully the feedback you receive and use it to improve where possible. It is also important that you plan your time so that you can benefit from receiving feedback. Some candidates find it difficult to commit to their planned observations, and cancel them. Obviously there are times when this cannot be avoided, but we know that often this is through bad planning or simply due to nerves at the thought of being observed. Candidates then have a cluster of observations towards the end of their observation period and don't really have the opportunity to act on any advice that may be given. Another reason is that your assessor may not write down the verbal feedback he or she gives you, and then you forget some of the key points. Your assessor should be recording the key points in some format but you may want to make additional notes yourself at the time, and check out your understanding with the assessor. If you try something that has been suggested and it doesn't work, then talk to your mentor or colleagues or your assessor and see if there are other avenues that can be explored.

Sources and purposes of evidence

Your choice of evidence to demonstrate how you meet the assessment criteria for a unit must meet the requirements of authenticity, validity, reliability and currency (see Unit 1). If you are discussing these selections with your assessor, perhaps as you negotiate your action and assessment plan for a unit, you are getting immediate feedback. Table 2.2 although by no means comprehensive, may provide you with some ideas on the variety of evidence you can use to demonstrate your competence as an assessor or internal IQA, both from present work roles and from previous experience or achievements.

The purpose of Table 2.2 is to prompt you as to what might be useful corroborative evidence when undertaking professional discussion in your workplace. We are not suggesting that you collect together lots of documents and put them into your portfolio. In fact, don't do this unless you absolutely have to. If you can show evidence to your assessor in your workplace, and the assessor can note down then and there what he or she has seen, where it is stored and what criteria have been covered, then the job is done.

TABLE 2.2 Types of evidence and their purpose

Evidence	Purpose
Action plans	To show details of initial assessment and review with your own candidates
APL documents	To show previous competence/experience and to infer current competence
Appraisal records	To indicate activities you have undertaken or planned that meet CPD requirements and/or assessment strategy
Assessment plans	To show you are supporting your candidates in the required way
Assignments (marked)	To show knowledge and understanding of your specialist subject, whether you are meeting deadlines and whether you are making accurate judgements
Audio recording	To provide a record of questioning or professional discussion between assessor and candidate
Briefing notes to staff	To show how you communicate relevant information
Candidate tracking documents	To show how you regularly record your assessment decisions
Certificates (original)	To provide evidence of your relevant qualifications
Costings (time, money)	To show you understand efficiency
Data printouts	To provide information for verification and quality assurance
Feedback sheets to candidates	To show how you give constructive feedback
Forms, pro formas	To show how you input information
Graphs	To show how you analyse quantitative data
Individual learning plans	To show how you plan achievable targets with candidates

TABLE 2.2 *continued*

Evidence	Purpose
Induction documents	To use, if completed, as a focus to show how you use candidate information to support their learning
Job specifications	To give a context to your discussion
Memos	To show how you communicate with others
Minutes of meetings etc	To use as a focus for discussion – only useful if they show how you have contributed in a way that meets specific criteria
Photographs	To show artefacts/products that assessors are not able to view themselves – but you need to be able to authenticate these
Policies and procedures	To use as a focus in professional discussion for explaining how policy impacts on own practice, but in themselves these say nothing about your knowledge, understanding or competence
Questions, written or oral	To show the techniques you use if answers are logged and recorded
Record sheets (completed)	To show your ability to track, eg monitoring of assessors, or candidate work
Reports (qualitative)	To show how you have carried out and evaluated your activities
Reports (quantitative)	To show how you have used data to analyse and summarize
Review sheets (completed)	To show how you are monitoring assessment progress with candidates
Sampling plans	To indicate your monitoring activities
Staff lists	To use as a discussion focus for showing your understanding of internal communications and operations
IQAs' reports	To show, if they include your name, how you have performed against awarding organization criteria
Videotapes	To provide evidence of professional discussion or workplace performance
Witness statements	To give validation of performance and product evidence not seen by your primary or observational assessor

07 **Presenting your work**

Recording your sources and avoiding plagiarism

Many candidates for QCF vocational and work-based qualifications are practical people. They often prefer 'doing' to 'reading and writing'. However, it is likely that you will need to broaden your knowledge, especially to satisfy requirements for continuing professional development, and the most common ways of doing this are by reading (trade journals, textbooks, internet articles) or by viewing (relevant television programmes, video clips, informational DVDs). It's sensible to make a note of what you used. It's also highly likely that, especially in a L4 qualification, your assessor will wish to check your sources. There are agreed ways of recording this information. The most commonly used method is called the Harvard system. If you turn to 'Supporting materials' at the end of this book, you will see the ways to record information. A quick click on 'Harvard referencing guide' in your search engine will take you through to lots of websites that will explain more about referencing and bibliographies. Get familiar with these before you start your course, and then you can keep a running list of what you use, which will save you lots of time in the end.

Plagiarism is a serious offence and occurs when you pass off information as your own without attributing it to the original author. Sometimes this is deliberate, and you may have read of cases where candidates have been asked to leave a course/institution or been told that they cannot have their qualification awarded. In other cases, it can be due to candidates being disorganized. If you keep a list as described above, for both websites and written material, and make notes as to which pages any direct quotes are taken from, the attribution of sources will not take up too much of your time, and you will find that you have a useful reference tool that you can use later.

Organizing your evidence

As you progress through your qualification you will use and accumulate a number of documents and products, such as assessor reports and feedback on your performance, recordings of professional discussion, photographs or samples of your own candidates' achievements, and written assignment feedback. This evidence of your work as a candidate-assessor or candidate-IV/IQA is generally presented for assessment in a referenced folder (digital or paper copy), often termed a 'portfolio'.

A familiar example of a portfolio is that of the art student who has a varied collection of samples of work. Items that are inappropriate for folder presentation, such as sculpture or ceramics, are often represented by photographs or by written reference to their location if, for example, they have been sold. Other examples are an actor's portfolio, representing the range of roles played, and the portfolios held by Cabinet ministers, which are the range of activities and responsibilities expected of them. Your own 'portfolio' is likely to be a collection of mixed evidence, much of which may not be in written form.

However, candidates have to be selective in choosing the appropriate evidence to include. When using paper-based portfolios it is vital to be selective in the evidence included, as the more evidence there is, the heavier it gets to carry. Your assessor is likely to have at least 20 candidates. Assessors who work in a college could have many more. Where are they going to put all this stuff? We have seen countless staffrooms over the years where desks and floors are covered with big files, often with very small amounts of paper in them. We also know staff who have been physically injured trying to carry bulky portfolios to their cars or, worse still, on public transport.

Most candidates opt to keep all the notes and supplementary information gathered as part of learning (but not as part of the assessment) in an A4 lever arch or box file. However, please don't use A4 lever arch files to hand in work to assessors unless you are specifically told to do so! Where possible, it can be much more time effective if documents are viewed *in situ* in a candidate's workplace, and acknowledged through assessor reports of assessed activities including video and photographic evidence. Candidates commonly give assessors irrelevant or superfluous material. Not only does this take up unnecessary space, but it alerts the assessors or IQAs to the fact that you may be unclear regarding the requirements of your assessment. You could therefore be advising your own candidates poorly and encouraging them to think that the process is about chasing paper rather than performing jobs in an informed way to particular standards.

Look at your collected works and de-clutter by asking yourself the following questions:

- Does this relate to my assessment plan?
- Is this evidence relevant to the unit(s) and, if so, to which element(s)?
- Does the evidence demonstrate competent performance, have I explained the context in which the tasks are done and/or does it demonstrate underpinning knowledge or understanding?
- Have I evaluated this policy document and showed elsewhere, for example in a learner statement or through professional discussion, how it is applied in practice?
- Is the evidence recent and authentic? In other words, does it prove that I am currently competent?
- Do I have sufficient examples of meeting performance criteria over time?
- Does this evidence need to be physically included in my portfolio, or would it be better to show it to my assessor during or following an observation, or during professional discussion?
- Has my assessor seen this already and made a decision on it? Can I replace it where it came from?
- Is my assessor asking me to put more documents into my portfolio because the assessor is not making assessment judgements when we meet? Would we be better meeting at my workplace instead of the assessor's and getting some assessment done?

If you are unsure, get advice from your assessor. The specifications from awarding organizations now give clear guidance as to the agreed evidence that you must show to your assessor, and if you follow this guidance you should have no problems with sufficiency or validity.

Remember – one of the signs of a good assessor, or candidate, is that he or she is able to identify relevant evidence that covers as many criteria as possible – holistic assessment. There is no positive correlation between large paper-based portfolios and good assessor or IV practice!

Electronic evidence and portfolios

Many centres are moving towards online systems for recording candidate achievement. The downside of this is that they can be a bit mechanistic, as well as requiring everyone to be fully familiar with the technology involved. The positive side is that necessary information can be scanned, and downloaded from mobile devices, and assessments and feedback can be entered all in one virtual space.

There are now a number of e-portfolio systems – electronic recording systems – being used by awarding organizations or available on the market that enable the assessor to capture all assessment activity on-screen. All necessary recording pro-formas are online. Candidate work may be scanned into the system. Feedback comments can be sent online to candidates. Assessment and verification records can be entered straight into the electronic system. Internal and external IQAs can access the system at any time to verify assessment activity.

The e-portfolio is, like any recording system, as good as those using it. Like a paper-based system, it relies on the assessor to enter data regularly and on the candidate to arrange appropriately timed workplace visits for observation and professional discussion.

08 Checking you are on track for certification

The major factors influencing the time you take to get your qualification are likely to be:

- *The support, advice and documentation provided by the awarding organization with which you register.* Make sure you have a registration number from the awarding organization as soon as you have been enrolled as a suitable candidate for an award. Check you have a full copy of the occupational standards and any helpful materials provided by the awarding organizations. The awarding organization and standards websites will be helpful here (see 'Supporting materials'). For NVQ (NQF) qualifications you have to wait a minimum of 10 weeks from registering before you can be entered for certification. This is known as the '10-week rule'. Some awarding organizations have regulations that require you to be registered within a certain number of weeks, say four, of the course start date. This means you may need to be sure that you can fulfil practical work-based requirements before you start the course.

- *The support, advice and documentation provided by the centre with which you enrol.* Check out the amount of time your centre has allocated for your support, and plan with your assessor at the outset how it will be used. Keep appointments, and let your assessor know in good time if you need to cancel visits. If you do have to cancel visits on more than one occasion, you may be jeopardizing your ability to complete the course on time. Ask what additional support the centre can provide, such as computing or library facilities. Make sure you have access to key documents, such as the candidate handbooks and unit specifications and the relevant awarding organization information. Reading these will help you to get an understanding of the issues around assessment and internal and external quality assurance and give you a broader perspective than that of your centre or awarding organization. Ask if you have any queries.

- *Your familiarity with the occupational standards relevant to your qualification.* Discuss these with other staff or candidates at your workplace. Make sure that your mentor, if you have one, is familiar with the standards. You need to get to the point where you have a good overview of your qualification, as well as understanding evidence required to meet the assessment criteria.

- *Your familiarity with the assessment and/or internal quality-assurance process.* The more experience you have of this and the closeness with which you are integrated into the centre's operation, the easier it will be to undertake the process as a candidate. Almost every course offered has some internal and external quality-assurance monitoring, and if you are teaching, training or assessing it is highly likely that you will be involved at several points during a typical year.

- *Your opportunities and abilities to meet the required standards.* If you are a candidate-assessor/-IQA, you will need to ensure that your own internal IV/IQA has included you in standardization activities and that you are able to carry out all the activities required by the standards. No simulation is allowed. If this is a problem, you need to take advice, as the assessor/IQA awards may not be appropriate for you, or your centre may need to review its processes if it wishes you to succeed.

- *The support of your workplace colleagues as, for example, witnesses or vocational observers.* Assuming your manager has suggested that you get the qualification, then hopefully the staff will be fully behind you and prepared to carry out observations or verify your practice as required. Even so, staff may well need to meet with you initially so that they are clear about your expectations. If you are taking the qualification on your own initiative, you need to think carefully about whom you will need to work with in the centre, their own work commitments, and what you can do to have your award seen as useful to the centre and those you are working with.

- *Your commitments in and outside work.* However well you plan, the unexpected often happens, so it can be worth thinking through some contingency plans, for example for when your candidates leave unexpectedly or there is a home crisis. Ensure you let your assessor and others who may be affected know as soon as possible in case they are able to help.

- *Your ability to select and present evidence clearly.* If you understand the occupational standards and can see that they represent a job broken down into its constituent parts, you will find it easier to select assessment opportunities that cover substantial parts of your required performance. The more clearly you are able to link your evidence to specific learning outcomes, the easier it will be for your assessor to make the necessary judgements. Your assessor should be looking to see that you have confidence in your role and that you understand what you should be doing and how you should be working.

If things go wrong

Your trainer, teacher or assessor will support you regarding your progress towards your qualification through his or her assessment and feedback. You will no doubt have one or two tutorials that will be focused on your workplace or academic progress. Your mentor, if you have one, should support you to develop your understanding of your specialist subject and its requirements. However, you all need to be clear about the extent to which these people should support you if you encounter problems that are not directly connected with their teaching, training, support or assessment (see Table 2.3). Find out what additional support your approved centre or workplace has, such as confidential counsellors or study staff who can support you with issues that are beyond the call of duty of your assessor or teacher.

TABLE 2.3 Examples of who to see if you need help

A candidate had relationship difficulties that were affecting her ability to get work done at home. She arranged to see a counsellor, to deal with that side of things, but also started to use the centre's study facilities to do her work.
A candidate had inadvertently booked a holiday that clashed with her workplace assessments. She let her assessor know early enough, and a substitute assessor was found who could observe her as soon as she returned.
A candidate fell behind with his work and had not completed by the end of the year. The centre arranged for him to pay additional fees so that he could receive additional tutorials and assessment the following year.
An anxious candidate used a lot of his allocated tutorial time talking about his concerns rather than discussing his work. The tutor suggested he use the specialist in the study centre to help him with structuring and referencing assignments, as well as with time management.
A candidate cancelled two workplace assessments for different work-related reasons. The workplace assessor arranged to see the internal IQA/iqa at the candidate's workplace, who was able to work with the candidate's line manager and arrange observation dates that would not be disrupted and that suited all parties.

Conclusion

Being a student, learner or candidate, whatever term you prefer, and whatever your age and experience, can be stressful. However, you will also have the opportunity to make friends, understand how your own learners or candidates feel – and get a qualification that might even change your life!

PART THREE
Guidance on units for assessment and quality assurance

Introduction: overview of the units

Here is the guide to the units for assessment and internal quality assurance.

Units 1 and 4 are knowledge-based units that can be taken by anyone who wants to know more about assessment and quality assurance.

Units 2 and 3 are competence-based units and only for those who are assessing registered candidates, and Unit 5 is only for those who are carrying out internal quality assurance for an accredited centre. No simulation is allowed for these units.

Unit 8 is a competence-based unit for those who manage teams. In this context, the 'team' is that of quality-assurance staff and assessors.

There are overlaps between some of the units. This gives the opportunity for a holistic approach to units. For example, some of your evidence for Unit 1 will also be applicable to Units 2 and 3 and vice versa. Through just one observation followed by questioning or discussion, you could show how you prepare, manage, decide and record assessments, and so maximize that opportunity to provide evidence. One effective witness statement, for example from an IQA/internal verifier could support your claims that you follow procedures.

Your centre and awarding organization will provide much of the assessment documentation you will use as evidence for these units, together with guidance on how to complete it.

Table 3.1 shows the combination of units for different qualifications, and following that, there is an outline of the learning outcomes of all the units, including those for Units 6 and 7 for external quality-assurance staff (Table 3.2).

TABLE 3.1 The qualifications for assessment and quality assurance

Qualifications for assessors

Level 3 Award in Understanding the Principles and Processes of Assessment (Unit 1)

Level 3 Award in Assessing Competence in the Work Environment (Unit 1 and Unit 2)

Level 3 Certificate in Assessing Vocational Achievement (Unit 1, Unit 2 and Unit 3)

Qualifications for internal quality-assurance staff

Level 4 Award in Understanding the Internal Quality Assurance of Assessment Processes and Practice (Unit 4)

Level 4 Award in the Internal Quality Assurance of Assessment Processes and Practice (Unit 4 and Unit 5)

Level 4 Certificate in Leading the Internal Quality Assurance of Assessment Processes and Practice (Unit 4, Unit 5 and Unit 8)

Qualifications for external quality-assurance staff

Level 4 Award in Understanding the External Quality Assurance of Assessment Processes and Practices (Unit 6)

TABLE 3.2 Learning outcomes for all units

Unit	Learning outcomes
Unit 1: Understanding the principles and practices of assessment	1 Understand the principles and requirements of assessment 2 Understand different types of assessment method 3 Understand how to plan assessment 4 Understand how to involve learners and others in assessment 5 Understand how to make assessment decisions 6 Understand quality assurance of the assessment process 7 Understand how to manage information relating to assessment 8 Understand the legal and good practice requirements in relation to assessment
Unit 2: Assess occupational competence in the work environment	1 Be able to plan the assessment of occupational competence 2 Be able to make assessment decisions about occupational competence 3 Be able to provide required information following the assessment of occupational competence 4 Be able to maintain legal and good practice requirements when assessing occupational competence
Unit 3: Assess vocational skills, knowledge and understanding	1 Be able to prepare assessments of vocational skills, knowledge and understanding 2 Be able to carry out assessments of vocational skills, knowledge and understanding 3 Be able to provide required information following the assessment of vocational skills, knowledge and understanding 4 Be able to maintain legal and good practice requirements when assessing vocational skills, knowledge and understanding

TABLE 3.2 *continued*

Unit	Learning outcomes
Unit 4: Understanding the principles and practices of internally assuring the quality of assessment	1 Understand the context and principles of internal quality assurance 2 Understand how to plan the internal quality assurance of assessment 3 Understand techniques and criteria for monitoring the quality of assessment internally 4 Understand how to internally maintain and improve the quality of assessment 5 Understand how to manage information relevant to the internal quality assurance of assessment 6 Understand the legal and good practice requirements for the internal quality assurance of assessment
Unit 5: Internally assure the quality of assessment	1 Be able to plan the internal quality assurance of assessment 2 Be able to internally evaluate the quality of assessment 3 Be able to internally maintain and improve the quality of assessment 4 Be able to manage information relevant to the internal quality assurance of assessment 5 Be able to maintain legal and good practice requirements when internally monitoring and maintaining the quality of assessment
Unit 6: Understanding the principles and practices of externally assuring the quality of assessment	1 Understand the context and principles of external quality assurance 2 Understand how to plan the external quality assurance of assessment 3 Understand how to externally evaluate the quality of assessment and internal quality assurance 4 Understand how to externally maintain and improve the quality of assessment 5 Understand how to manage information relevant to external quality assurance 6 Understand the legal and good practice requirements relating to external quality assurance

TABLE 3.2 *continued*

Unit	Learning outcomes
Unit 7: Externally assure the quality of assessment	**1** Be able to plan the external quality assurance of assessment **2** Be able to externally evaluate internal quality assurance and assessment **3** Be able to maintain and improve internal quality assurance processes **4** Be able to manage information relevant to the external quality assurance of assessment **5** Be able to maintain legal and good practice requirements when externally monitoring and maintaining the quality of assessment
Unit 8: Plan, allocate and monitor work in own area of responsibility	**1** Be able to produce a work plan for own area of responsibility **2** Be able to allocate and agree responsibilities with team members **3** Be able to monitor the progress and quality of work in own area of responsibility and provide feedback **4** Be able to review and amend plans of work for own area of responsibility and communicate changes

Unit 1
Understanding the principles and practices of assessment

LEARNING OUTCOMES FOR UNIT 1

1 Understand the principles and requirements of assessment
2 Understand different types of assessment method
3 Understand how to plan assessment
4 Understand how to involve learners and others in assessment
5 Understand how to make assessment decisions
6 Understand quality assurance of the assessment process
7 Understand how to manage information relating to assessment
8 Understand the legal and good practice requirements in relation to assessment

U nit 1 provides the knowledge and understanding you need to put assessment into practice. Here you will find detailed information about what you need to know to assess QCF qualifications, including competence-based qualifications and NVQs (which still exist although they are being phased out). This unit is also taken by teachers on PTLLS, CTLLS and DTLLS courses.

Work-based assessment is concerned with the assessment of occupational competence, whereas vocational assessment takes place in non-work education and training settings and has a more theoretical and knowledge base. We give practical examples to help you understand some of the key concepts and ideas in assessment generally, and then for work-based (Unit 2) and vocational assessment (Unit 3)

LEARNING OUTCOME 1: UNDERSTAND THE PRINCIPLES AND REQUIREMENTS OF ASSESSMENT

ASSESSMENT CRITERIA

1.1 Explain the functions of assessment in learning and development.

1.2 Define the key concepts and principles of assessment.

1.3 Explain the responsibilities of the assessor.

1.4 Identify the regulations and requirements relevant to assessment in own area of practice.

1.1 Explain the functions of assessment in learning and development

'Assessment' is judging performance against an agreed standard. In this process, a learner gets feedback on learning, and teachers can see where they need to make changes to help learner development. Assessment is used for a number of different purposes, which affect the types and methods of assessment chosen.

Here are some typical functions of assessment:

- to assess whether the learner has met required standards/criteria;
- to assess occupational competence;
- to find out the learner's current level of knowledge and/or skill in a vocational area;

- to find out what support the learner might need in order to be successful in learning;
- to find out what methods of teaching and learning would be most appropriate for the learner;
- to provide the teacher with information about what the learner is learning during different stages of the course (initial, formative, summative) and how he or she can be helped to improve;
- to provide the learner with information about what he or she is learning and what help the learner thinks he or she needs to improve;
- to motivate the learner to continue/try to do better;
- to motivate the teacher to try different ways of helping the learner learn;
- to provide the teacher and learner with evidence of what the learner has learnt through both formal and informal methods;
- to provide other stakeholders (eg awarding organization, parents, potential or existing employers, universities) with evidence of what the learner has achieved;

and also:

- *to provide data that can be used for quality-assurance and improvement purposes;*
- *measure cohorts of learners' achievements against standards/ performance criteria/assessment criteria;*
- *measure achievements against national benchmarks or targets.*

As an assessor, what you do fits into a far larger picture. The last three points show there are wider purposes of assessment related to quality assurance within an organization and, potentially, to education and training policy in the UK.

Many skills are involved in the assessment process. You need to be able to plan assessment, make judgements against assessment criteria on the evidence produced by the candidate and record decisions accurately and unambiguously, using the documentation required by your organization or the awarding organization. All of this needs to take into account relevant legislation, regulations and procedures. Having an awareness of these functions and processes can help make sense of some of the detailed record keeping and paperwork that is required of today's assessors.

Categories of assessment

From the list of functions of assessment, the main functions of assessment can be categorized in three ways – initial, formative and summative assessment. Each of these categories has a different purpose (see Table 3.3).

TABLE 3.3 Three categories of assessment

Assessment category	Purpose
Initial assessment	Finding out about the individual learner at the beginning of a course or unit
Formative assessment	Helping the learner towards his or her learning goals by providing ongoing feedback on their performance (see also Table 000)
Summative assessment	Measuring what the learner has achieved at the end of a course, unit or period of study

Initial assessment

The idea of initial assessment is based on the following:

- In order to help someone to learn more, both teacher and the learner need to be aware of what the learner knows and can do already, and what he or she still needs to learn. This will also help in deciding when the learner is ready for formal assessment.

- Both teacher and learner need to be aware of how the learner likes to learn. In other words, people learn by building on the knowledge and skills they already possess, and people like to learn in different ways. Initial assessment can provide important information in both these areas.

The term 'initial assessment' means what it says – that is, assessment at the beginning of something – but the term can be used to reflect different situations, and this can sometimes be confusing for the new teacher/assessor. It is important that you know the various ways the term is used, and are clear how it is being used in your own work context.

Examples of initial assessment:

- A candidate in the workplace goes through an initial assessment process with an adviser to determine what level he or she is working at and whether any RPL might be appropriate.

- A learner is guided onto a course by a specialist advisers at an FE college, having taken an initial assessment which included information about the learner's interests and abilities as well as identifying any general issues of support necessary for this learner. As the learner already knew s/he was dyslexic, then this was recorded straight away and taken into account during the guidance and discussion on what extra support the learner might need.

- A learner takes an entry test designed to test this applicant's ability to deal with a plumbing course. As the course requires the ability to solve problems, the initial assessment was designed to represent situations and problems that would be met in the work for the actual course and tested the learner's potential to deal with these.

- A group of learners are given an initial assessment exercise at the start of their health and social care course, to help them and the teacher identify their current level of knowledge and skills in that vocational area and also to identify any additional support needs.

In vocational education and training, a key aspect of initial assessment includes assessing the functional skills of English, mathematics and information and communications technology (ICT) to ensure that, where necessary, the correct specific support is put in place for the learner. English assessment would probably include assessment for both reading and writing skills as these are essential for most courses. However, in some cases, the teacher might decide to focus on certain aspects of a learner's ability during an initial assessment and assess other aspects of his or her ability on an ongoing basis during the first few weeks of a course. One example of this would be where a teacher decides that a learner's ability to read a certain level of information needs to be assessed straight away, because without that ability he or she cannot even begin the course, but that the learner's writing ability can be assessed more naturally during the first piece of written work.

Confusion between 'initial' and 'diagnostic' assessment

You may encounter the terms 'initial assessment' and 'diagnostic assessment' being used in different ways. This can be confusing, but unfortunately there is no clear and consistent way that these terms are used!

- Initial assessments are used to 'diagnose' learners' needs, and so sometimes the terms 'initial assessment' and 'diagnostic assessment' are used to mean the same thing.

- Sometimes the two terms are used together: 'initial diagnostic assessment'.

- Sometimes they are used to mean different stages of the same process, where the initial assessment provides a certain level of information, but a diagnostic assessment provides a greater level of detail. An example of this is where a teacher carries out an initial assessment and identifies that the learner has problems with writing. The learner is then referred to a literacy specialist, who carries out a diagnostic assessment that identifies the problem areas in specific detail.

The only advice we can give here is always to check out what the terms mean in the context where you meet them.

Formative assessment

Every time candidates receive a judgement on their performance that will cause them to alter certain aspects of it, they are receiving formative assessment:

that is, an assessment that 'forms' their development towards a certain desired goal, just as a metalworker 'forms' a hot piece of metal towards a certain desired shape.

This type of assessment takes place on a continuous basis – sometimes formally, but very often informally. Formative assessment that is carried out helpfully and sympathetically can play a large part in motivating candidates, particularly those unsure of their own abilities. The recording of outcomes by the assessor will lead to a gradual build-up of confidence towards assessment of competencies and/or knowledge and understanding, which will give candidates clear guidance as to what aspects of performance they still need to work on.

In competence-based qualifications this is fairly straightforward – formative assessment is geared to helping learners develop the knowledge and skills required to meet performance criteria. However, the examples below show how formative assessment may serve different purposes in the range of qualifications and contexts in the lifelong-learning sector (LLS).

Examples of formative assessment in the LLS:

- A joinery teacher walks around the workshop in a private training organization while learners are carrying out a specific joinery task. The teacher observes each student and stops where necessary, pointing out how the students might improve what they are doing or correcting mistakes. The purpose here is to provide immediate and ongoing feedback to help learners in the task they are actually performing. In this case there is little distinction between formative assessment and teaching.

- A candidate studying for her Certificate in Teaching in the lifelong-learning sector receives formative feedback on her reflective journal, which she writes up on a weekly basis along with reflections on her teaching sessions. This feedback, given six weeks into the course but before the candidate has any formal assignments or been assessed in the workplace. It enables her to prepare better for the future assessments by alerting her to the fact that she must improve her written English and the writing of session objectives, and develop the range of methods she is using with her own learners.

- A teacher on a foundation degree in educational administration offered in an FE college receives the first draft of a learner's written assignment. The teacher sends back the first draft accompanied by a completed formative assessment sheet that includes specific comments on how to improve academic writing skills. The purpose here is to provide clear and detailed guidance on how to improve, giving the learner an opportunity to read the feedback in his own time and ask for clarification on any points he does not understand.

- A functional skills teacher working in a community centre has a progress tutorial with a learner, where they look in detail at the initial learning goals identified in the ILP. During this process the learner identifies what she thinks she has achieved so far and, in discussion with the learner, the teacher gives formative feedback on the learner's development and what she needs to do to improve or develop further. The purpose here is to provide clear guidance and action planning for further development, but also to model a process in which the learner is actively involved in her own assessment.

Formative assessment also provides candidates with information about when they will be ready for summative assessment:

Example

A candidate for a competence-based QCF diploma in food and beverage service, working in a restaurant, is constantly receiving feedback on his performance by the head waiter. From the simple reminder 'You've forgotten the table napkins' to a full debriefing on how the candidate served at table on a busy Saturday night, the head waiter is providing feedback that will shape the candidate's future performance to the desired goal of being the perfect waiter. This formative assessment, linked to the required assessment criteria, will also give him an indication of when he will be ready for a formal end (summative) assessment.

As well as providing learners with information, it is also important to remember that formative assessment also helps teachers to evaluate their own teaching/assessment practice and how they may need to adjust, clarify or even radically alter their approach.

Summative assessment

Whereas formative assessment relates to development, summative assessment is a formal 'summing up' of what has been achieved at a particular point or at particular points in a course of study. The main purposes behind summative assessment are to:

- measure the learner's performance against an expected standard;
- draw conclusions about how well he or she has performed.

Summative assessment also provides the evidence for certification of the learner's achievement. This will be used when applying for a job or further study to inform employers or HE/FE institutions about the applicant's current level of skills/knowledge.

Sometimes summative assessments occur at various times during a course, as for example in end-of-unit tests or assignments. However, it is important to remember that, even at the end of a course, summative assessment is not really 'the end', in that it can provide information for learners to decide on their future learning and directions for development.

In the case of many vocational qualifications, summative assessment will take place at the completion of each unit. The assessor will make a final judgement on the whole of a unit after a series of assessments on different tasks. The results of this assessment will be recorded to stand as a statement of the candidate's competence at the time of the summative assessment. Academic qualifications usually have a series of assignments and/or projects. Summative assessment will occur on the completion of each of these pieces of work. However, the final summative assessment, which indicates the overall grade achieved, cannot be given until all parts of the qualification have been completed.

Other examples of summative assessment include:

- end-of-year/end-of-course examinations;
- end-of-unit tests for craft certificates;
- the final grade given to completed projects or assignments;
- an online test;
- an observed practical activity or task.

1.2 Define the key concepts and principles of assessment

Relationship of assessment to teaching, training and learning

In a vocational education setting such as an FE college, it is very likely that the assessor would also be the teacher who has taught the learner – the teacher/assessor. In workplace education, the assessor is quite likely to be independent from the training process.

Assessment is part of a cycle of development. There are a number of different models for the teaching/learning/assessment process, but, although the terms may vary from one model to another, the essential stages are similar in nature. They all have the following features and these are reflected in the contents of the assessor units. Different activities take place in each stage of the cycle as described in Table 3.4.

Principles of good practice in assessment

Good practice in assessment is based on the idea that everyone has the capacity to improve. As far as possible, the type of assessment should take into account the needs of the individual learner, as well as the requirements of the course/qualification. In the assessment process the learner should be actively involved in his or her own assessment as far as possible. Both the teacher and the learner should be clear on what is being assessed and how it is being assessed through the use of well-expressed assessment criteria. It is essential that every effort is made to make the assessment fair and unbiased and that the learners have every chance to perform well as

TABLE 3.4 Stages of teaching/learning/assessment cycle

Stages of teaching/ learning/assessment cycle	Description of stage
Initial review and assessment	Diagnosis of what the learner already knows or can do, compared with what he or she needs to demonstrate and learn.
Planning for learning/assessment	Decisions are made and agreements are reached on what the outcomes of learning should be, how the learning/assessment is to take place, what methods and resources will be used and what timescale is appropriate; this is done with regard to cost-effectiveness, health and safety and equality and diversity agendas. An added requirement is that the training/assessment must be appropriate for the needs of each learner.
Implementation	The learning programme or assessment process is put into practice.
Assessment	The results of learning are assessed, formatively and summatively.
Evaluation and quality assurance	A variety of techniques is used to gain quantitative and qualitative information on the overall effectiveness of the process, from candidate performance and satisfaction, evaluation of assessor performance to success in meeting organizational targets.

NOTE: 'Evaluation' is judging the *value* of what has been experienced or achieved – whether it has been *worthwhile* for the candidate involved but also worthwhile for other stakeholders involved, such as employers, sector skills councils, awarding organisations, parents, teachers, assessors, funding agencies or relevant government departments. Evaluation considers a range of sources of information, including the candidate's views, the assessor's views and the opinions of other stakeholders, as well as practical outcomes, such as assessment results to determine the value of what has been undertaken and achieved.

long as they have the required knowledge and skill. This means the assessor has to be aware of any potential barriers for learners that might prevent fair access to assessment.

There have been changes to how assessment is understood and carried out in the last decade that have impacted on successive qualifications for assessors:

- Previously assessment was often carried out in small chunks that measured separate criteria. Now the emphasis is on holistic assessment where a number of criteria could be met through one assessment task.

- Previously, the emphasis was on a few highly standardized methods of assessment that were applied to everyone. Now the emphasis is on exploring a whole range of different types of assessment and trying to fit the assessment not just to the purpose but to the learner and learning situation.

- Previously, only the teacher/assessor was involved in assessing the student. Now, wherever possible, the learner is involved in his or her own assessment.

Key concepts

Five key concepts underpin the principles of good practice in relation to assessment. They are used in planning, implementing and judging, which need to become second nature to any assessor. The concepts are validity, reliability, sufficiency, authenticity and currency:

- The type of assessment used and the evidence provided should be fit for the purpose for which it is intended (validity).

- The assessment should be consistent and reliable (reliability).

- The evidence being assessed should be sufficient for the assessor to make a judgement on the learner's knowledge and/or skills against specified criteria (sufficiency).

- There should be no doubt that the evidence is genuine and has been produced by the candidate (authenticity).

- The evidence can prove that the candidate is up to date on current methods, skills and knowledge in the chosen vocational area (currency).

Let us look at these key concepts in more detail.

Validity

The type of assessment used and the evidence provided should be fit for the purpose for which it is intended.

It would not be valid to assess whether a cook could bake a cake by asking him or her to draw a picture of one! Nor would it be valid to assess whether a gardener could plant bulbs by watching him or her sow seeds. Valid assessment implies that the method or methods used are the ones most likely to give an accurate picture of that individual's performance within a particular area. Over the last few decades, an emphasis on validity – finding methods that are fit for the purpose of assessing particular knowledge and skill – have resulted in much more imaginative assessment practice. Old-fashioned methods of assessing a student's skill in a foreign language often lacked validity. It is amazing to think that a person's ability to communicate in French used to be tested by completing a series of written grammatical exercises rather than by whether they could actually speak and be understood!

As an assessor you may have some help in the design of valid assessments. In QCF qualifications, awarding organizations may provide standardized assessment briefs, to be used by centres, containing a range of assessment tasks considered to be valid means of assessment for specified criteria. If assessment briefs are not provided, the awarding organization usually offers guidance on how to make assessment valid. In many vocational qualifications, assessment tasks are prepared by the teacher/assessor drawing on examples or advice from the relevant awarding organization. Those used for summative assessment, such as assignment briefs, will be approved by the internal verifier and records of approval of assignment briefs will be part of the documentation required from the centre by the awarding organization.

Competence-based qualifications assessed in the workplace and based on portfolios of evidence, such as NVQs, may involve some negotiation between the assessor and the candidate about the evidence required to meet specified criteria. Some awarding organizations, such as HABIA, produce very comprehensive record books that specify in detail the evidence required for their hair and beauty therapy qualifications. Other qualifications, especially those at higher levels, might rely far more on negotiated evidence. In this situation, it is important to grasp that no evidence is automatically valid or not valid. It also involves the candidate's interpretation of that evidence – by effective justification of its relevance the candidate can convince the assessor that it is valid.

If this evidence is not valid – in other words, it is not an appropriate means of demonstrating their skills or knowledge – candidates will have to be reassessed using different, or additional and more relevant, evidence. Your skills as an assessor in the planning stage, using your knowledge of valid assessment to advise the candidate, can help to avoid this scenario.

Example

A photograph of the candidate and another person could be presented as evidence. By itself that photograph has no meaning. However, if the candidate says: 'This is a photograph that appeared in my firm's newsletter showing me receiving a prize for apprentice of the year,' the photograph takes on a meaning and becomes valid evidence (as long as the candidate can prove that the statement is true). This is why explanatory statements related to any documentary evidence presented are important, as they can give the reasons why the candidate believes a particular piece of evidence to be valid.

TABLE 3.5 Different types of validity

Type of validity	Description
Construct validity	The method is as close as it can be to testing what it is intended to test – it is 'fit for the purpose' of testing performance against the specified criteria.
Content validity	Covers a relevant sample of the overall knowledge and skills expected to have been learnt (ie it tests some aspects of the syllabus).
Face validity	'On the face of it' the test looks all right, seems suitable for the purpose and fits in with the culture of the teaching/training/work environment; eg a written examination would not fit in with a workplace culture, but would fit in with a school culture.
Predictive validity	The method has some capacity to predict future performance (eg in another environment), not only current performance.

Invalidity would also be possible if a candidate provided witness statements from colleagues who were also candidates for the same NVQ award. If these colleagues were very experienced in the area, but had just never converted that experience into a qualification, their evidence might well be valid. If, however, they did not really have the depth of knowledge or experience to warrant acting as a witness, the validity of the evidence could be questioned.

The most usual definition of validity relates to its 'fitness for purpose', sometimes called 'construct' validity. But as Table 3.5 shows, the concept of validity can be broken down even more and all of these aspects can usefully be taken into account when deciding on the method and relevance of the evidence produced against the specified criteria.

Reliability and fairness

The assessment should be consistent and reliable (ie can be relied upon).

As an assessor of a national qualification, it is important that your judgements are consistent with those of other assessors of the same qualification across the country. For an assessment to be reliable it needs to have the following characteristics:

- The assessment judgement confirms that the candidate's performance will be of a consistent standard in a range of different contexts.

- The same assessor would make the same judgement about the candidate on a number of different occasions.
- Other assessors would make the same judgement about the candidate.

Reliability and fairness are closely linked. Candidates must have confidence that they will be treated fairly by assessors, that they are not going to have a harsher assessment from one assessor than from another, and that other candidates are not going to be assessed more leniently. Candidates are entitled to feel confident that they will be treated fairly when working towards their qualification. This means that the assessment process should be free from bias or discrimination. Candidates need to be sure that they will not be discriminated against through the subjective judgement of the assessor because of some personal prejudice or personal interpretation of the assessment criteria.

One way that subjective judgements can cloud the objectivity of an assessment is in the 'halo and horns' effect, where a candidate is considered 'good' or 'poor' by the assessor and all evidence is judged on that basis, as opposed to being judged on its own merit. Probably the most effective safeguard that can operate here is the assessor's own awareness of where he or she might be biased or have personal preferences, plus a strict adherence to the requirements of the outcome and criteria being assessed. However, subjectivity will also be reduced by the moderation/verification processes put in place within your centre, where other assessors' judgements can confirm or amend the judgements of all assessors in the team.

Most of us would probably agree that people may interpret guidelines and assessment criteria differently or consider some aspects of work more important than others. These can all affect our judgements and make them different from candidate to candidate, and different from those of someone else doing the same assessment. Hence measures that ensure consistency – training on making assessment judgements, comparing judgements with other assessors and being involved in major quality-assurance processes such as moderation, standardization or verification – are essential if we are to be fair to the candidate. Consistency in assessment is also essential for employers or educational institutions. These will be asked to accept that a qualification gives a clear and accurate picture of how someone can perform in employment or in preparation for a higher education programme. These stakeholders will need to rely on the quality and consistency of the judgements being made.

Many vocational qualifications are practically based, so reliable assessment of occupational skills is crucial. Inaccurately assessing a candidate as competent, say in construction or motor vehicle repair, could have potentially fatal consequences. Some competence-based qualifications still use independent assessors as a double check on the assessment process. An experienced assessor, independent of the candidate, who may never meet him or her, assesses some of the candidate's evidence. Some awarding organizations stipulate exactly what the independent assessor will assess; others request that 'a significant part' of the candidate's work is independently assessed.

Sufficiency

The evidence being assessed should be sufficient for the assessor to make a judgement on the learner's knowledge and/or skills against specified criteria.

In some contexts, learners will be asked to complete assignments or carry out written tasks to meet the learning outcomes and assessment criteria for a unit. There will usually be a word count associated with that piece of work. This will be decided by the teacher/assessor or the awarding organization on the basis that the word count needs to be sufficient to allow for full coverage of the subject at the level required. In practical tasks, learners need to be given sufficient time and opportunity to meet the specified criteria.

With portfolio-based assessments, insufficient evidence may mean not enough evidence but also not enough relevant evidence. This can result from a 'shopping trolley' approach to the assessment, where all sorts of documentary items are collected in the vague hope that they will provide something of substance. If being assessed is to be meaningful for candidates, an essential part of the process is the thought required in discussing their own performance, in assessing their own strengths and areas for development and in working out what they need to do, make or explain to demonstrate competence appropriately. Without this disciplined identification and selection, candidates will remain unaware of what it is that they do or know that enables them to perform a particular work role. Here are some examples of evidence that is not sufficient:

- a letter (as a witness statement) from an employer that does not refer to the specific competences performed by the candidate;
- a document without any explanation as to its relevance;
- a practical activity with no record of questioning to show that the candidate has the underpinning knowledge;
- evidence of competent performance on just one occasion or within a very limited time span;
- an assignment answer that asks for three examples of an application to the candidate's work practice, in which the candidate only gives three generalized examples;
- an assignment that needs referencing and evidence of a range of sources that the candidate has not referenced accurately and has referred to just two standard textbooks.

Authenticity

There should be no doubt that the evidence is genuine and has been produced by the candidate.

Some vocational assessment methods, such as end-of-term examinations, provide safeguards to prevent cheating by candidates. An independent invigilator watches them while they write their answers, and there are rules about what items of equipment can be present and strict rules of secrecy about what they might be required to answer. Candidates who have to present written work, such as assignments, will receive information about their centre's policy on malpractice, such as plagiarism.

Plagiarism is a deliberate attempt by candidates to pass off someone else's work as their own. Unfortunately, the widespread use of the internet has increased opportunities for people who are tempted to cheat in this way. Assessors often can spot plagiarism, as they become familiar with the writing styles and abilities of their candidates, but luckily there is now very effective software designed to identify unacknowledged or wrongly attributed passages lifted wholesale from other sources.

The knowledge requirements for vocational qualifications may be assessed by a variety of methods such as externally assessed written tests, examinations, or assignments, or by written answers to pre-set questions marked by a centre assessor. In all these cases, the assessor should apply the appropriate safeguards against copying or cheating.

Some awarding organizations have developed extensive banks of randomly generated online questions that can be accessed via the internet by candidates at any time or place to suit them. The random nature of the questions helps to deter cheating.

In competence-based qualifications, determining whether performance evidence is genuine will be straightforward if you, as the assessor, are observing the candidate doing something at work. However, the assessor has to be sure that any end product presented by the candidate as 'one I made earlier' really has been produced by that candidate.

Example

If a candidate in catering showed you a cake he had prepared, you might ask him to describe how he had made it, what ingredients he had used and the temperature he had used while cooking it. In fact, you should ask as many questions as you need to ask to feel sure that he knows what he is talking about. You still might not be satisfied, so you might ask to talk to his supervisor, who could confirm that the candidate had made the cake or, if that was not possible, review a witness statement that stated that the cake was the normal standard of work of the candidate.

Assessors should check especially carefully any evidence, such as product evidence or RPL, that has not been assessed and certified as achieved by an accredited assessor.

Assessors will need to have confidence that witness statements are genuine, and will need to look at original certificates where candidates are claiming that they have prior qualifications. Documents included by candidates may not be their own work. This may be innocent, in that candidates may not have realized that they need to show their understanding and application of policy rather than including a copy of a company document. Assessors do need to be on the lookout for documentation that seems to come from a candidate but has differences in spelling, sentence structure and/or grammar from other documentation that you know is the candidate's own work.

Awarding organizations now generally require candidates to sign documentation confirming that what they have submitted is all their own work. Always check that this has been signed and return it to candidates to sign if they have omitted to do so. In that way the candidate takes explicit responsibility for confirming that this evidence is authentic.

Currency

The evidence can prove that the candidate is up to date on current methods, skills and knowledge in the chosen vocational area.

Here are some examples where an assessor would have to decide currency:

- A candidate for a certificate in business administration worked in an office 10 years ago. Would this provide evidence that the candidate could work in an office now?

- A candidate for a diploma in learning and development has a teaching qualification obtained in 1992. Would this provide evidence that the candidate could work in a training environment now?

- A candidate for an NVQ in aircraft maintenance engineering has been off work for two years because of an accident. Would the candidate still be up to date with the skills and technology required?

There are no hard-and-fast rules here. Obviously every vocational area is different, and some change far more quickly than others. However, as a general rule, areas that deal primarily with people can use evidence that dates back over a greater number of years than occupational areas where rapid changes in technology are likely to make skills obsolete – even those acquired only a few years before.

Obviously, if a candidate is applying for recognition of prior learning and/or achievement, the currency of their knowledge and skills will need to be taken onto account.

Assessment theories

A theory is a framework that helps us in understanding, explaining or predicting some area of interest or concern. Understanding relevant theory can help assessors choose appropriate methods, justify the reasons why they take a particular approach to assessment and reflect more effectively on assessment experiences and how to improve their practice.

Theories of assessment are usually concerned with exploring the different types and purposes of assessment and how various types and methods of assessment can help or hinder those purposes. A helpful distinction here is between assessment that is for testing learning or performance (assessment *of* learning) and assessment that is mainly for helping learning (assessment *for* learning). Paul Black and Dylan Wiliam have written extensively in this area, looking at effectiveness in formative assessment (1998) and ways of putting 'assessment for learning' into practice (Black et al, 2003).

Using ideas from the research of Black and Wiliam, the UK Assessment Reform Group (1999) identified five key principles of assessment for learning:

- the provision of effective feedback to students;
- the active involvement of students in their own learning;
- adjusting teaching to take account of the results of assessment;
- recognition of the profound influence assessment has on the motivation and self-esteem of pupils, both of which are critical influences on learning;
- the need for students to be able to assess themselves and understand how to improve.

These have been influential in changing approaches to assessment and this is reflected in the new QCF assessor qualifications, which have a stronger focus on knowledge, understanding and learning than previous assessor awards. Learning processes are sometimes discussed in terms of different learning domains – cognitive (mental skills, knowledge and understanding), affective (related to feelings/attitudes), psychomotor (manual or physical skills). These are based on work last century by Benjamin Bloom (1956) that continues to be highly influential in the development and planning of learning and assessment.

Some assessment theory may be closely linked to other types of theory, including:

- *Theories of learning*: behaviourist, cognitivist, humanist, social learning theory, situated learning theory. So, for example, if you favour a humanist theory of learning, where learning is about the development of the whole person, you are likely to consider types of assessment that help develop the learner/candidate's critical thinking and self-confidence.

- *Theories of intelligence*: one example here is Gardner's theory of multiple intelligences. If you accept that people have different types of intelligences, then you will consider how different types of assessment might be used to test or develop those intelligences.
- *Theories of motivation*: good assessment practice can motivate learners. If you accept this idea, then considering different types of motivation, as well as barriers to learning, could also help with deciding appropriate types of assessment.
- *Theories of communication*: good assessment involves good communication. Examples include clear instructions, good negotiations, accurate recording of decisions, sensitivity to individual needs and use of appropriate language.

TABLE 3.6 Learning domains and assessment

Domain	Issues to take into account in assessment
Cognitive (mental skills, knowledge and understanding)	• the level of knowledge and understanding being assessed; • the appropriate level of task/activity/questioning; • use of formative assessment to stretch and challenge learners; • improve performance and ability to achieve higher grade; help develop critical thinking skills.
Affective (feelings, attitudes)	• encourage the learner's ability to self-assess; • develop confidence and progress towards learning goals; • keep motivated to achieve the best possible result.
Psychomotor (manual or physical skills)	• the skills being assessed and the most valid way of them being demonstrated; • 'real-life' scenarios which allow occupational competence in the workplace; • the knowledge and understanding which underpins those skills which may require additional forms of assessment.

Different types of assessment

Criterion-referenced assessment

All QCF qualifications use 'criterion-referenced' systems of assessment – that is, the candidate is assessed against a set of pre-established criteria based on national occupational standards. The assessment criteria represent a consensus of opinion over what forms the basis of an 'acceptable' standard.

In a sense, all occupational areas are already based on criterion-referenced systems. For example, if your car was having its brakes mended, you would want to feel confident that the mechanic was working to an acceptable set of standards within the motor industry. Similarly, a patient being looked after by a nurse would want to feel that the nurse was performing duties to a standard required by any hospital in the country. The creation of sets of national standards for different occupational areas reflects what has traditionally occurred in practice, although there is always professional controversy over whether the standards contain the right criteria.

In competence-based assessments in qualifications such as NVQs, made against performance criteria, there are two possible outcomes for a candidate. The candidate can be judged either competent against the criteria or not yet competent against the criteria. In competence-based qualifications such as NVQs, there is no limit to the numbers of candidates who can be judged competent, as long as they meet the full requirements of the standards.

Example

In vehicle body repair, a candidate fitting replacement body panels either does or does not position the replacement components according to the vehicle manufacturer's specifications. In the first case s/he is competent against that criterion, and in the second case s/he is not yet competent against that criterion.

Unlike competence-based qualifications, where there are only two judgements against criteria – competent or not competent – many QCF qualifications allow for grading of performance with grades of pass, merit and distinction. This system is linked to 'norm-referenced' assessment, which allows for the measurement of performance against others and against national benchmarks.

Norm-referenced assessment

Traditional academic programmes are based on norm-referenced systems where the achievement of the candidate is judged in comparison to the achievement of other candidates. Hence in programmes such as A levels

FIGURE 3.1   Performance distribution curve

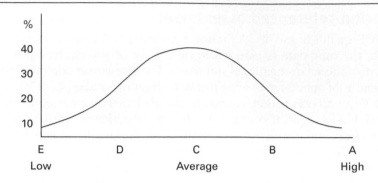

and GCSEs, candidates who get an A grade are judged to be better than candidates who have obtained a C grade. Norm-referenced systems have their basis in the idea that a few will do well, most will do averagely and some will do poorly. That means there is an expectation that a few people will get A* or A grades, a large number of people will get C grades and some will get E or even F grades. This 'normal distribution' is usually represented by a 'bell shaped curve' (see Figure 3.1).

If one year it turned out that an unusually large proportion of candidates obtained high grades, the system would be studied closely and revised. Either the examinations would be made more difficult or the examiners making the assessments would be told to assess more strictly. Hence there is no real notion of 'fixed' standards.

Most years, when A level and GCSE results are published and the numbers passing the examination increase, you will read articles and letters in newspapers about whether educational standards are falling. It could be that improved teaching methods and revision support help more candidates to do better (not forgetting the effectiveness of the 'A' level AS/A2 system at identifying those who are counselled out of A2 due to the risk of under-achievement). However, only a certain number are expected to get top grades and norm-referenced assessment acts as a way of distinguishing high from low achievers. As more candidates with higher grades can, for example, make it more difficult to get into particular universities because there are more students than places, government education policy will have an overall influence on the number of high grades that can be awarded year on year.

Use of national benchmarks

A potential problem in the norm-referenced system is that if the comparison is between poor performance and even poorer performance, then overall standards will be low. Let us consider our previous example of the patient being looked after by the nurse. It would be no consolation to the patient that the nurse was the best in the country if the general standards of nursing care nationally were inadequate and the nurse was merely the best out of a very poorly skilled profession. The problem, then, with norm-referencing is that comparisons only suggest that someone is better or worse in a particular group and do not suggest what the minimum standard for performance or achievement actually is. That is why there are national benchmarks for acceptable levels of performance based on national standards.

Employers and educational institutions such as universities do place an emphasis on the achievement of high grades, and one argument put forward for norm-referencing is that it provides a means of identifying the highest performers or those with the best potential. The problem arises when so much emphasis is placed on high grades that other positive aspects of an individual's performance are overlooked. For this reason, the use of student profiles that summarize their achievements and strengths after a course of study or training are growing in popularity.

1.3 Explain the responsibilities of the assessor

The assessor's obvious responsibility is to support the candidate through the assessment process. However, this takes place in the context of the organization and awarding organization's requirements, so assessors need to be mindful of the vital part they play in, for example, the effectiveness of the quality-assurance process.

Practical responsibilities of the assessor

- Plans assessments with the candidate.
- Makes accurate judgements against agreed criteria.
- Records judgements on approved documentation.
- Gives feedback to the candidate and ensures this can be remembered (so written notes are advised).
- Keeps records of candidate details such as registrations and dates of assessments, and makes these available to IQA/IV.

Assessor responsibilities to others

- Keeps up to date with the occupational area, and undertakes required professional development.
- Implements appropriate centre and awarding organization procedures and policies.
- Attends training and standardization events.
- Gives accurate reports on time to relevant persons such as internal verifiers, parents and employers.

See Unit 4 for additional information on roles.

1.4 Identify the regulations and requirements relevant to assessment in own area of practice

In a national system, it is inevitable that there will be a number of different bodies responsible for monitoring standards and compliance with the legislation and regulations that impact on your work as an assessor. See Appendix 3 for a brief overview of some of the major national bodies concerned with quality assurance in education and training and some of the main legislation that impacts on your assessment practice. You can find more detail about all of these by looking them up on the internet.

All centres need to show that they are aware of the relevant regulations and requirements as a condition of approval, but the important factor is that these regulations and requirements are implemented.

Here are some typical examples that apply to all assessors, who must:

- conform to awarding organization requirements (eg for quality assurance, documentation, access to assessment);
- meet centre requirements (eg ensuring all candidates are correctly registered, using the correct documentation, following the requirements of the data protection and copyright acts, reporting health and safety issues, wearing a name badge);
- meet workplace requirements when assessing (eg wearing protective clothing, following rules for signing into buildings).

Regulations and legislation

There is a whole range of legislation that might impact on you as an assessor, including occupation-specific legislation that you would be expected to know. Each awarding organization will have many regulations and policies, related to their responsibilities identified in the Table in Appendix 3). Your own organization will also have extensive policies and procedures. All of these are too numerous to mention here, but you need to be aware of them and ensure you are up to date. If in doubt, check with your internal quality assurer.

Here is a list of the key legislation that those who assess need to take into account both in the workplace and in vocational education and training establishments. Assessors need to ensure that their own practice and their candidates' practice conform to all legislative requirements. Further details will be found in Appendix 2.

- health and safety legislation;
- equality and diversity legislation;
- public sector equality duty (PSED) 2011;
- safeguarding children, young people and vulnerable adults;
- The Data Protection Act (1998).

LEARNING OUTCOME 2: UNDERSTAND DIFFERENT TYPES OF ASSESSMENT METHOD

ASSESSMENT CRITERION

2.1 Compare the strengths and limitations of a range of assessment methods with reference to the needs of individual learners.

2.1 Compare the strengths and limitations of a range of assessment methods with reference to the needs of individual learners

Introduction to assessment methods

Previously we covered the functions and purposes of assessment – *why* we assess. This outcome deals with *how* we assess – the methods used and how appropriate they are for assessing different learners. As this is an area where new assessors often need a lot of information, we go into considerable detail for this outcome. For example we provide a lengthy section on oral and written questioning – an important method used in a range of contexts.

When assessing QCF or NVQ qualifications in the work-based context, certain methods for producing evidence, such as direct observation, are expected to be used. However, in QCF qualifications offered in an education and training context, covering broader areas of knowledge and understanding, a wider range of assessment methods may be appropriate. We will evaluate a whole range of methods that can be used for assessment purposes – oral, written and audio-visual. We will then cover in more detail the specific methods identified in the QCF assessor units, as shown in Table 3.7. As can be seen, some of the methods are similar; for example both contexts must offer recognition of prior learning (RPL). Whilst the terminology and the context for assessment might be different, some of the methods used will be very similar. For example, when assessing a candidate producing a meal, the activity being observed will be similar and the product of work is going to be the meal, whether it has been produced in a real or a simulated work environment.

TABLE 3.7 The specific methods of assessment identified in the QCF assessor units

Methods of assessing occupational competence (see Unit 2)	Methods of assessing vocational knowledge and skills (see Unit 3)
Observation of performance in the work environment	Assessment of performance in simulated environments
Examining products of work	Skills tests
Questioning the learner	Oral and written questions
Recognizing prior learning	Recognizing prior learning
Discussing with the learner	
Use of others (witness testimony)	
Looking at learner statements	
	Written assignments/tasks
	Projects
	Case studies

Note on functional skills

Currently in the LLS, some qualifications take into account the requirements of functional skills (FS) in the core subjects of English (E), mathematics (M) and information and communications technology (ICT) when designing assessment tools. From 2011 functional skills replaced key skills as a mandatory component of all apprenticeship frameworks. Although functional skills are embedded in revised programmes of study in these core subjects, they can also be developed more widely by being integrated across the curriculum.

Whilst the needs of the learner have to be taken into account when deciding on the methods of assessment, in practice the extent to which this can address individual needs will vary to some extent according to the context:

- When assessing occupational competence in the work environment, the assessor may work mainly with individual candidates and so the methods can be focused on each candidate's circumstances.

- In an education and training context, the teacher will often have to use the same assessment method with a group of learners, as being more time-efficient and more likely to achieve consistent and reliable assessment. This will be especially true for summative assessments. However, in initial assessments, and particularly in formative assessments, it may be more appropriate and less difficult to customize the assessment method to the individual learner, and the teacher may think of creative ways of finding out what the learner has learnt.

Table 3.8 evaluates different types of assessment methods – (a) written (b) oral and (c) audio/visual. It also indicates the potential of different methods for including functional skills (FS).

You can see from the table that there are a vast range of methods to choose from and you would be able to find out more on these methods through reading or internet research.

Assessment methods and the needs of different learners

When taking into account the needs of individual learners we need to consider:

Is the learner being assessed as an independent candidate or as part of a group of learners who will all complete the same assessment activities?
Some of these methods will be relevant to assessment in the work-environment, customized to individual candidates; some will be suitable for assessments of groups of learners (and may enable learners to work and be assessed in groups).

In a vocational setting, such as an FE college, there is a broader educational perspective and a need for preparation for future employment in a variety of different settings.

In this setting there is a strong emphasis on the personal development of the learner, for example an increase in independence, confidence, communication and interpersonal skills. Hence the methods chosen in that setting may also encompass the development of the 'softer' skills such as those represented by QCF Personal Learning and Thinking Skills.

What is the purpose of the assessment; for example is it initial, formative or summative? Is it to test occupational competence or a broader set of skills and knowledge?
Initial assessment: Certain methods are effective in initial assessments because they can be carried out and assessed relatively quickly. Certain types of skills tests are a common form of initial assessment.

TABLE 3.8 Comparison of different types of assessment method

Type of assessment method	Strengths	Potential for functional skills (FS)	Limitations
(a) Written assessments	*Can give learners more time to think before answering* *Can give opportunity for learners to explore a subject in depth* *Provide a clear record of evidence* *Can be verified/moderated*	*Depending on task, all FS could be covered*	*All require relatively high levels of literacy to do well* *Dyslexic students disadvantaged*
Examination	Knowledge, understanding of concepts and ideas, factual recall, ability to provide clear and logical written answers in strict timescale	E; M	Strict timing Stressful situation
Examination – 'open book'	Knowledge, understanding of concepts and ideas, ability to construct a logical argument, ability to provide clear and logical written answers in strict timescale	E; M	Strict timing Stressful situation But being able to take in notes/ books can reduce stress
Short answer test, online knowledge testing (eg multiple choice)	Knowledge, factual recall, superficial understanding of concepts and ideas	E; M; ICT	Limited in testing understanding of complex ideas
Skills test	Paper-based or online Set of short tasks/activities Test skills such as literacy, numeracy, ICT	E; M; ICT	Generally unsuitable for testing understanding of complex ideas
Essays	Knowledge, understanding of concepts and ideas, factual recall, ability to construct a logical argument, ability to provide clear and logical written answers	E; ICT	Requires good writing skills – formal structure may not suit everyone

TABLE 3.8 *continued*

Type of assessment method	Strengths	Potential for functional skills (FS)	Limitations
Assignments	Knowledge, understanding of concepts and ideas, ability to research different types of information, ability to organize material, ability to manage own time	E; M; ICT	Need to organize time and manage information can be challenging, especially for young learners
Writing articles	Knowledge, understanding of concepts and ideas, ability to summarize for a specific audience	E; M (eg statistics); ICT	High-level literacy skills needed to summarize and synthesize information
Case studies	Allows time to consider written or video 'real-life' scenarios, make judgements and decisions, and solve problems	E; ICT	Can be time-consuming Need to ensure enough information provided for decisions to be made
Writing leaflets, producing leaflets in electronic formats	Knowledge, understanding of concepts and ideas, ability to summarize for a specific audience, ability to lay out information in a way that is easy for others to understand	E; ICT	Danger that the products are very superficial Need to be clear about standard of presentation required
Online discussions, blogs	Knowledge, understanding concepts and ideas, ability to present an argument, ability to interact online with other people, ability to present information, ability to use ICT for online discussion	E; ICT	Could degenerate into anecdotes and 'chat' Could be difficult to moderate for IQA

TABLE 3.8 *continued*

Type of assessment method	Strengths	Potential for functional skills (FS)	Limitations
Portfolios, e-portfolios	Evidence of skills, knowledge, ability to organize and present verbal and visual material in an accessible way; e-portfolios – use of ICT	E; ICT	Could be lots of little bits of evidence rather than holistic
Learner statements	Ability to put evidence in context and provide rationale for actions	E; ICT	Difficulty in knowing how long these should be – can often be far too sketchy in detail
Reflective journals	Ability to evaluate own and others' practice and to use information and ideas from practical experience to develop and improve	E	Could be superficial and over-descriptive rather than evaluative
(b) Oral assessments	*Good test of learners' ability to communicate* *Can provide immediate evidence of achievement/knowledge and understanding* *Helpful for learners with literacy difficulties*	*Depending on task, all FS could be covered*	*Learner may have to respond immediately without time to think* *Harder for learners lacking confidence* *Assessor needs to assess, observe and listen at the same time*
Learner answering questions	Factual knowledge, knowledge of processes and procedures, ability to give answers quickly and clearly	E	Assessor would need to ensure there are no 'leading' questions
Learner devising questions to ask someone else	Factual knowledge, understanding of scope of topic, ability to consider level of audience	E; M	Learner could ask irrelevant questions, leaving assessor with problem about what to assess

TABLE 3.8 *continued*

Type of assessment method	Strengths	Potential for functional skills (FS)	Limitations
Learner presentations	Knowledge, skills in presentation, ability to construct a logical sequence of ideas or information, ability to summarize, ability to consider level of audience, ability to construct interesting visual resources	E; ICT (eg Powerpoint)	If working in a group, assessment would need to take into account not only group presentation, but individual contribution
Simulations	Ability to carry out often complex skills and problem solving in 'real-life' situations usually using real objects/equipment	E; M; ICT	Need to be very carefully prepared Can be resource and time intensive
Role plays	Ability to take on a 'real-life' role when it is not possible to assess in a real-life situation; ability to put self in place of others	E (oral)	Can be stressful Learners can be self-conscious
Participation in group discussions	Ability to put forward ideas or arguments orally, ability to listen to others	E (oral)	Assessor would need to think about how to define constructive participation and what they would look for to assess
Debates	Ability to construct and deliver a logical oral argument from a particular viewpoint; ability to argue against others' ideas, ability to use emotive language	E; M (eg statistics)	Could disadvantage learners lacking in confidence
Song, rap lyrics	Ability to use language creatively, ability to link words and music, ability to use language to suit a particular audience	E	Could disadvantage learners lacking in confidence

TABLE 3.8 *continued*

Type of assessment method	Strengths	Potential for functional skills (FS)	Limitations
(c) Audio/visual assessments	*Opportunities for assessor to see/hear the candidate carrying out practical task/work activity and for candidate to demonstrate practical competence* *Test learner skills in presenting information visually; translating verbal information into visual information*	*Depending on task, all FS could be covered*	*If occurring in the workplace, possibilities that disruptions or cancellations could occur* *Can be very stressful for candidates* *Reliant on all resources being available – can be time-consuming and costly* *Need to produce audio/visual evidence could disadvantage learners lacking in artistic skills*
Observation: Practical task/ work-related activity assessments	Practical activities – being observed by assessor carrying out tasks/ work-related activity and where appropriate resulting product(s) being assessed	E; M; ICT	Could be difficult to arrange, time consuming Could be disruptive and not give a true reflection of performance
Practical demonstrations	Practical skills, oral skills, ability to present practical skills so that other people can understand	E; M	Could disadvantage learners lacking in confidence
Project work, community-based work, event organizing	Research skills, organizing skills, skills of working with others, verbal and oral presentation skills	E; M; ICT	High level of organizational and communications skills required May be too challenging for some learners

TABLE 3.8 *continued*

Type of assessment method	Strengths	Potential for functional skills (FS)	Limitations
Poster displays	Knowledge, ability to summarize using a combination of visual and verbal media, ability to create an interesting display for a particular audience	E; M; ICT	Quite advanced ICT needed Could disadvantage learners lacking access to printing facilities
Art work – drawings, paintings, graphics, 3D designs	Practical skills, ability to use visual media creatively, ability to create an interesting display for a particular audience, spatial ability	M (eg calculations); ICT	Could disadvantage learners lacking in artistic skills
Art or design objects	Practical skills, spatial ability	M (calculations)	Could disadvantage learners lacking in artistic skills
Photographs, using camera or mobile phone	Practical skills, ability to use visual media creatively, ability to summarize using visual rather than verbal media	ICT	Could disadvantage learners not having everyday access to equipment
Production of DVDs or videos	Practical skills, ability to use visual media creatively, ability to summarize, ability to produce for a particular audience	E; ICT	Could disadvantage learners not having everyday access to equipment
Interactive whiteboard displays, web displays	Practical skills, ability to use visual and verbal media, ability to summarize, ability to produce for a particular audience, presentation skills	E; M; ICT	Quite advanced ICT skills needed

TABLE 3.8 *continued*

Type of assessment method	Strengths	Potential for functional skills (FS)	Limitations
Production of radio programmes, podcasts, group texts using mobile phone	Practical skills, ability to use verbal media, ability to summarize, ability to produce for a particular audience, presentation skills, ability to use ICT	E; ICT	Could disadvantage learners not having everyday access to equipment
Production of piece of music	Creative skills, ability to produce for a particular audience	M (musical notation, rythym); ICT	Some learners would be far more comfortable with this than others due to experience outside class
Observation: Practical task/ work-related activity assessments	Practical activities – being observed by assessor carrying out tasks/ work-related activity, and where appropriate resulting product(s) being assessed	M	Could be difficult to arrange, time consuming
Practical demonstrations	Practical skills, oral skills, ability to present practical skills so that other people can understand	E; M	Could disadvantage learners lacking in confidence
Project work, community-based work, event organizing	Research skills, organizing skills, skills of working with others, verbal and oral presentation skills	E; M; ICT	High level of organizational and communications skills required May be too challenging for some learners

---

Examples

- Learner might undertake online skills tests to establish their current level of ICT. This can test practical ICT skills such as developing or editing an electronic presentation.

- A learner just beginning a Level 2 certificate in controlling parking areas might be given a knowledge test to find out what s/he knows already about the legal requirements and constraints for those operating in this area of work.

Formative assessment: We need to make sure that the chosen method(s) will help the learner to practise and develop the skills/knowledge they will need to perform well in their summative assessment.

Summative assessment: We need to make sure the method allows the candidate to meet the specified assessment criteria and that it operates within awarding organization guidelines. We also need to take a 'holistic' assessment approach where the learner has an opportunity to meet a number of outcomes/assessment criteria, rather than carrying out piecemeal assessments.

In assessing occupational competence, there are accepted methods for assessment, as identified in QCF Unit 2. In assessing vocational knowledge and skills, teachers may draw from a whole range of methods to give more opportunity for valid assessments and more opportunity to develop a broader range of knowledge and skills in their learners. This is where the context of the assessment becomes very important. In the workplace, the employee being assessed needs to be competent to perform their job. Although appraisal systems will identify future training needs and potentials for job enhancement or promotion, these are all within the context of that particular organization.

What are the time/cost constraints?

Assessors in the work environment may need to factor in travel time to carry out workplace observations and may need to observe for quite a lengthy period to see a whole process being carried out. It makes sense to maximize the opportunity by using a range of complementary methods so the candidate can produce substantial evidence against a number of outcomes.

The focus of the assessment may be on the process of performing a practical task such as electrical wiring or greeting a new customer at reception. When deciding on the assessment method(s) consider whether the assessment would provide the opportunities for addressing a number of assessment criteria. So a practical assessment combined with oral questioning might assess not only practical skills but some criteria related to the learner's knowledge of what they are doing. This links to the QCF emphasis on holistic assessment, where the assessment can take into account practical skills and the knowledge underpinning specific skills.

In a vocational education and training context, teachers/assessors with learners studying as a learning group also need to use methods that are valid and reliable, and as time-effective as possible. Assessment can be extremely time-consuming. For example, a teacher could easily spend 15 hours marking written assignments from a group of 30 learners, and as many teachers/assessors know, this means evenings and weekends sitting with a pile of work rather than relaxing or catching up with their household chores! However, the plus side of assessments of groups is that teachers have more opportunity to use interesting assessment methods, for example those involving peer-assessment, small group projects and learner presentations to peer groups.

Example

The assessment for learners on a QCF diploma in automotive maintenance and repair might involve completing a project on common problems with different makes of car. Although the learning outcome and assessment criteria would be the same for everyone, individual learners could decide on which type of car interested them most and focus on that particular make. They could then present their findings to the rest of the group.

Timescales

Assessments of learners on QCF qualifications in vocational education and training contexts will often have to fit in with the institution's academic year, including the quality-assurance cycle and the deadlines for reporting and confirmation of results. Externally set end tests or examinations are usually set at specific dates or times of the year. For example, as summative assessment, City and Guilds offers Global Online Assessment (GOLA) at scheduled dates and times that have a strict timeframe. So candidates for the Level 2 certificate in gardening can only access their online 30-minute end test for up to four hours before or after the scheduled time. City and Guilds also provide GOLA practice tests that can be used for formative feedback and indication of readiness to proceed with the end test.

Personal or professional circumstances might also dictate an especially tight timescale. One example from our experience involved a candidate who was pregnant and would be taking maternity leave from work. In this situation she wanted to have achieved the qualification before taking the leave, as she would be otherwise occupied in the following months!

You will also need to consider the cost involved with different methods. Finding out what someone knows through professional discussion may be more time-consuming and less cost-effective for the assessor as it can take a considerable time for the assessor to reference the discussion to the outcomes and criteria met by the activity, though careful planning with the candidate, prior to the discussion, can help. However, professional discussion is likely to be quicker for the candidate. A written multiple choice test administered to a group of candidates will probably be cheaper and quicker for both candidate and assessor, but there might need to be further assessment to fill in any 'gaps' in evidence.

Methods identified in the QCF assessor qualifications

We will now consider in more detail the QCF methods identified at the start of this section, which appear in Table 3.8. We will also discuss the use of reflective journals as they are a popular method for providing evidence of evaluation, learning and improvement, used in many different contexts. We will consider the methods in the following order:

a) Observation of performance in the work environment and in simulated environments.

b) Questioning the learner: oral and written questions.

c) Examining products of work.

d) Skills tests.

e) Discussing with the learner.

f) Using statements from others (witness testimony).

g) Learner statements.

h) Written assignments/tasks.

i) Case studies.

j) Recognizing prior learning.

k) Reflective journals.

a) Observation of performance in the work environment and in simulated environments

The processes for observation, particularly if the vocational assessment observation takes place in a busy environment with paying clients, such as a college hairdressing salon, will be similar. The main differences are that in a workplace environment the candidates' colleagues are likely to be qualified workers, and the candidate will actually be at work – with the potential pressures that this involves. The focus here will primarily be on assessment. In a simulated training environment, the learner/candidate's colleagues will be their fellow learners and the focus will be on learning as well as assessment.

Observation of performance in the workplace

This is the main method by which occupational competence (ie can the person do the work properly!) should be assessed and involves either observation of performance or examination of the end product. Many people in work will have been involved in informal assessment of performance by observing and making judgements about how effectively someone is doing his or her job. Instructors or trainers will be used to watching how an individual trainee learns or behaves, and will make mental notes on areas of strength and areas where the trainee may need help. These observations also need to be recorded in writing, preferably using a checklist derived from the required competencies, with a space for detailing the evidence that has been observed.

In order for observation to be effective, the assessor should keep the following in mind:

- Ensure that the candidate has been involved in the planning process and clearly understands what will happen.

- Be clear about what is being assessed and the processes involved.

- Use a checklist to record judgements and comments.

- Try to give the candidate some control over the conditions; for example ask the candidate's opinion on the best place for the assessor to stand or sit and, if feasible, respect his or her wishes. If not familiar with the place of assessment, try to visit it beforehand.

- Keep out of the eyeline of the person being assessed.

- If the candidate's work involves interacting with clients or colleagues, keep out of their eyeline and workspace. Avoid becoming involved in what is being observed.

- Ensure the candidate knows that the needs of any client should take precedence over the needs of the observing assessor (though hopefully, by following occupational standards, both will be accommodated).

- Make sure that anyone else involved is informed and reassured about the presence of an observer.

- Whenever possible, find time after the observation to give immediate feedback and discuss what has been observed and achieved.

- Ensure that all external visitors to the candidate's workplace (eg assessors, verifiers) comply with the requirements of the organization and with relevant legislation, such as the Health and Safety at Work Act.

Observation of the learner in simulated environments

A simulated environment is set up to mirror as near as possible the conditions and activities related to a real-life situation.

Examples in vocational education and training

- a training restaurant;
- a training hairdressing and beauty salon;
- a training garden centre;
- a training motor repair workshop;
- a training animal care centre.

In these examples, learners will be trained and assessed to standards expected in the workplace. They will have contact with clients and, according to their level of study, will gradually have an increasingly complex range of tasks and duties to perform under supervision. The simulated environment will expect learners to pay attention to timescales and economic ways of carrying out tasks, as well as being able to carry out tasks effectively. They will also need to fulfil any legal requirements and regulations, including health and safety procedures and wearing of protective clothing. The teacher has ample opportunity to give formative assessment in this context, as well as preparing learners for summative assessments. A significant part of the assessment will involve the same methods as assessing occupational competence, such as observation of work-related performance and the products of work.

Observations: Example of initial, formative, summative assessment in simulated environments

- *Initial*: An initial assessment for learners on a certificate in food preparation takes place in one of the first sessions in the college training kitchen. Learners can select from a range of ingredients to make a sandwich for their lunch. They are asked to identify one source of carbohydrate (the bread), one source of protein and at least one salad item to include in the sandwich (initial assessment of basic knowledge about food components). They are then given time to prepare ingredients and make the sandwich. By observing and questioning, the teacher/assessor can assess each learner's current skills and knowledge on sandwich preparation.

- *Formative*: In the next practical session on sandwich making, the learners are reminded of the assessment criteria prior to beginning and the teacher walks around giving individual formative feedback against these criteria – inviting the learner to self-assess against the criteria first. The process may become more complex so as to incorporate more assessment criteria relating to a simulated 'real' work environment, time constraints and customer service. Learners will also become more aware of how the grading process works and the criteria used to determine grades. Formative feedback will give them information that they can use to improve their grades.

- *Summative*: The summative assessment involves each learner/ candidate making different sandwiches under real life pressures, for example serving in the training café at the college. By the time of the summative assessment, the learners should be very clear about the assessment criteria used by the assessor and what these mean in practice. There should be no surprises!

b) Questioning the learner: oral and written questions

Questioning can be a very effective way of finding out what a learner knows or understands.

In most work contexts the testing of knowledge and understanding in assessing occupational competence will normally be oral rather than written. For example, a supervisor will ask an employee why s/he has increased the speed of a manufacturing process, how s/he intends to use the new floor polisher in a safe manner, or what the ratio of sand and cement is to water for a particular mix of concrete. Every occupation has its underpinning knowledge and understanding requirements, which are used as a basis for assessment. In order to carry out an oral assessment, assessors need a thorough knowledge of the standards, so that they are able to ask appropriate questions.

The use of questions, either oral or written, is the main method for establishing whether the candidate has knowledge and understanding across a range of contexts and contingencies. This is vital, as, without knowing what exactly he or she is doing, why and what the possible alternatives are, there is little possibility that an individual will be able to transfer any skill from one situation to another. Instead of the desired highly skilled and flexible workforce, we might end up with a nation of robots.

Questions can be used in:

- *Initial assessment*: they can provide the teacher with immediate feedback about an individual learner's or a group's current level and range of knowledge.

- *Formative assessment*: questions provide both teacher and learner with information about how the learner is progressing in their understanding of a fact, task or concept, in order to correct misunderstandings or move on to more complex material.

- *Summative assessment*: well-constructed, valid questions can establish whether a learner has reached the required standard in a task or activity.

An assessor could ask questions at appropriate times during an observation or set aside a separate time after the observation to ask all the necessary questions together.

It is obviously important to choose questioning methods appropriate to the activity being tested. The next sections will consider the different types of oral questions that can be used.

Open and closed questions

Questions can be closed or open. Closed questions have a restricted response such as 'yes' or 'no' – for instance: 'Is Paris the capital of France?' – or one correct answer (for instance: 'What is the capital of France?'); open questions can elicit a variety of responses like 'What do you think of higher education tuition fees? or 'Why might a child not want to play?'

Open questions associated with prompt words such as 'How?' and 'Why?' offer the opportunity for candidates to respond fully and in their own words. Closed questions are associated with phrases such as 'Do you think...?', where the candidate can only respond with 'Yes' or 'No', and with prompt words such as 'What?' and 'Where?', when the candidate is required to respond with specific factual information.

Choosing the right type of question

Assessors need to be clear on why they are asking the question and what answer or answers will be acceptable. At Levels 1 or 2, it is likely that questions will be simple and closed because specific factual knowledge is being tested. For example, a candidate taking a Level 2 in construction might be asked 'Can you give me five examples of construction work that would need to be protected against the weather while other work was being finished?' The assessor will know the range of acceptable answers and will accept any five of these answers from the candidate. Some more open questions may also be appropriate, for example asking the candidate why he or she is using a particular process or piece of equipment. It is likely that the answers to these questions will be fairly short and simple.

When deciding on the questions to ask, you need to be aware of the functions of different types of questions (see Table 3.9).

For higher level qualifications, the question-and-answer process will inevitably become far more complex. For example, a middle manager who is a candidate on a QCF Level 5 management and leadership qualification may need to show that he or she has an effective management style. The candidate's underpinning knowledge of why he or she has adopted a particular style over others could be assessed by a variety of techniques. These could include questioning and discussion between the assessor, the candidate and the candidate's colleagues, and demonstration by the candidate that his or

TABLE 3.9 Different functions of questions

Function	Example
Set at ease	'Would you like a coffee?' 'What sort of journey have you had?'
Ask for general information	'What were your responsibilities as...?' 'What have you been doing in the past year?'
Ask for specific information	'What is your name?' 'How do you save data onto a memory stick?' 'Precisely what does that entail?'
Ask for further information	'Could you tell me some more about that?' 'Can you give me some more details?'
Ask the reason or justification	'Can you tell me why you used that particular technique?' 'Why is ice put in the glass before pouring the drink?'
Ask for opinions, ideas	'What do you think of this product?' 'Do you believe in positive discrimination?'

her chosen style results in positive outcomes from the candidate's staff and the achievement of corporate objectives. This would be far more useful and valid than asking the candidate to write a report or assignment on 'Comparing and contrasting different management styles, with special reference to the work situation'.

Questioning skills
Effective questioning involves considerable skill on the part of the assessor. Some of the skills are identified below:

- Putting the candidate at ease. It goes without saying that candidates are likely to be nervous, and the assessor needs to be sensitive to this. The more confident candidates feel, the more likely it is that they will be able to give a true representation of what they really know. It usually helps if candidates actually know what the procedure will be, know that they can ask for a question to be repeated and know that they can take their time answering.
- Ensuring the language is at the right level and can be understood. Be clear as to what is being tested and avoid using over-complex

language if this is not necessary. Be aware of what candidates' normal range of vocabulary is likely to be and take that into account when phrasing questions. Distinguish between essential technical jargon that candidates will need in their vocational area and unnecessary use of over-sophisticated vocabulary.

● Not asking leading questions. Assessors should be careful not to use questions that could lead candidates by giving them a clue to the right answer (see examples in the box below). Assessors should also be aware of any preferences or opinions they might hold that could affect the way they ask questions. It is just as easy to lead candidates by the tone or inflection of voice or by some facial expression or body movement. One assessor we know would automatically purse her lips and lean forward slightly if the answer she was getting was incorrect. However difficult it may be, a neutral but pleasant expression is the ideal.

Examples of leading questions are:

● 'Your client seemed a bit uncomfortable, didn't she?'

● 'Don't you think you should have cleaned the floor before varnishing it?'

● 'Why would you say UPVC was better than wood?'

Each question should be specific, easy to understand and not phrased in such a way that an answer has been suggested or a bias on the part of the assessor is indicated. For example, a question such as 'Don't you think you should have cleared the work area before you began the next job?' is hardly a question at all, but an indication that the assessor thinks that the candidate has done something wrong. The evidence produced through the candidate's answer to this question would not allow the assessor to make a fair judgement on the candidate's understanding of a process.

If you are a new assessor, it is worthwhile practising oral questioning techniques and asking for feedback from colleagues or your internal verifier.

Questions can also be at different levels

Bloom's (1956) taxonomy, although developed a long time ago, has been very influential in providing a means of categorizing levels of difficulty of questions and is still used today in the development of educational objectives and in distinguishing between low and high level questions. Bloom identified three domains of learning – cognitive (thinking); affective (feeling); psychomotor (doing) – and six levels in the cognitive domain of learning,

TABLE 3.10 Levels of difficulty of questions

Cognitive domain	Types of question words	Example of question
Knowledge: recalling information, facts	Define; list; what…?; where?	What are the main ingredients of Yorkshire pudding?
Comprehension: understanding the main aspects of an idea or process	Describe; explain; discuss; How does…?	How does a car engine work?
Application: applying existing information in practice	Apply; demonstrate; use; what would happen if…? What could happen if…?	What could happen if you didn't put on your safety helmet at a building site?
Analysis: breaking down information/ideas into component parts in order to be able to offer suggestions/draw conclusions	Analyse; give reasons why…; what is the cause of…? Why…?	What are the reasons why the plants in the greenhouse did better than the plants left outside?
Synthesis: pulling together lots of information/ideas to develop general principles/theories/creative approaches to solve problems	Design; create; plan; offer solutions to; 'How would you deal with…?'	How would you deal with an angry customer who wouldn't leave the office?
Evaluation: judging the value of information, ideas or actions	Criticize; compare; evaluate; 'Which is the best…. and why?'	Which of the following products offer the best value for money? Give your reasons why.

with 'knowledge' (that is, being able to recall information) being the lowest level, and 'evaluation' (that is, ascertaining the value of information/ideas) being the highest level. The six levels are shown in Table 3.10).

Types of written questions used in tests
There are a number of different types of written questioning used within vocational qualifications, and the choice of the appropriate test format depends entirely on what level and complexity of knowledge and understanding need to be demonstrated. The main ones are:

Yes/No or True/False response. A statement is followed by either a Yes/No or True/False response to be ticked or circled.

> Example: A larch tree is an evergreen. True/False

Objective tests (multiple choice). A question is asked followed by several alternatives, out of which one must be selected.

> **Example**
>
> A chronological filing system is one where files are arranged according to:
>
> - geographical area;
> - initial letter of surname;
> - date received;
> - reference number.

Gapped statements. A statement or longer piece of text is given, with a space or spaces left for the candidate to complete.

> Example: Foods that are high in fibre include... and...

NB: Sometimes the candidate is free to write any appropriate word and sometimes the word or words can be selected from a given list.

Short answer tests. These give a series of questions that require answers of a few words or a few lines.

> Example: Explain briefly how a colour correction filter works.

Essays. These cover set topics, usually with a defined number of words, often involving research through reading and including the structuring and development of ideas.

> Example: Discuss how different learning theories can be used in planning training programmes.

Reports. These cover a set subject with clearly defined objectives based on practical research and laid out with headings, following a conventional report structure.

> Example: Write a report on the procedures for employee appraisal within your organization, with recommendations for improvement.

Setting tests

This book cannot go into the depth required on this broad subject. Many awarding organizations now have substantial guidance and examples on setting tests. One crucial factor in setting tests are that they have validity in relation to what needs to be assessed, for example they have construct validity ('fitness for purpose') and content validity (they test relevant parts of the syllabus). In order to be valid assessments, test questions need to be designed so candidates cannot guess the answers – this seems obvious, but poorly designed multiple choice tests may enable candidates to guess the answer.

As an example, look at the following multiple choice test designed as part of a test on nutrition.

Multiple choice example: Original version
Name the odd one out:

1 Mandarin.

2 Satsuma.

3 Grapefruit.

4 Clementine.

The answer is 'grapefruit' (because it is alkaline rather than acidic). However, a lucky guess might have occurred because a candidate looked at the colours of the fruit and all were orange, except the grapefruit, which is yellow!

Multiple choice example: Amended version

1 Mandarin.

2 Satsuma.

3 Grapefruit.

4 Clementine.

5 Lime.

By the addition of lime, another fruit that is not orange, the opportunity for a lucky guess becomes less. Hence the multiple choice becomes a more valid test of someone's knowledge of acidity and alkalinity in fruits.

Marking criteria

The marking criteria for a test would be based on the assessment criteria in the unit. If the test was summative, there would be a pass mark identified based on the number of correct answers. In tests devised by the awarding organization this is the case; in centre devised tests, the pass mark will be agreed within the assessment team.

Candidates would need to be clear about the criteria used and the basis on which a pass would be awarded or if the test is graded, the marks associated with different grades.

c) Examining products of work

Work products are very satisfying to assess as they often show the culmination of a learner's training. Examples are memos or reports, assignments or photographs produced by the candidate, items the candidate has made, such as a cake, a painted wall, a graphic design, a repaired tyre; a plan of work; an assessment plan.

Holistic assessment planning would cover both the process of production and the final product so that authenticity is assured.

Other examples of products of work could be the records of a process, such as checklists for patient care, health and safety checks, MOT checks. They may be documents produced as a result of a process, such as an MOT certificate or a health and safety report, or documents that show communication with others, such as letters or memos. Other products of work may be written assignments or photographs, graphs, charts and other materials produced by the candidate.

d) Skills tests

The term 'skills tests' covers a number of different tests and is used in different ways according to the context. Some awarding organizations use the term 'skills tests' to refer to specified vocational assessments, often devised by the awarding organization, which test a whole range of practical skills, often by direct observation. For example a C&G qualification in practical horticulture skills has skills tests where the assessor observes candidates: 'prune shrubs for winter stem colour, prune hedges by hand, prune rose bushes, dead head rose bushes'.

However, the term 'skills tests' is also used to refer to interactive tests, formerly paper-based but now often accessed online. These are usually to test job skills, job or career preferences or key/functional skills. They offer a variety of different testing types: multiple choice/multiple answer; true/false; fill in blanks; essays (usually short); comment boxes (eg for commenting on given extracts), as well as interactive tasks for certain vocational areas, for example an 'in-basket' prioritizing exercise in a course on office skills. Online skills tests can use a variety of media such as pictures, graphs, sound files, film clips. The tests can be time constrained and designed for private or public access. Teachers can access the responses and view the results. A major advantage for teachers using this type of assessment is that learners can work individually, but all the results can be collated and made available to the teacher. Hence they have the potential to be time- and cost-effective.

Initial assessment. You might decide to give learners a skills test to give you information as a teacher about how best to support each learner and whether they need any additional support needs.

Formative assessment. Skills tests might be used formatively. For example in a literacy skills test, formative assessments from a skills test bank, where questions at a particular level are designed to be of equivalent standard and difficulty, would give the learner and teacher an indication of improvement as a result of specific teaching input or additional support.

Summative assessment. Practical skills tests form a major part of the summative assessment of some vocational qualifications.

e) Discussing with the learner

Assessments can be made by using evidence elicited through discussion: by having a planned, recorded discussion where the candidate is prompted to talk through his or her role and activities, and shows supporting evidence (ideally captured on video) to validate the knowledge and performance claims being made.

This method gives the candidate an opportunity to talk through, demonstrate, show and clarify aspects of his or her work that still need evidencing and/or for which other types of assessment are less appropriate. This also gives opportunities for the offering and protection of confidentiality and security and the demonstration of complex competencies, knowledge and understanding.

The discussion must be recorded in some way. An audio recording is unobtrusive and gives proof of the discussion without interfering with the activities of either candidate or assessor. The assessor can take photographic evidence to augment the recorded conversations. There is no necessity to transcribe the conversation. If the camera can record date and time, this is often a more acceptable form of recording 'live' evidence than is video, and sits well alongside an indexed audiotape. A video recording can be used where it would cause no disruption to normal work activity and where the candidate feels it would aid his or her demonstration of competence. It is important that permission to be recorded is obtained from anyone else who might be involved. The third method of recording, taking down the discussion verbatim, is the most difficult to do, as the assessor is less able to give full attention to the candidate, and the discussion can become stilted owing to the need to write everything down exactly as it is spoken.

f) Using statements from others (witness testimony)

Another method for the candidate to provide evidence is to use statements from other credible individuals or organizations that confirm aspects of the candidate's competence against particular learning outcomes and criteria. This is sometimes called 'witness' testimony, a term that has the ring of the courtroom about it. This is a useful to bear in mind when deciding who is likely to be a credible 'witness' to someone's competence – this would not be a close relative or friend, and not someone who would have had little opportunity to see in any detail the candidate's working practices. The statements should provide relevant evidence from past activities and situations when the witness has seen the candidate carrying out work to the required standards. The assessor will review and check statements from credible witnesses, matching them to assessment criteria.

g) Learner statements

Learner statements are important in helping the assessor to understand the context and background for the evidence provided and the rationale for including that evidence. In a learner statement learners can explain the thinking behind their decision to take a certain approach or why they decided to change aspects of a task or activity. Learner statements are also a means for the candidate to provide a commentary that links holistic pieces of evidence to specific outcomes and criteria. Awarding organizations or different education/training organizations may provide pro-formas that provide a structure for the learner statements.

h) Written assignments/tasks

A written assignment or task is a very familiar form of assessment in educational settings and has considerable 'face' validity, as written work is an expected form of assessment in that context. In vocational education and training, an assignment is likely to be used as a summative assessment, drawing together the learning from a range of classroom/workshop-based activities. However, it is likely that the teacher will build in at least one opportunity for formative assessment of a part or draft of the assignment.

An assignment differs from an essay in that its focus is practical – an investigation into something or a report on a particular subject, whereas an essay has a theoretical focus. A written assignment would be considerably longer than a single written task undertaken during the same course of study. It might also include supporting materials such as photographs, charts, graphs, leaflets, visual displays or CDs. However, assignments may be built up through learners completing a series of written tasks that together make up the assignment. In this case, it would be expected that learners must pass all the tasks within the assignment, although they may be given one opportunity to repeat the task to improve their grade.

Awarding organizations often produce standard assignments for their qualifications, although they may offer more than one version of the assignment so it can suit different learner's circumstances. Written assignments cover set topics, usually entailing some practical research and written explanation and analysis of what has been discovered. They may also include tasks that are short answer or multiple choice tests.

When setting assignments, you need to give very clear instructions (see box below).

Example of assignment instruction

'Choose one specific client group in the community, eg young mothers, pensioners, etc. Find out what services are provided for them and their opinion of these services. Compare local to national provision. Present your information using both written and visual means.'

Examples of assignment tasks

Learners taking a C&G advanced certificate in floristry complete an assignment on diverse flower and plant care. This involves them completing a series of tasks prescribed by the awarding organization. One task involves them being shown 10 pot plants and being asked to identify them in writing on the pro-forma provided, using the correct botanical name and completing other details such as the genus and species of the plant.

On the same course, learners have to design four different planted containers, each suitable for a different micro-climate. They have to sketch the designs and provide appropriate supplementary information for each, including the botanical names of the plants, the plant groups to which they belong, the environmental conditions necessary for each design and the reasons behind their choice.

Learners on a BTEC Level 2 certificate in sustainability skills, complete an assignment devised with the Woodland Trust, where they have to audit all the types of trees in a given area, devise questions and interview local people for their views on the benefits and importance of trees, and then present their findings in the form of a poster or a presentation.

Assignment documentation

Unless provided by the awarding organization, centres will devise their own documentation to present assignment briefs. Completed briefs will be approved before use by the internal verifier. Typically, the following information will be included:

- *Assignment cover sheet*: candidate name; course; year; unit number(s) and title(s) (for holistic assessment, we would expect a number of units to be covered through the one assignment); tutor name; brief number, brief title, start date; hand-in date; date submitted, date returned; assignment instructions. There may also be a section to agree an extension – agreed extension date; signed tutor; date; signed candidate; date.
- *Assignment briefing sheet*: detailed instructions to students on what the assignment entails, identifying clearly what they have to do, the timescale for the work, what needs to be submitted as evidence of planning or progress.
- Suggested resources to be used for the assignment.

The evidence learners need to present should be clearly identified against the relevant units and criteria. If grading is used, then the unit(s) and evidence should be identified together with descriptions of the criteria for pass (P), merit (M) and distinction (D) for each item of evidence. Each centre will have its own system or documentation to record this, whether devised by the centre or provided by the awarding organization.

Feedback for assignments

Formative feedback might be given orally with a brief record sheet of feedback, action plan and date for each learner, or there might be more detailed written feedback given to the learner, which might need to be included in the final submission.

The summative feedback sheet for each unit will identify the unit title, outcomes and criteria and, if graded, the criteria for achievement at pass, merit and distinction with columns for evidence provided and areas for development. There will be space for the final grade to be identified.

Projects

The terms 'assignment' and 'project' are often used interchangeably and this can be confusing for the new assessor. We have seen both terms used on the same assessment brief given to learners. As usual, we suggest you clarify with colleagues how the term is understood in your own context. Projects are highly practical forms of assessment, covering substantial knowledge and work-related skills. Especially at higher levels, these can be substantial pieces of work.

Examples

- Learners on a Level 3 diploma in production arts learn about stage lighting and sound, video projection, stage management, set construction and painting, technical maintenance and electrical installation. For their assessments they may be involved in a major project working with a theatre group putting on a whole production.

- Students on an IT National Diploma course have to liaise with a real organization and work with them to design a website or a database that would be of use to them. They need to complete progress reports and present the final design to the client. They then have to write a report on the project.

Because projects assess a whole range of practical skills and can take a considerable time to complete, students are often given project briefs quite early in the academic year so they have time to prepare. Major projects often form a significant part of the summative assessment for a course. Some projects are externally set by the awarding organization.

The briefing documentation for project briefs and feedback might be very similar to that for assignments.

i) Case studies

Case studies are written descriptions of specific situations that prompt discussion and analysis of real life issues, dilemmas or problems. They may be based on actual (but anonymized) circumstances or they may be fictional, but based on knowledge of issues and problems likely to occur in the relevant occupational area. Case studies often involve the learner in making a decision or decisions on a particular course of action, based on the information provided. They may also involve the learners making judgements on other people's decisions as presented in the case study. Responses may be oral – individual or group – or written, usually on an individual basis. Case studies can be used for both formative and summative assessment. For example, case studies are sometimes used as the main focus in open book examinations.

j) Recognizing prior learning

Applicants for a course in a vocational setting, such as an FE college, will have the opportunity to use RPL towards part of the qualification. They would go through the process with a college advisor. This would involve looking at the units, outcomes and criteria for the course, and matching evidence from prior learning and experience against these. Some courses contain units of different levels, for example some at Level 2 and some at Level 3. An applicant for a course at Level 3 may previously have completed a qualification at Level 2 in the same vocational area. In this case, the units from the Level 2 qualification would be counted towards the Level 3 course, and s/he would be given RPL against those units.

Once the evidence is reviewed, the assessor needs to decide whether it proves that the candidate has met the required criteria, and the scope and/or range of the unit or assignment.

k) Reflective journals

Another major form of evidence for assessment in vocational education and training, especially for qualifications that involve working with people, such as learning and development, childcare, youth work, is the use of reflective journals.

Reflective journals are a way for learners to chart their personal/professional growth and development on a regular basis over a course of study. In QCF qualifications the reflection is also geared to how well the learner is progressing in relation to the relevant national occupational standards. Reflective practice is an important part of professional/vocational development and is strongly embedded in professions such as teaching and nursing.

At the most basic level, reflection involves the learner asking questions such as: 'What happened? How did I deal with it? How did I feel? How did others react? What did I do well? What would I do differently next time?' At a more advanced level, reflection can involve complex thinking and analysis. Roth (1989) gives a comprehensive summary of possible reflective processes. These include:

- questioning what, why and how one does things and asking what, why and how others do things;
- seeking alternatives;
- keeping an open mind;
- comparing and contrasting;

- seeking the framework, theoretical basis and/or underlying rationale;
- viewing from various perspectives;
- asking 'what if...?'
- asking for others' ideas and viewpoints;
- using prescriptive models only when adapted to the situation;
- considering consequences;
- hypothesizing;
- synthesizing and testing out ideas/actions;
- seeking, identifying and resolving problems.

(Roth, 1989)

There are problems with using reflective journals as summative assessments, in that they can be highly personalized accounts of learning from experience. However, they can provide evidence of, for example, candidates' ability to self-assess, self-evaluate and improve their performance, knowledge and understanding related to practice, reasoning behind choices and decisions, and learning from contact with others, such as colleagues or internal quality assurers. They can also show the processes behind practice, for example how work plans are developed, how meetings with learners are approached and so on, as well as learning from experiences. As a candidate assessor, some of your evidence could come from a reflective journal, where you reflect on aspects of your work and role, such as experiences with your own candidates, learning from standardization meetings and how you approach assessment planning.

LEARNING OUTCOME 3:
UNDERSTAND HOW TO PLAN ASSESSMENT

ASSESSMENT CRITERIA

3.1 Summarize key factors to consider when planning assessment.

3.2 Evaluate the benefits of using a holistic approach to assessment.

3.3 Explain how to plan a holistic approach to assessment.

3.4 Summarize the types of risks that may be involved in assessment in own area of responsibility.

3.5 Explain how to minimize risks through the planning process.

3.1 Summarize key factors to consider when planning assessment

Planning (see Table 3.11) is the first part of five stages of the assessment process:

1 Planning for assessment.
2 Carrying out the assessment.
3 Judging all evidence against agreed criteria.
4 Recording assessment decisions and giving feedback.
5 Contributing to quality-assurance processes.

Planning for assessing different stages of learning

Initial assessments may use standardized assessment documentation produced by the centre or awarding organization, for example to assess the level of literacy and numeracy of a learner at the beginning of a vocational course. However, it may be up to the individual teacher/assessor to devise an appropriate initial assessment for their vocational area (see Outcome 2). This might plan to use one or more of a number of methods, including:

- an initial knowledge check where learners answer written questions, such as multiple choice questions;

TABLE 3.11 Factors to consider when planning for assessment

Vocational

Before the course begins, work through the assessment specification and check your understanding of what is required from candidates with colleagues, administration and examinations staff, including dates for registering candidates for the qualification.

Decide when and how you will give candidates an overview of the assessment requirements of the qualification. There is a dilemma here – some may be frightened by the amount of 'work' they see (though they should have been told the full requirements before enrolling for the course/ qualification), but to give only a partial picture means that candidates will not be able to plan their study/work/life arrangements appropriately.

Prepare an assessment timetable to cover the programme, which needs to be shared with other staff working on the same qualification who may have their own assessments to give, so that assessments are spread evenly for candidates.

Decide how candidates will access the assessment specification – via the awarding organization website, or will you e-mail them copies, or will there be hard copies? Will you adapt anything to suit your candidates (for example, font size) but without altering the requirements.

Check that all candidates understand the terminology used in the assessment specification and the grading critiera.

Plan 'mock tests' and times to introduce candidates to external test conditions or requirements.

Work-based

Review the assessment guidance, qualification units and learning outcomes. Check that candidates are registered for the qualification, and know the dates for internal quality assurance and the documentation required.

Review the qualification units and their assessment requirements with your candidate. Identify areas for RPL. Discuss holistic approaches the assessment for the qualification.

Negotiate assessment plans with your candidates that cover the assessment criteria, using holistic approaches, and identify the methods for assessment. Identify some prospective dates for assessment. Plan when oral feedback will be given and make dates for this if it will occur at separate times from the workplace assessment. Decide who is responsible for liaising with the workplace about the assessment visit.

Inform your IQA of the planned assessment dates.

A week or so before the first check the readiness of your candidate for assessment, and whether the arrangements are in place. Let your IQA know if there are changes.

- an initial practical assessment of a particular skill, for example checking how well carpentry students can use a range of woodworking tools;
- an initial self-assessment by each learner, identifying strengths and areas of development.

Planning for formative and summative assessment

If you are a course leader you will have to work with the course team to produce a course plan that includes the nature and timing of formative and summative assessments. This includes timings for examinations/end tests and quality-assurance processes, such as verification. Learners also need to be given an overview of assessments for the course and it would be expected that they would be given a course timetable that indicates the timings and spread of formative and summative assessments throughout the year.

Planning for summative assessment may involve designing and presenting assignment or project briefs for learners. It will certainly involve planning how to fit in the teaching of a subject whilst allowing enough time for assessment, feedback and submitting results to meet awarding organization deadlines.

Questions to consider when beginning the planning process

a) Do I have any freedom in what the assessment activity will be, or do I have to follow a prescribed assessment activity?

Prescribed activities: If you have to follow a prescribed assessment activity, you need to understand the assessment method(s) required and the conditions under which the assessment needs to take place, such as the location and amount of supervision required. If you are using an assessment activity devised by an awarding organization, there should be written guidance on how it should be carried out, so that all assessors across the country carry out the activity in the same way.

If your learners/candidates have to do an online test (sometimes called 'onscreen' tests) through an awarding organization, make sure you have the information about the test well in advance. This can be found on the relevant website with a list of onscreen tests available, the number of questions and the time limit for each test. So, for example, Edexcel's test for 'Key principles of team leading' has 25 questions and lasts 45 minutes. Your planning for an end test needs to ensure that learners are well prepared and ready to take the assessment (and that all the necessary registration procedures have taken place).

Freedom to design assessment: If you do have some freedom to design the assessment, check if the awarding organization or other organizations have produced ideas/suggestions to help you in your planning. Experienced colleagues or those involved in internal quality assurance can be an invaluable source of advice and help in designing assignments. Ask them to show you examples of previous assessments – not only the assessment activities, but also feedback and how the results are recorded. This will help you get a sense of the 'shape' of the whole assessment process.

b) What regulations/standards must I take into account?

You will need to take into account the awarding organization's and centre's regulations very carefully, as well as any relevant national occupational standards. You also need to be clear about the level of the qualification and what that means in terms of the level of difficulty of the assessment. Other regulations you will need to take into account relate to health and safety, safeguarding, equality and diversity (See Unit 1, Outcome 1).

c) What competences or criteria will be assessed?

QCF qualifications have clearly identified learning outcomes and assessment criteria for each unit. NVQs have elements and performance criteria. You need to decide which outcomes and criteria need to be met through a particular assessment. Some QCF qualifications are graded, so in those cases planning will take into account the grading criteria and ways in which formative assessments and feedback can help learners/candidates develop and improve their grades.

d) How will they be assessed?

There are a whole range of assessment methods available depending on the knowledge/skills that need to be assessed. You should consider the learning domain(s) being assessed (See Unit 1, Outcome 1 and ensure the methods are the most appropriate. Some key methods of assessment have been discussed in Unit 1, Outcome 2). In both Unit 2 and Unit 3, assessments will need to provide opportunities for recognition of prior learning. Your planning for the assessments will need to take into account timing, location, organization of the assessment, the resources that will be required and any requirements for supervision of the assessment. For example, if an examination needs an invigilator, has the examinations officer made the necessary arrangements?

e) Who will be involved in the assessment?

Apart from the assessor and candidate(s), other people (such as employers) may be involved. As the assessor, you will make the majority of assessments, but you may be assisted in this process by:

- other assessors with whom the assessor may need to coordinate, for example across a course team or to help the candidate transfer learning from one qualification to another;
- second assessors to confirm a mark or a grade;
- credible witnesses, who will need to write statements;

- an independent assessor to make a specific specialist assessment;
- internal verifiers/IQAs to sample the assessments.

Also, some of these might be involved:

- employers, line managers or supervisors, who may wish to be involved with feedback;
- technical staff, to make sure the appropriate facilities are available;
- quality coordinators or managers, who may need reports;
- candidates' colleagues or their own learners/candidates who may be affected;
- centre examinations officer;
- administration staff, for processing registrations and certification requests;
- caretakers and car parking and security staff.

Many of these other people will not need support as such, but will be involved as part of the quality and administration process surrounding assessment.

f) When will they be assessed?
All assessment planning will need to:

- take into account any dates of external tests/examinations (see Table 3.12);
- take into account dates when results need to be reported;
- the centre's annual verification schedule, which will determine when samples of the assessed candidate's work, together with feedback need to be available;
- overall internal/external quality-assurance schedule.

g) Where will they be assessed?
For work-based NVQs and QCF qualifications, the assessments must be in a workplace setting. In a vocational education context, practical assessments will usually take place in a simulated work environment such as a construction workshop or a training salon for hairdressers, set up to give work experience in a college. Written knowledge assessments may take place in the classroom or, if assignment-based, would be completed by the learner mainly outside classroom time and then given in to be marked by the teacher. For lower level qualifications in education and training environments, the teacher/assessor should make class time for learners to work on assignments in a supported environment.

h) When and how will feedback be given?
Different methods and purposes of assessment are linked to different kinds of feedback. In formative assessment taking place in a classroom, workshop

TABLE 3.12 Timings of assessment

Assessments of occupational competence in the work environment, timing of assessments:

- decided between the assessor and the individual candidate
- certain amount of flexibility available
- fit in with employer requirements, candidate's work commitments as an employee and assessor's availability
- take into account circumstances related to the vocational area, for instance in a horticulture qualification, the timing of the assessments would need to correspond to the performance evidence generated at different seasons of the year

Vocational education and training, timing of the assessments:

- appear in course plan/scheme of work
- may be assessments relating to whole group rather than individuals
- affected by the length of the school/college terms
- teacher/assessor's other work commitments
- space and resources available
- take into account dates of external tests/examinations

or workplace setting, oral feedback might be given when a task had been completed, to give learners confidence in what they were doing right and immediate points for development where they needed to improve. Supportive formative feedback also might be given on an ongoing basis while a learner was in the process of carrying out a task or activity. For example, 'You're doing really well with "x"; now just try and improve "y" by doing...'.

Summative assessments may involve immediate feedback and recording of results when observing practical tasks followed by questioning. Summative assessments of written work, such as assignments, will need to be marked by the teacher. Most organizations have a maximum 'turnaround' time for work to be marked and returned. This timescale needs to be taken into account when planning.

i) What special learner requirements need to be taken into account when planning the assessment?
Assessors must be mindful during the planning process that individuals are not excluded from access to assessment and that requirements related

to disability, culture, religion, gender or domestic/personal circumstances are taken into account.

There are many different kinds of problems that people might face, and all assessors will have their own examples. Table 3.13 gives a few from our own experience and the measures taken to combat them.

Special reasonable adjustment and special considerations

Your awarding organization will have a policy and procedures for 'special reasonable adjustment and special considerations' for candidates being assessed. You will need to be aware of this. There will also be a special request form that will need to be completed by the centre manager (with information supplied by the assessor) and sent to the awarding organization. These will either involve a temporary adjustment of assessment to take into account a specific circumstance such as a learner being ill and unable to attend for an examination, or they will relate to a more permanent circumstance that needs to be taken into account for assessments, such as hearing impairment or mental health issues. Evidence such as medical notes would need to be included with the applications.

Planning to assess occupational competence in the work environment

Planning for workplace observations

When planning for observations, involving candidates' supervisors in the planning process should enable candidates to plan work-based assessment opportunities into their normal work routines with as little disruption as feasible. This should help the candidates' performance to be as natural as possible and give them the opportunity to demonstrate the outcomes and criteria agreed in the assessment plan.

Having an assessor around is likely to alter the dynamics of situations and increase the nerves of candidates (and potentially their own learners/clients if the qualification is process- rather than product-based, for example working with children, patients, customers). If you need to be very close to the candidate for particular operations, perhaps to observe what s/he is doing or saying to a client, discuss this with the candidate in the planning meeting.

The candidates will need the opportunity to discuss the proposed assessment plan with workplace colleagues and their own candidates, but before they do this both of you need to clarify what is or is not negotiable in terms of the assessment. Rearrangement of time or place, choice of different units for candidates (and even of different candidates), materials to be used, types of evidence and witnesses are all negotiable. It is important to note that there will probably be non-negotiable aspects. For example for QCF qualifications, there are specified evidence requirements that detail the number of plans, reviews, records and statements to be provided by the candidate-assessor.

TABLE 3.13 Problems of learner-candidates and ways to help

Problems faced by learner-candidates	Measures taken to help
A candidate in information technology who developed arthritis	A special keyboard overlay was obtained for the computer that helped her to hit the keys accurately
A candidate in residential care who could only work on the night shift	A qualified assessor from a different team was found who was prepared to conduct an assessment observation during this time
A candidate in an engineering firm who broke his writing arm the week before having to take a written examination	The awarding organization allowed a scribe to be used for his answers in the examination
A visually-impaired candidate wanted to submit her work in braille	The assessor checked the awarding organization's guidance and reassured her that this was allowed without even having to apply for 'special reasonable adjustment'
A young girl who had been in care since she was a child was placed on an apprenticeship programme working with animals	She was given a good deal of encouragement and a very slow and gentle introduction to the process of assessment by giving her feedback on an informal basis When her supervisor was certain she had a good chance of being successful, she suggested that the girl be assessed against one unit of the qualification Success in this increased the girl's confidence and she could soon be assessed against other units
A candidate wanting to be assessed for commercial harvesting was told by the assessor where he worked that he would have to wait until June to harvest the strawberries This was because candidates had always been assessed harvesting strawberries	When it was pointed out that it was just as possible to assess the candidate harvesting another type of crop, the assessor realized that the candidate could be assessed almost straight away – harvesting winter broccoli!

Planning to assess products of work

Assessment planning should take into account the products of work that will provide the necessary evidence against criteria and organize how these will be made available for the assessor to see in real life or incorporated into the evidence portfolio. For example, planning will take into account how the candidate will document some of the evidence that cannot be viewed through observation.

Planning for questioning the learner

You will need to ensure that the candidate is clear about the purpose of questioning following observation: namely, to provide evidence that they have the required knowledge and understanding of what they are doing. As part of your planning for the actual assessment, you will need to select appropriate questions from an existing question bank and/or devise an appropriate set of questions.

Planning for discussion with the learner

Planned discussion can contribute substantial evidence against assessment criteria. It can be used either to 'fill' gaps in evidence or as a way of identifying gaps in understanding. The formative assessment and subsequent plan for the discussion need to be agreed with the candidate, who can then prepare properly. Discussion should ideally be workplace-based and candidate-led. The assessor also needs to plan how the discussion will be recorded – audio recording, a video recording or writing down the discussion as it takes place. The assessor then needs to log the criteria achieved against the discussion evidence. The selection of the appropriate method needs to take into account the need to gain permission from anyone else who may be recorded as part of the process, for example the candidate's colleagues or trainees.

Planning for witness testimony

In the assessment planning, evidence gaps or need for further supporting evidence may be identified that could be filled through effective use of witness testimony. The candidate should have the opportunity to discuss possible sources of witness testimony and to discuss their suitability with the assessor. If suitable, these should be identified on the plan, together with the relevant outcomes/criteria. If the candidate is not in regular contact with the 'witness', they should discuss their actions and timescale to get the appropriate witness statement(s).

Planning for learner statements

You need to ensure that the candidate knows the purpose of learner statements and has the opportunity to discuss how these should be structured. If there are required pro-forma for these statements, then make sure the candidate is familiar with these and given guidance about the amount of detail expected.

Sharing the plan with others

Once candidates understand what is and is not negotiable, the plan needs to be shared with everyone who may be affected. The assessment plan should state clearly what will be assessed, how it will be assessed and when it will be assessed. Only after this can the plan be finally agreed. Signing and dating by both parties is the convention used to denote agreement. It is important that this signing and dating is done as soon as the plan has been agreed. The other people who could be affected by the planned assessment will vary according to the work situation, but they might include:

- supervisors in the workplace who might need to adjust staffing rotas;
- witnesses who may be required to provide written statements;
- other tutors or trainers who need to coordinate their assessments with yours;
- technical staff, to make sure that the appropriate facilities are made available;
- the internal verifier, who will need to include you as an assessor and your assessments in his or her sampling plan;
- candidates' colleagues who might be affected by the presence of an assessor.

Planning for assessing vocational skills, knowledge and understanding

In vocational education and training contexts, a significant amount of the planning will have taken place before the learners/candidates are involved, in that course plans will have been produced, assessment schedules will have been agreed within the course team and any centre-devised summative assessments – for example assignments – will have gone through an approval process. However, there will be opportunities to involve learners/candidates in the detail of how the assessments will take place.

Observing learners/candidates in a simulated work environment

Teachers/assessors will have discussed with their learner group how observations of practical skills will take place and answered any queries from their learners. They will plan to observe all learners/candidates individually and this will form part of the records relating to each individual. Observations for formative assessment will take place on an ongoing informal basis whilst teaching in the workshop/training environment; observations for summative assessment will form part of the assessment schedule and the course plan and in some instances will all have to take place within a particular timeframe. However, within that framework there is likely to be some flexibility, with planning for assessment taking into account how ready a learner/candidate is to take a formal assessment and agreeing with the individual precisely when an assessment will take place and the outcomes and criteria to be evidenced.

In some situations candidates will be used to being observed on a regular basis. In a motor vehicle workshop, for example, supervisory staff will be moving around all the time checking on work being done. Similarly, in an open-learning workshop, candidates will be used to staff circulating and being available for consultation. In situations such as these, candidates are less likely to be disturbed than in a situation where they are not used to being observed; for example, a candidate being assessed as a trainer may never have had an observer with him or her in the training situation.

Skills tests

As discussed earlier in Part 3, many vocational skills tests will use observation as a major method of assessment, so the same approach and time constraints are likely to operate as identified above.

Planning for online or paper-based skills tests will involve discussion with learners/candidates about what these entail and identifying opportunities for formative assessment on 'dry runs' of the types of questions used before agreeing dates and times when any summative assessments will be undertaken.

Oral and written questions

Where oral questioning is involved, for example following observation, the teacher/assessor will have discussed this method with learners/candidates, planned questions and allocated sufficient time for oral questioning. In the planning process, the learner/candidate will have discussed the outcomes and criteria that may be met through the oral questioning.

Planning for the use of written questions may follow the pattern for oral questioning with the learners being given the opportunity to discuss and clarify and the teacher devising or using pre-set written questions. However, there may be different ways that these are used. For example they could be:

- Written questions given to each individual learner/candidate to answer, the written responses to which they will put in their portfolio. These would not be factual questions, as the authenticity of the answers could be in doubt, but they might be specific to the candidate's own work or workplace (so could not be answered by anyone but the candidate).

- Written questions given to the whole learner group in a classroom, which they will have to answer within a limited time period. In this case, the teacher/assessor will have planned to allocate the time to do this within their session planning.

Assignments, projects and case studies

These may sometimes be centre-devised assessments (as opposed to those devised by the awarding organization) that take into account local conditions and context and need to go through a formal approval process by the awarding organization; the timescale involved needs to be taken into account in your planning. There will be a series of planning documents you are required to complete and have signed off. Your internal verifier will be required to check your assessment brief against certain criteria and confirm to the awarding organization that this has been done. A sample of these assessment briefs will be sent to the EQA. The criteria used by the internal verifier in the approval process will include:

- accuracy of details;
- clear deadlines;
- appropriate timescale;
- appropriate language and presentation;
- assessment criteria listed;
- grading criteria addressed if appropriate to qualification;
- a list of criteria addressed by each task;
- confirmation that the task enables the specified criteria to be addressed;
- clear identification of evidence required;
- relevance and appropriateness of activities;
- link to work-related context and skills;
- fitness for purpose.

Planning for recognizing prior learning

In both assessment contexts, the planning of assessments for recognition of prior learning (RPL) before a candidate begins a qualification will follow organizational procedures. The processes involved may be set out by the awarding organization. In some organizations, the assessor's role may initially be taken by a special RPL advisor. Generally the candidate and the assessor will have an initial meeting, where the extent of the candidate's prior learning and experience is discussed and the units where RPL might be possible are identified. The candidate will then be responsible for putting together evidence for RPL against specific unit learning outcomes and assessment criteria. This will then be produced on an agreed date to be assessed. This planning will be recorded using the appropriate RPL documentation, and signed and agreed by assessor and candidate.

Candidates wishing to gain recognition for prior learning must be helped to plan the evidence they need to provide. When candidates wish to use evidence from RPL, an issue to consider is the currency of their evidence of competence. A candidate producing a computing qualification dating from the late 1970s will not be providing evidence of current competence in modern computer technology, whereas a qualification that is only one year old may well be acceptable. Currency of competence is obviously particularly important in areas where technology is in use; however, there may be other areas, such as the care sector, where a qualification obtained a number of years ago may still be judged appropriate and sufficient. In the planning process, you and the candidate need to check with the relevant internal verifier whether the awarding organization has set time limits on past experience and achievements. Witness statements and testimonials referring to past competence need to identify clearly the criteria the candidate has met. Original certificates for qualifications will need to be produced by the candidate. It could be that the discussion with the candidate could be planned to allow him or her to explain the evidence from prior assessments, experience or learning. Candidate and assessor need to discuss whether this evidence is likely to give proof of performance competence or of knowledge, and how it is likely to correlate with the required performance criteria and knowledge.

3.2 Evaluate the benefits of using a holistic approach to assessment

Holistic means 'capturing the whole or wider situation'. Applied to assessment, it means that the assessment (whether of a written assignment, test or observation) will cover as broad a range of natural performance or related assessment criteria as possible.

Although QCF qualifications are organized into units, these do not usually have to be assessed separately (except where only one unit is being taken). One task or activity may be used as evidence for learning outcomes and assessment criteria belonging to more than one unit, although the evidence for assessment criteria in each unit needs to be identified individually. It is here that clear and comprehensive mapping of evidence against criteria is essential.

Planning for holistic assessment will take into account what a candidate would be expected to do in practice and the requirements of the units being assessed by:

- identifying the substantial activities and naturally occurring evidence from the candidate's work;
- analysing different aspects of the work to establish which learning outcomes and assessment criteria can be met;
- considering other forms of assessment that can generate evidence against additional criteria on the same assessment visit;
- collaboration with other members of the qualification or assessment team, which might mean that assessments can be planned that cover multiple units taught or assessed by other team members.

A holistic approach to assessment allows the assessment process to be meaningful and more related to 'natural' activity rather than performing 'to the test', providing the opportunity for the candidate to provide evidence against a significant number of criteria. Planning using a holistic approach can also minimize the time and costs associated with visits to the work environment – helping assessor and candidate to decide whether assessment of non-performance evidence and professional discussion is likely to be more cost-effective if done at the candidate's workplace, close to his or her documentary evidence and possible witnesses, or at the assessor's premises. It is important to estimate in advance the time that each assessment is likely to take and the range of criteria that will be assessed, so that neither party is disadvantaged by cost or by an unplanned, lengthy or – just as bad – too short visit.

A holistic approach also allows for 'natural performance' to be assessed. For example, think of an occupation such as health and social care. There are many skills involved, such as carrying out health and safety procedures correctly, being involved in patient care and deciding when to call for expert help. There are also 'soft skills' such as making a patient feel at ease, communicating with the patient and the family, and dealing with highly sensitive emotional situations. The knowledge required to perform in a skilled and professional manner is complex – including knowledge on manual handling, knowledge about hospital procedures and interpersonal knowledge about how to interact effectively with staff and patients. It would not be valid to assess relatively complex knowledge and skills by a series of short assessments. A much more realistic assessment of competence would be to observe the candidate actually caring for a patient. As this involves a wide range of skills and knowledge, the process would encompass a large number of criteria, probably across a number of units.

A key advantage of holistic assessment is that planning to use naturally occurring workplace evidence, or obviously vocationally relevant assessment, as near 'real life' as possible, is likely to be viewed by the candidate as more meaningful than tasks just designed to meet the criteria. This can increase learner involvement and motivation, rather than the demotivating sense experienced by some learners that they are jumping through hoops to achieve a qualification.

3.3 Explain how to plan a holistic approach to assessment

In workplace assessment, a holistic assessment approach, several aspects of a unit or of several units could be covered in one well-planned direct observation visit. If products of work are assessed as well, and the candidate is questioned following the observation, then both skills and knowledge can be assessed on the same visit. A holistic plan could start with a task to be assessed in the normal course of work and then identify which assessment criteria this might cover over a number of units. The assessments should be done as part of a normal working shift, when the candidate is naturally carrying out performance tasks. Observations should be planned to cover as many outcomes and assessment criteria as possible, and the candidate needs to estimate the time likely to be taken.

Example

A candidate on a healthcare pathway has an apprenticeship as a healthcare support worker in a hospital geriatric ward. The assessor and candidate have a planning meeting where they look at the units, outcomes and criteria involved and discuss how these can be addressed through a combination of direct observations, questioning, witness testimony and learner statement, where knowledge and performance are linked together.

The assessor plans to observe the candidate caring for a particular patient with dementia – helping the patient get dressed and washed, serving food and changing bed linen. Following the observation the assessor will question the candidate. In the planning meeting assessor and candidate also agree evidence to meet the substantial knowledge requirements of the unit. The candidate will investigate some of the legal requirements of the work context such as equality and inclusion, safeguarding, health and safety and how that affects the role of the healthcare support worker working with dementia. The candidate will then produce a written report on the project findings. Table 3.14 shows how this holistic planning approach based on observation of natural performance could provide evidence across a number of units in a health and social care qualification.

TABLE 3.14 Example of holistic planning

Mandatory units	Potential for Coverage
Introduction to communication in health and social care	
Equality and inclusion	x
Introduction to duty of care in health and social care	
Principles of safeguarding	x
Health and safety	x
Role of the health and social care worker	x
Professional development	
Option units include:	
Dementia awareness	x
The person-centred approach to the care and support of individuals with dementia	x

Mapping of a substantial 'real-life' task against unit learning outcomes and assessment criteria would show any gaps in evidence that might need to be filled by another, and possibly smaller, assessment task. Where grading criteria are used, these also need to be mapped and designed to ensure there are opportunities for the candidate to achieve a grade higher than pass.

3.4 Summarize the types of risks that may be involved in assessment in own area of responsibility

The risks associated with assessment can be divided into:

1 Organizational or legislative processes such as health and safety and safeguarding.
2 Those related to the assessment process, for example problems carrying out the assessment or making assessment judgements.

Risk assessment documentation may be one form of product evidence from the candidate that will help the assessor plan to minimize potential risks.

1 Health and safety risks could include dangers inherent in the activity being assessed (to either the candidate or the assessor, or both), such as observations taking place in industrial environments where heavy machinery or equipment is used, agricultural settings with farm machinery or large animals, or work environments where toxic substances are used or where there is danger of infection. Health and safety risks in relation to the occupational area would also include risks to others involved: for example, risk assessments for children in a play group, if the candidate was a playworker.

Safeguarding risks could involve assessments in environments with children, young people or vulnerable adults. They could also relate to certain timescales not being met, for example the length of time for a CRB check to be made, which could prevent the assessment taking place.

2 Risks in carrying out the assessment could relate to the work environment or the evidence required. Examples include:
   - where employers or supervisors are not willing for the candidate to have proper time to be observed and questioned;
   - where the candidate is not supported in finding opportunities to meet the assessment criteria;
   - where an observation has to be cancelled at the last minute because of work priorities;
   - where something happens that prevents some/all of the evidence being produced, such as a breakdown in equipment, a patient being moved to another ward or a supervisor being off sick and not producing a witness testimony in time;
   - where learners have been given a project that involves an outside visit or interview and they are unable to complete it due to lack of availability/cooperation of outside sources;
   - where the assessment may cause disruption in the workplace;
   - frequent changes to practice, for example ICT or technology or any industry undergoing standards review.

3 Risks in the assessment process could include issues related to the assessor:

- a new assessor unsure of the amount/standard of evidence required;
- assessor bias, for example assumptions being made about candidates who are colleagues;
- the candidate believing the assessor has been biased, and complaining of this;
- lack of consistency between assessors;
- assessor and candidate being colleagues or friends.

More general risks could occur with:

- poor assessment planning leading to inadequate evidence, costly and time-consuming assessment;
- candidates who are not motivated, who do not keep in regular contact and who are in danger of dropping out;
- poor monitoring and record-keeping;
- awarding organization timescale not being met, so qualification cannot be achieved within intended timescale;
- assessor not being up to date with information/procedures;
- too heavy a workload for the assessor with the risk they will not be thorough.

3.5 Explain how to minimize risks through the planning process

Careful planning may not be able to eliminate all risks, but should attempt to minimize them. Talk to your IQA to see when monitoring will take place, and discuss any concerns you may have. We have given some suggestions below that you, as assessor, could take to minimize risks prior to the actual assessment:

- *Health and safety*: ensure that any health and safety risks are identified prior to assessment and that discussions take place about how to deal with them/minimize them, for example discussing where it would be best for the assessor to stand to observe. Assessors need to have the required occupational competence to assess, so they should know about health and safety within that occupational area. They need to be clear about any special equipment/procedures for that particular work environment. The assessment environment must meet the requirements of the Health and Safety at Work Act. All participants in the assessment have a responsibility for reporting any unsafe environment, equipment or practices. The assessor must conform to any additional health and safety rules determined by the workplace. The only time you, as assessor, should interfere with an assessment you are observing is if you, the candidate or his or her own candidates appear to be at risk. You will need to plan accordingly to address any potential safety aspects. For example, if the candidate is inexperienced, you may need to prompt them to discuss arrangements for you to have suitable protective clothing if appropriate.

- *Safeguarding*: ensure that any requirements for CRB checks are met; follow any rules of confidentiality required by the work environment. In planning discussions, discuss with the candidate any particular sensitivities related to the work context. You will need to ensure you can gain access to the workplace. This may include processes for signing in or any regulatory requirements regarding safeguarding that you will need to address prior to being allowed entry. Make sure you have all the necessary identification with you on your observation visit; for example you may be required to produce an identity card.

- *Work environment and evidence*: wherever possible in workplace assessment, involve employers/line managers/workplace mentors in the planning process, helping them become aware of the requirements (and benefits) of the qualification and how they can support the candidate. Candidate and assessor need to clarify whether there are any sensitivities surrounding the assessment, such as difficulties with staff, premises or other organizations, that need to be addressed prior to the assessment. Create back up plans if it is likely that assessment might have to be cancelled or the focus of performance assessment might have to be altered because of a last-minute change in work activity. As assessor, think ahead; be prepared to adapt to circumstances, suggest additional criteria to the candidate that you have observed due to the change in activity and devise extra questions or suggest additional evidence if appropriate, to fill the gaps in what has been observed. The assessments should be organized so that candidates demonstrating their competence do not experience unnecessary disruption to their work routine. Assessors need to be conscious of the work environment and ensure that feedback and questioning following assessment keep within planned timescales.

For vocational projects involving outside sources, it is generally a good idea to contact these people in advance and ensure their cooperation and availability before setting the learners onto the project. This will minimize the risk of learners/candidates not having access to the information they need to complete the work and meet the planned criteria.

Plan to avoid difficulties or disagreement

Discussion during this planning stage should reduce the likelihood of difficulties or disagreement. Candidates need to know what procedures and systems are in place to ensure confidentiality on sensitive issues. It is important that the assessor is clear about what is or is not negotiable, and candidates should be made aware of this. For example, if the awarding organization requires a written test, candidates must complete this even though they may be unwilling to do so. The only viable response here is basically: 'Do it, because if you don't you can't get the qualification.' However, you would obviously take into account whether a candidate is objecting because he or she needs encouragement or more guidance in order to provide this sort of evidence. It may be that you cannot resolve the difficulties yourself. You may suggest another assessor to the candidate or suggest that he or she talks to the internal verifier. You may feel that it would help if the candidate talked to other candidates who have been through the process. If assessments have to be cancelled by either party, there must be clear lines of communication and guidelines to minimize disruption and to facilitate the earliest possible reassessment opportunity. The most likely problem will be that the candidate disagrees with the assessor's judgement or that the assessor and candidate cannot find common times to carry out assessments. Both parties need to be clear about the options available, for example whether the use of another assessor is possible. The complaints and appeals procedure is there as a last resort.

LEARNING OUTCOME 4: UNDERSTAND HOW TO INVOLVE LEARNERS AND OTHERS IN ASSESSMENT

ASSESSMENT CRITERIA

4.1 Explain the importance of involving the learner and others in the assessment process.

4.2 Summarize types of information that should be made available to learners and others involved in the assessment process.

4.3 Explain how peer and self-assessment can be used effectively to promote learner involvement and personal responsibility in the assessment of learning.

4.4 Explain how assessment arrangements can be adapted to meet the needs of individual learners.

4.1 Explain the importance of involving the learner and others in the assessment process

If we want a learner to become independent, then we need to think about how assessment can help that process. In many types of assessment, it is someone else who decides how well the learner has performed – for example the person marking GCSE scripts for an examination board, the work-based assessor watching a practical task being carried out or the teacher assessing an assignment. In these cases, we could say that assessment is being 'done' to the learner, rather than the learner having a chance to take part and begin to learn to understand the standards required. In QCF qualifications, the learners should be involved in various ways:

- They should understand the assessment requirements by being given opportunities to discuss and clarify what is needed.
- They should be involved in aspects of assessment planning related to their own role and participation in the assessment.
- They should understand the terminology (candidates on a graded business studies course only started getting distinctions once they had been told what 'evaluate' meant!)

- They should be supported in pacing themselves so that they produce the evidence for assessment on agreed dates and within the necessary timescale.
- They should take part in self and/or peer assessment.

Note down on the assessment plan everything that has been agreed and discussed. If there are activities the candidate needs to do that are pre-assessment (eg training or research), these can go onto an action plan.

Keeping in touch and reviewing progress

Even at the initial planning meeting, it is important that the learner-candidate is aware of the 'shape' of the whole assessment process, including agreeing how arrangements for reviewing progress are approached. Reviews are usually best done following feedback sessions from each assessment and may be done face to face, by telephone or via e-mail contact. These reviews will result in the assessment plan being physically updated, with new dates and actions. If the candidate is not physically present at the review, but has verbally agreed or responded to e-mail, the assessor will need to send an updated copy of the assessment plan to the candidate as soon as possible. Reviews should always be documented in some way and any revision of assessment plans recorded on them, and be signed and dated by both parties at the time, as evidence of agreement.

One of the problems with working on assessments with candidates who are on a programme dependent on the progress and cooperation of others, possibly on different sites from the main assessor, is the danger that they will feel isolated or let other work take priority. Assessors need to be aware of this and develop a system for keeping in contact, regularly and reviewing progress. The way you decide to do this will depend largely on the experience of the candidate and the amount of support and motivation he or she needs from you.

Assessors will also need to ensure that any other people who will be involved in the assessment process are fully informed. For example there may be mentors who can provide some formative assessment and feedback or provide supporting evidence such as witness statements. Apart from mentors, contributors might include other assessors on the qualification, workplace supervisors and also those people – such as clients, customers, students or patients – receiving a service from the candidate that will form part of the evidence for assessment.

Self-assessment

Teachers can help learners to learn how to self-assess so that the learners can take ownership of the standards they need to achieve. The eventual aim is that they will become independent learners with the ability to become self-directed in developing new skills and knowledge. This self-assessment needs to achieve three goals: It needs to:

- be realistic;
- be accurate;
- recognize strengths as well as areas for improvement.

Important aspects of increasing learner involvement include the following:

- Making sure that learners can understand the processes of assessment, by sharing how you approach it and what you look for when you are assessing.
- Making sure that the assessment tools are as relevant and fair to learners as possible.
- Taking the learners' views seriously. So, for example, if they self-assess, discuss their ideas with respect rather than immediately imposing your own. They may have important perceptions about what constitutes good practice that can help the learning and assessment process. If their self-assessment is very different to your assessment, explore why this has occurred – it could provide important information for you to help them.
- Avoiding throwing learners 'in at the deep end'. As with any other learning process, you should devise strategies to increase their levels of responsibility gradually, moving from quick informal assessments to more detailed evaluative reflections. With inexperienced learners/ candidates, help them to make choices by the use of structured alternatives, such as 'Would you prefer... or...?'

Peer assessment

We have already mentioned the different purposes of assessment and have emphasized that assessment is about helping people to learn as well as about measuring the standard they have achieved.

Involving learners in peer assessment through providing opportunities to assess each other's work can also help to develop independence from the teacher and, if done in a constructive and cooperative way, can be a rewarding experience. If handled badly, however, peer assessment can sometimes be a demotivating and damaging experience for particular learners.

Teacher/assessors can help to make peer assessment a positive experience in the following ways:

- Give plenty of opportunities for learners to become aware of good practice in assessing and giving feedback. This can be done through teachers presenting a model of such good practice themselves, but also by drawing learners' attention to the principles of giving constructive feedback.

- Give some opportunities for practice in giving helpful feedback under supportive and controlled conditions, before allowing full peer assessment to take place.
- Set down clear ground rules for peer assessment.
- Carefully choose the composition of the pairs or groups that will peer-assess.
- Create structures for giving feedback that build-in comments on strengths as well as areas for improvement.
- Ensure that feedback focuses on the work and not the person.
- Praise and value good skills in peer assessment and giving feedback.

See also the section on feedback in Unit 1, Outcome 7.

4.2 Summarize types of information that should be made available to learners and others involved in the assessment process

Assessment should hold no surprises for candidates or teachers/assessors. Sharing information enables participants to understand what is expected from them, and gives them the opportunity to perform to the best of their ability.

Below are some examples of different types of information that should be available from those involved:

- *Awarding organization*: occupational standards, specifications, prescribed assessments, grading criteria, appeals procedures, access to assessment information, specific documentation and how to use it.
- *Centre*: times and places for assessments, complaints procedures, costs, dates of any award ceremonies.
- *Assessor*: assessment schemes, assessment plans agreed with candidates, evidence required, results of assessments, feedback.
- *Candidate*: particular requirements because of specific needs such as dyslexia; previous learning and related achievements, registration information.

4.3 Explain how peer and self-assessment can be used effectively to promote learner involvement and personal responsibility in the assessment of learning

A major aim of any education and training process is to enable people to become independent learners. In order for lifelong learning to be genuinely 'lifelong', learners need to develop the capacity to evaluate their own and others' performance, rather than leaving it solely to the teacher/assessor (who will not be with them once the course is over).

Examples: encouraging self and peer assessment

- In the induction for a BTEC Level 3 diploma in travel and tourism, the teacher talks through with the whole group how they will be assessed, the criteria that will be used and how feedback will be given. The teacher also talks briefly about how the units will be graded. The teacher then carries out a pair-work activity where each pair is encouraged to use Post-its to jot down any questions about the work they will have to do and how it will be assessed. The teacher then collects the Post-its, sticks them up and answers each of them in turn, making sure that all the learners' queries are answered fully.

- In a City and Guilds Level 2 plumbing course, learners have to self-assess their practical work before the teacher assesses it, using an assessment sheet that they have helped devise based on the awarding organization criteria. By doing this, they are given the opportunity to look at their own work with a critical eye and also have the chance to correct any mistakes before the teacher is involved.

- In the first module on a foundation studies degree for teaching support assistants, the teacher carries out an exercise where learners have to 'mark' two short sample (fictional) assignments – one poor and one excellent. They then discuss with the teacher how they judged the assignments. This exercise raises a number of issues about standards in academic writing and provides a model of good practice that can help the learners to become aware of the standards they should aim for themselves.

4.4 Explain how assessment arrangements can be adapted to meet the needs of individual learners

Assessors must ensure during the planning process that individuals are not excluded from access to assessment and that any special requirements are taken into account.

The centre's assessment systems and staff need to be flexible enough to take account of a variety of different needs. The fairness and reliability of assessment judgements can be affected by not taking into account the characteristics of the candidate and the situation in which he or she is working. Let us look at four different cases and briefly identify some considerations in the approach to the assessment of the individual candidates.

QCF Level 1 – work-based horticulture

The candidate is working on a Level 1 qualification in horticulture. He has learning difficulties and a tendency to get worked up under pressure. However, he has shown a real aptitude for gardening and could hold down a regular job. The assessor should try to be friendly and natural, making as little of the assessment process as possible in order to give the candidate the best chance of demonstrating his ability.

QCF Level 2 – instructing exercise and fitness diploma

The candidate is 21 years old, in employment, and working part-time towards this qualification at college. The assessor finds that written assignments are well below the standards indicated by the candidate's oral responses. It is discovered that the candidate has problems with organizing written material, and additional support is given via the college learning support staff, who are familiar with the assessment requirements of the course. The candidate is able to renegotiate hand-in dates for assignments.

QCF Level 4 – health and social care

The candidate has worked for a number of years in voluntary service, where she held a position of some responsibility. She then began work in a hospice, where she is dealing with patients sympathetically and effectively. The assessor would need to be aware of the sensitivity of the situation and might consider it appropriate to take the lead from the candidate about how to carry out the assessment. In particular, the feelings of the patients would need to be a major consideration. Witness statements from qualified staff who work closely with the candidate and understand the demands of the QCF qualification could form a large part of the evidence, along with carefully planned professional discussion.

QCF Level 5 – management and leadership

The candidate is a senior manager in a local authority. At this level the assessor would expect that the candidate should be well used to pressure and responsibility, but recognizes that the candidate is very busy. The main consideration would be to help the candidate to utilize all opportunities for work-based and holistic assessment, ensure that the assessments do not take more of the candidate's time than is strictly necessary and use RPL and recorded professional development as a way of cutting down paperwork for the candidate.

LEARNING OUTCOME 5: UNDERSTAND HOW TO MAKE ASSESSMENT DECISIONS

From reading the guidance on Outcome 1, you should be familiar with the key concepts underpinning assessment. In this outcome you need to show that you understand how these apply in practice. You should be able to justify any assessment decision, if required, to other assessors, IQAs and verifiers, EQAs and to the candidate. Your careful recording of what you have assessed matched to the relevant criteria, together with written feedback to the candidate explaining your decision could provide evidence here.

ASSESSMENT CRITERIA

5.1 Explain how to judge whether evidence is sufficient, authentic and current.

5.2 Explain how to ensure that assessment decisions are made against specified criteria, valid, reliable and fair.

5.1 Explain how to judge whether evidence is sufficient, authentic and current

It is normal to worry about whether your judgement is accurate and you must not hesitate to ask for advice about the regulations and requirements of your awarding organization, the regulations in your own organization and the relevant national standards. You need to attend the internal quality-assurance events in your own organization, such as those for standardization or moderation, and consult with colleagues who are experienced in assessment.

Having planned and carried out the assessment(s), teachers/assessors have to make certain decisions on the evidence provided:

- Has it met the specific outcomes and criteria identified in the assessment planning?
- Is it at the appropriate level for the qualification?
- Is it sufficient, authentic, current, valid?

TABLE 3.15 Sufficiency, authenticity, currency in the decision-making process

Is evidence	Making decision
Sufficient?	The evidence is sufficient to meet all the necessary regulations and requirements.
	The evidence is sufficient to meet all the learning outcomes and assessment criteria identified in the assessment plan.
	The evidence is understandable: ie presented clearly, logically. (There may be a lot of evidence but it will never be sufficient if it is incoherent, so you can't understand it or its relevance!)
	The evidence is sufficient to prove achievement at the appropriate level.
Authentic?	You have confirmed that the evidence is the candidate's own work.
	The candidate has completed any necessary documentation to confirm it is his or her own work.
	You have checked for plagiarism.
	You have checked that any statements from others, eg witness testimonies, come from credible and trustworthy sources.
	If in doubt about any of the above you have taken steps to check more closely before making decision: eg questioning the candidate more fully; confirming someone's position in an organization if you have doubts whether they are in the correct role to give a valid witness testimony; running written work through plagiarism software; consulting with your internal verifier.
Current?	The evidence conforms to the awarding organization's policy on currency; eg is there a time limit after which any prior qualifications become unacceptable as evidence?
	The evidence has been produced/submitted within the time constraints discussed in the assessment plan.
	The evidence shows that the candidate is up to date in his or her knowledge and skills related to the outcomes and criteria agreed in the assessment plan. (It could be that some criteria, eg those related to good interpersonal skills are not time-constrained in the same way as other criteria, eg ability to use most up-to-date equipment, or awareness of current legislation impacting on the occupational area.)

They also need to be sure that the result will be reliable and fair to the learner/candidate. We have already discussed key concepts and principles in assessment in Unit 1, Outcome 1 and given some examples of how these concepts might relate to practice. Table 3.15 gives some points to check when you are making an assessment decision.

5.2 Explain how to ensure that assessment decisions are made against specified criteria and are valid, reliable and fair

We have discussed validity, reliability and fairness in some detail in Unit 1, Outcome 1.

Questions to check your own assessment practice include:

- *Have the assessment criteria been identified and discussed with the candidate and recorded in the assessment plan?*
  You need to be very familiar with the units, outcomes and criteria that are being used for the assessment, as well as the appropriate methods for assessment.

- *Has the assessment deviated from the agreed specified criteria?*
  It is important to remember that you must not deviate from the agreed criteria when making your judgements. Even if you are convinced that receptionists should smile at their clients, if this is not included in the standard, then it is invalid and unfair to use it as a criterion for making an assessment decision. Make notes of any performance that appears to be beyond the requirements of the standards (eg smiling, in the case of the receptionists). This will be good for positive developmental feedback and may form good evidence for the candidate for another unit, or even evidence for a future assessment at a higher level.

- *How can you tell that the candidate would meet this standard on other occasions?*
  Has the candidate given additional evidence through product evidence, witness statements, formative assessment, discussion or questioning?

- *Has the reliability of your decisions been confirmed, for example through standardization processes such as double marking, moderation, verification? (Or are you confident that they will when the work is brought to verification?)*

- *What, if any, special learner requirements have been taken into account in the evidence required? Have they been addressed within the awarding organization's regulations?*

- *What measures have you adopted to ensure that your decisions are fair and without bias?*

  Assessors need to be sure that they are being fair by judging all learners/candidates according to their evidence against the identified criteria and not against what the assessor thinks they can do or thinks they should do. It is easy to want to give candidates 'the benefit of the doubt', because most of us want learners/candidates to succeed, especially if we have invested a lot of time and effort into helping them learn, but the assessment decision needs to be accurate in relation to the evidence provided. Just as unfair would be refusing to accept that a candidate is competent because of the lack of a skill that may not be required for the competence being assessed. Legibility of handwriting and the ability to speak fluently might be crucial to the achievement of competences for a candidate in administration, but might not be part of the competences required in a highly practical subject.

LEARNING OUTCOME 6: UNDERSTAND QUALITY ASSURANCE OF THE ASSESSMENT PROCESS

ASSESSMENT CRITERIA

6.1 Evaluate the importance of quality assurance in the assessment process.

6.2 Summarize quality assurance and standardization procedures in own area of practice.

6.3 Summarize the procedures to follow when there are disputes concerning assessment in own area of practice.

6.1 Evaluate the importance of quality assurance in the assessment process

An awarding organization must meet rigorous external quality-assurance systems in order to be approved by Ofqual. Accredited centres for the QCF qualifications are approved only after proving they can carry out internal quality assurance to national standards.

QCF and NVQ qualifications are nationally recognized and, as such, need to represent a consistent standard. All stakeholders need an assurance that all awards for each vocational area at a particular level are of the same quality, wherever the assessment has taken place and whoever was involved in the assessment. This means a candidate in Wolverhampton being assessed on a Level 2 diploma in food production and cooking will be assessed against the same criteria and at the same level as a candidate for the same qualification in Plymouth. Effective internal quality assurance is crucial in identifying any risk so that participants have confidence in the assessment process.

In every vocational area, awarding organizations are approved by Ofqual to offer qualifications, and have the responsibility for developing and monitoring quality-assurance procedures for their own awards and for providing comprehensive guidance to all centres offering their qualifications. They need to provide a clear quality-assurance structure involving assessors, internal quality-assurance and external quality-assurance procedures in order to ensure consistency of standards and of quality across a number of centres. This also involves clearly identified assessment procedures and record-keeping and ongoing monitoring of quality. At a national level they need to manage the training of their external quality assurers (EQAs) and also offer training updates for all involved in delivering the awards. (See Unit 4 for more on internal quality assurance.)

Wider purposes of quality assurance of assessment

Quality assurance of assessment should result in reliable data that gives information to benchmark the quality of a qualification or a course. The results of formal assessments are seen as an indicator of the course and qualification quality. For example:

- If a large number of students achieve certification, then the course has a good chance of meeting its targets for retention and achievement. These results feed into the results for organizational targets, which have been set to meet government targets, and these results in turn affect the future funding received by the organization.

- If a high proportion of students achieve qualifications, then it is seen as one indication that the course is being taught well and the learners are learning effectively.

- The results of assessments also enable organizations to monitor the overall quality of what they offer, avoid risks to the integrity of the qualification and identify ways to improve.

- In many organizations, the course leader writes an end-of-course review, which is received and monitored by a member of senior management or by a review panel. Student results will form part of the end-of-course review and will give an indication of whether there needs to be any radical intervention or whether there could be anything done to improve already good-quality provision. The appropriate person (people) will then take action, and this action will be reported and monitored.

- In most organizations the external moderators' or external examiners' reports are considered in detail, and actions are identified and implemented via staff development and training.

- Results can be used for marketing and publicity purposes.

6.2 Summarize quality assurance and standardization procedures in own area of practice

Unit 4 goes into detail about quality assurance and Appendix 3 will provide you with an overview of some of the bodies involved in quality assurance.

Most assessors have two areas of practice because of the need to comply with assessment and quality-assurance standards. The first is their own vocational subject, such as travel and tourism, and the second is lifelong learning/learning and development. Standard internal quality-assurance practice means that as an assessor you will have to, for example:

- report to the IQA for your allocated candidates who will oversee your assessments (your IQA may also be involved in allocating candidates);
- meet requirements for CPD, including updating on national occupational and assessment standards;
- attend standardization meetings;
- keep records according to centre regulations and requirements;
- know about internal quality assurance, and what happens and when throughout the assessment cycle.

All teachers/assessors have a responsibility to keep up to date with the assessment requirements on all their courses and for all their learners. You can get some of this information from more experienced colleagues, but beware! Assessment regulations and procedures can change, and it is important that you have the latest information. Most awarding organizations send out regular newsletters and updates to those on their mailing list. There are also websites you can access, but in some cases there can be a time lapse between a new assessment procedure or regulation and its appearance on a website.

Although teachers/assessors complain (with some justification) about the number of documents they need to complete the accurate recording of assessments is extremely important. This is important both for learners, who in most cases will have invested considerable time and effort in trying to achieve success, and for the organization, which is accountable to a range of outside bodies.

An internal quality assurer should manage you in your organization (and may work across a number of small organizations). S/he should be regularly sampling all types of assessment decisions and should also hold standardization sessions where you will have the opportunity to check that you are making the same decisions on evidence as would other assessors. Often these sessions use anonymous photocopied unit evidence from real candidates, which is judged independently by each member of the assessment team. The results of the assessments are then compared and discussed, allowing differences of interpretation to be resolved. Your organization could have, say, three audit points in a year. Internal verifiers will need to know how you are progressing with your workload on a regular basis and will request quantitative and qualitative data from assessors.

Many centres have their own system of recording feedback, assessment decisions and candidate progress. Relevant details are then transferred across to meet external awarding organization requirements. All assessors should be included within the process. Contributions to the process could include attending meetings, providing qualitative and quantitative data, being observed, discussing decisions and completing documentation accurately and promptly. Assessors may be asked to submit assessment decisions for sampling or for standardization purposes at any point during candidates' progress. An annual centre verification schedule will also be produced. You should be familiar with this as it will determine the timings of your assessments and when you need to provide candidate's work for verification and submit your assessment records.

Whatever the quality-assurance process used for verification by a centre, it should have been agreed with the relevant awarding organization for each qualification offered.

6.3 Summarize the procedures to follow when there are disputes concerning assessment in own area of practice

Each organization should have its own complaints and appeals procedure, and you should make sure you read and follow this. Your learners/candidates should also have been informed of these procedures in their induction and in the centre documentation provided. In addition, awarding organizations will have their own complaints and appeals procedures, which should also be understood by candidates and assessors. These will be used if matters cannot be resolved locally.

Familiarity with and meticulous following of assessment procedures should keep disputes to a minimum; however they may still occur. From our experience, the most common disputes are:

- disagreement over an assessment decision;
- where a candidate's work appears to have been lost by the centre;
- where work is not returned to candidates on time;
- cases where plagiarism is suspected and the candidate disputes this;
- candidate complaints about the assessment procedures or discriminatory practice.

You should know the procedures you are required to follow, as well as being really clear about the impact of any relevant regulations or legislation on your practice. You should familiarize yourself with these before any issue actually occurs, because any deviation from the proper procedures in dealing with a dispute could make yourself or your organization vulnerable for further complaints and disciplinary action. Take care to:

- Avoid having ongoing informal chats with no one else present with a candidate once they have made a complaint.
- Keep meetings formal, with the necessary representatives present and with proper written records of what has been said.
- Follow procedures to the letter. There may be different levels of seriousness of offence and these may trigger a new set of procedures.
- Make sure all stages of procedures are fully recorded, dated and show agreement/disagreement (usually through signatures of those involved).
- Make sure all relevant documents are stored safely for the required time period, eg 18 months.
- At every stage, keep good communication with your verifier/IQA.

A typical appeals procedure would go through different stages, each with defined timescales:

1 Informal stage: discussion between assessor and learner/candidate if there is a dispute over assessment decision. If unresolved, go to the next stage.

2 Involvement of internal verifier/lead IV/manager who reviews assessment decisions. Learner/candidate notified of decision in writing. Responds, in writing, to agree or disagree. If unresolved, go to the next stage.

3 Appeal hearing chaired by senior management at centre. If unresolved, go to the next stage.

4 External appeal: awarding organization deals with the appeal. Fee may be involved. Grounds for appeal and supporting evidence need to be provided within strict time limits.

Centre management should monitor the implementation and effectiveness of the appeals process as part of quality assurance and improvement.

LEARNING OUTCOME 7: UNDERSTAND HOW TO MANAGE INFORMATION RELATING TO ASSESSMENT

ASSESSMENT CRITERIA

7.1   Explain the importance of following procedures for the management of information relating to assessment.

7.2   Explain how feedback and questioning contribute to the assessment process.

7.1 Explain the importance of following procedures for the management of information relating to assessment

Like so many aspects of the assessment process, the management of assessment information will be governed by legislation such as the Data Protection Act, and by regulatory requirements such as those identified by the awarding organization and by accredited centres. The Data Protection Act 1988 not only protects existing information but requires it to be accurate and, where appropriate, updated. All information needs to be treated carefully and within legal requirements.

Records also need to meet organizational requirements and conform to regulations on storage of information. In normal circumstances, the Data Protection Act 1998 prevents information about individual assessments being released to any outside stakeholders, such as employers. The major exception here is students who are under the age of 16, where information about assessments can be released to the parents or legal guardians. External stakeholders connected with education and training such as the Skills Funding Agency (SFA), the Young People's Funding Agency (YPFA), BIS, DfE and Ofsted all have a legitimate right to gain statistical assessment information from the organizations involved, and each organization must have proper systems in place to ensure that accurate and comprehensive statistical information is received by these stakeholders.

Assessors need to know their legal position regarding record keeping. For example if they:

- Lose a laptop with personal data – could this lead to prosecution, and how could this be avoided?
- Fail to upload assessment information to a remote server at the end of the day – could they be disciplined by their organization?
- Place candidate assessment information where it can be read by others, altered by others or stolen – what complaints might be made against them?
- Are self-employed rather than an employee – do they need to take out any insurances or data registrations?
- Work from an organizations computerized record system – do they have to seek necessary permissions to share data, or do they have this as a matter of course?

The answers to these questions should be able to be answered by the person(s) who administers the software, as well as your IQA and centre managers.

Assessment records

Many awarding organizations have now developed comprehensive electronic recording systems, which enable results to be inputted through a secure online process. There should be clear guidelines on the protocols to use for inputting, storing and accessing information, and it is important to follow these – not only so that you manage the information properly, but so that there is no ground for candidate complaints. Some software packages incorporate straightforward ways for the learner to give permission for their data to be viewed. The protocols should include how to correct any recording errors. Your centre will have developed its own system of back-up for electronic records. However, we have found that many assessors still keep their own paper records as personal back-up in case of any problems with the electronic system.

Handwritten records must be legible. Any mistakes made in the recording should be altered clearly and signed to indicate the error has been corrected by the assessor and not altered without authority. Results should be recorded at the time the judgement is being made. Paper records might need to be transferred to electronic recording systems; this should be done as soon as possible, and the original paper record should be kept until at least after the next audit and after the candidate has received his or her certificate. Many accredited centres and awarding organizations recommend that file copies be kept for three years before destruction.

Records should be passed on promptly, as not doing this could hold up a candidate's assessment, especially if the observational assessor records form just part of a candidate's unit assessment. Records also provide the evidence for the sampling and monitoring activities carried out by the IQA/internal verifier and hence must be kept up to date so that internal verification can take place throughout a candidate's progress. Records are also needed in cases where there is a candidate complaint or appeal. Each organization should have its own complaints and appeals procedure, and both candidate and assessor should be familiar with this. In addition, awarding organizations will have their own complaints and appeals procedures, which should also be understood by candidates and assessors. These will be used if matters cannot be resolved locally.

Candidates need to know what arrangements the assessor will make to keep their work safe and provide secure storage, for example specific locked filing cabinets, or locked rooms where art work is displayed for assessment purposes. The demands of legislation will need to be followed. Both parties will need to comply with the Data Protection Act and the Mental Health Act regarding the disclosure of information about candidates, and decide how to assess necessary documentary evidence that cannot be removed from the workplace, while meeting the requirements of the Copyright Act.

7.2 Explain how feedback and questioning contribute to the assessment process

Feedback

As discussed in Unit 1 effective assessment contributes to development and improvement. However, candidates can only improve if they understand what they have done correctly, what they have done wrong or not to the level required, and what they need to do to improve.

The skill of giving constructive and helpful feedback is at the heart of successful assessment. If this skill is used, candidates will not just be clear on what they have achieved, but they will be clear on what they need to do to develop or maintain performance. They will also be motivated by the feedback to try to improve on their performance. Some examples of situations where feedback could be given (and received) are:

- an assessor giving feedback to a candidate who has just had a workplace observation;
- an RPL adviser discussing a candidate's first attempt at a portfolio of evidence;
- a teacher/assessor giving written feedback on an assignment;
- an assessor receiving feedback from an EQA or IQA.

In every case, badly delivered feedback can destroy confidence and trust. This is particularly important if the candidate has not been able to demonstrate competence or achievement and might be tempted to give up and not try again. It is crucial to be sensitive to how the other person is responding to what is being said. In oral feedback you will have immediate information on the candidate's response. With written feedback there may be some delay between work being submitted for summative assessment and it being marked and returned, but the teacher should always build in an opportunity for individual learners to discuss written feedback. An important aspect of written feedback, in particular, is to think carefully about the main audiences for the feedback. It is obviously directed at the learner/candidate, but it will also provide evidence for IQAs/EQAs that your judgement is carefully considered and justified by the comments you write. Clear explanation of why someone has passed/been given a particular grade, or clear explanation of why they haven't passed and what they would need to do to pass, gives confidence that you are basing your judgement on a good understanding of the unit requirements.

Although Table 3.16 focuses on points to consider when giving oral feedback, most of these points should also be taken into account when giving written feedback.

Wider purposes of feedback

As well as being a vital component of learning and development, feedback is also important in improving assessor and verifier performance and in improving the overall quality of assessment and verification. This can be through receiving and acting on information including:

- feedback from IQA to assessors/verifiers;
- feedback from EQA to IQA/centre managers;
- feedback from candidates to assessors;
- feedback from employers;
- feedback from others involved in national occupational standards/ vocational education and training.

TABLE 3.16 Points to consider when giving oral feedback

Giving oral feedback

1. Let the candidate have the first say

Give candidates the chance to say why they think they have been given their particular result. If they are competent, build on their understanding. If they haven't achieved competence, it is possible they will know why and this will help them to 'own' the feedback they receive.

2. Give praise before criticism

Most people will find it difficult to try to improve if they feel they are failures. Generally, by focusing first on their strengths and telling them why you think these are strengths, you can help them to understand what you as the assessor are looking for. They can learn a lot by finding out what they do well and seeing how they have met specific criteria. Then, by helping them to recognize their weaker areas, you can give candidates enough confidence to deal with anything that needs to be improved.

3. Limit what you cover

Don't try to cover everything. Focus on two or three key areas for development.

4. Be specific, not vague

Try to avoid general comments that don't help candidates to identify the issue. It's not very useful to say to someone: 'Your writing isn't very good.' It is much more useful to say: 'It was difficult to read what you had written, because your writing is rather small and you crowded all your information together without leaving any spaces between the different sections.'

5. Concentrate on things that can be changed

For feedback to be useful it must allow for the possibility of improvement. If there are intrinsic or extrinsic factors that you know cannot be changed, feedback relating to them is a waste of time. It is far more useful to concentrate on what can be changed. Again be specific and clear about what needs to be done to improve in a particular task or activity.

6. Give the candidate time to think and respond

Successful feedback involves a 'dialogue' between two individuals committed to improvement. If you have given the candidate a new perspective on some aspect of competence it could take some time for him or her to absorb it. Only when the candidate has absorbed it and then responded can the planning for improvements take place.

7. Keep to the learning outcomes and assessment criteria

As teacher/assessor you must distinguish between when the candidate has done something differently from the way you would do it but has still met the criteria, and when he or she has not performed to the required level of competence. You might draw the candidate's attention to this difference but be clear as to whether it is acceptable in relation to the standards or not.

8. Make sure the candidate understands

Think of the language you are using and ensure it is the right level and tone. If possible, give the candidate an opportunity to ask questions to clarify any points made in the feedback.

9. Listen to how the feedback is received

Be aware of how candidates are reacting to your feedback. Look for non-verbal cues that they are confused or that they don't agree. You might ask them directly whether they agree/understand.

10. End on a positive note

You should end the feedback session by agreeing some positive action to address areas for development as identified through the assessment. Try to help learners to identify for themselves what they will do to improve, rather than it being led entirely by you as the assessor. End with some encouragement. Good feedback should leave the candidate wanting to improve, not giving up in despair!

Questioning

There are many skills involved in developing and using appropriate questions and questioning techniques for assessment purposes. Questioning is an important part of the assessment of occupational competence and vocational skills and knowledge in that it can provide:

- Evidence that the candidate knows and understands what s/he is doing in practice.

- A means for the assessor to explore the candidate's reasons for approaching a task or a person in a particular way and help the candidate explain the rationale behind decisions s/he has made. Hypothetical questions such as 'What would you do if...?' can also enable the candidate to demonstrate what they would do in situations that are outside the scope of the observation but are important in building up a body of evidence that proves occupational competence.

- An effective form of ongoing formative assessment, whereby the candidate learns both from the assessor's questions (which act as a guide to what is important to know) and the assessor's responses/ corrections to the candidate's answers.

We have gone into types of questions and questioning skills in detail in the guidance on Unit 1, Outcome 2.

LEARNING OUTCOME 8: UNDERSTAND THE LEGAL AND GOOD PRACTICE REQUIREMENTS IN RELATION TO ASSESSMENT

ASSESSMENT CRITERIA

8.1 Explain legal issues, policies and procedures relevant to assessment, including those for confidentiality, health, safety and welfare.

8.2 Explain the contribution that technology can make to the assessment process.

8.3 Evaluate requirements for equality and diversity and, where appropriate, bilingualism in relation to assessment.

8.4 Explain the value of reflective practice and continuing professional development in the assessment process.

8.1 Explain legal issues, policies and procedures relevant to assessment, including those for confidentiality, health, safety and welfare

NB: A list of relevant legislation can be found in Appendix 2.

All relevant centre policies and procedures will be identified in the centre's approval process. The centre will have copies of the awarding organization's relevant policies and procedures. They may also be available on websites. Assessors need to understand how each policy and procedure affects the assessment process and themselves and their candidates. They may include:

- Confidentiality: systems for safe recording and storing, restricting access to assessment information.

- Health and safety, organizational health and safety policy, risk assessments to be taken into account when carrying out assessments.

- Occupational area H&S policies and procedures when assessing your candidates' competence in their occupational area.

- Observing candidates in a safe environment: the assessment environment must meet the requirements of the Health and Safety at Work Act. All participants in the assessment have a responsibility for reporting any unsafe environment, equipment or practices. The assessor must conform to any additional health and safety rules determined by the workplace, such as the wearing of protective clothing. The only time you, as assessor, should interfere with an assessment you are observing is if you, the candidate or his or her own candidates appear to be at risk.

- Safeguarding: signing in policies, CRB checks – which could impact on how you plan and carry out assessments.

- Access to assessment: ensuring candidates with special learning requirements have these taken into account where they would be otherwise disadvantaged in an assessment.

8.2 Explain the contribution that technology can make to the assessment process

We are all aware of the enormous impact new technology has had on our everyday lives. Here are some examples from our own experience of technology in assessment:

- Mobile phones used in formative assessment: the teacher texts a question to the mobile phones of learners in a class. Learners have to text back an answer quickly. The teacher selects texts at random to see if the response is correct (but can then look at all texts after the class to see who didn't get the answer).

- Mobile phones with cameras used to take photos/short videos of a candidate carrying out a process or of a finished product.

- Online banks of multiple choice questions to test knowledge and understanding of a particular topic (sometimes from the awarding organization). The results can be accessed immediately.

- Online initial diagnostic test for literacy/numeracy indicates which level the learner has achieved (eg Level 1) and indicates areas to work on in order to achieve a higher level.

- Creation of a 'wiki' on caring for a new baby, by a group of learners on a childcare course. Although it was a group project, individual contributions could be monitored by the tutor.

- Individual learners each keeping a reflective blog on what they were learning on their work placement.

- Learners submitting their work online through a system that uses plagiarism detection software.

- E-mail and PDAs by which those in the assessment process can communicate effectively.

- Electronic portfolios: candidates' work for some qualifications can now be presented through an electronic portfolio where all evidence is stored and accessed electronically. Like any recording system, the e-portfolio is only as good as those using it. Like a paper-based system, it relies on the candidate to include the appropriate evidence, whether in scanned, photographic or video format, and on the assessor to make judgements that are matched against the evidence and criteria for the qualification. Feedback comments can also be sent online to candidates. This means the assessor will have all the necessary records to hand and these may also be accessed and monitored for quality-assurance purposes.

- Electronic systems for storing assessment data that can, given the right permissions, be accessed by candidates, assessors, quality-assurance staff and administrative staff. Over the last few years, many awarding organizations have moved over to electronic registration and recording systems. There will be some public areas that can be viewed by anyone on the awarding organization's website, but the majority of the system will be secured and can be accessed only by approved and registered personnel. Assessment and verification records can be entered straight into the electronic system.

- Online documentation, such as quality-assurance reporting forms or training materials for assessors. Technology can be used not only in registering students, tracking student progress and recording data, but also in the collation of data and statistics. In the current education and training climate, with ongoing monitoring of recruitment and targets, technology can be used to collate the extensive data and statistics required.

8.3 Evaluate requirements for equality and diversity and, where appropriate, bilingualism in relation to assessment

The two terms 'equality' and 'diversity' are often used together and are closely associated, although they do not mean the same thing. There has been increased emphasis on the way that equality and diversity issues are handled in education and training, and also on the importance of staff development in these areas.

The term 'equality' refers to the importance of treating people equally and giving people the same opportunities, whatever their background, age, ethnicity, religion, gender, disability (mental or physical) or sexual orientation. However, treating people equally does not mean dealing with people in exactly the same way. The term 'diversity' refers to the differences between individuals, and the importance of appreciating those differences and acting accordingly. So you may want to give learners equal opportunities to achieve a qualification, but because of their diversity you may have to offer each of them different kinds of input or support for them to achieve the same eventual goal.

All awarding organizations have equality and diversity policies that can be found on their websites. You need to become familiar with these and make sure you put them into practice. As an assessor you should be aware of all the different dimensions of equality and diversity. This does not just mean sticking to the 'letter of the law' by conforming to the relevant regulations and legal requirements; it means understanding and trying to put into practice the principles and values that underpin this legislation.

Assessors of qualifications must meet good practice requirements in relation to equality and diversity, based on equal access to assessment irrespective of age, gender, religion, ethnic group, disability or geographical location. In our experience, there is still a lack of awareness regarding the circumstances in which discrimination can occur. Knowledge about equality and diversity issues, the policies of their own organizations and the legislation that exists can help those involved in assessment to become more aware of what they need to address. However, good assessors need to move beyond obeying legislative requirements to actively ensuring that a respect for equality and diversity is present in all they do. One of the most powerful means of preventing unfair discrimination is by an open-minded examination of one's own beliefs and prejudices and how they may affect one's judgement. The subject of equal opportunities is far too extensive to be covered here in any detail; however, here are some examples of how discrimination might affect judgement:

- an assessor being prejudiced against someone because he or she thinks the person is too young to have the required skills, rather than objectively viewing the evidence;

- an assessor in childcare being particularly hard on a male candidate because the assessor does not think that this is 'man's work' so wants to discourage him;

- an assessor undervaluing the practical skills demonstrated by a candidate whose first language is Urdu, because the candidate's command of English is not perfect;

- an assessor being over-generous in his or her assessment of a candidate who is a wheelchair user.

Some of these may strike a chord in the reader. If not, dig deeper. The majority of us have at least one significant prejudice that could affect our ability to assess fairly! Honest reflection of our own values and beliefs and how they might affect our judgements is an important skill to develop.

Bilingualism

The term 'bilingual' implies that someone is proficient in two languages. The UK is a multicultural society and a significant proportion of people living here speak two or more languages. Welsh is the first language in some parts of Wales, some schooling takes place in Welsh and many public offices require employees to speak and write Welsh. In QCF qualifications, learners may be assessed using the Welsh language, and hence arrangements may need to be made for assessment tasks to be produced in Welsh and marked by a Welsh speaker. Similarly, observation of competence in the work environment may need a Welsh-speaking assessor.

There are many other languages spoken in Britain, including Urdu, Punjabi, Hindi, Cantonese Chinese, Mandarin Chinese and many Eastern European languages such as Polish. Many of these language speakers have been born here and grown up speaking English at work or school and speaking the language of their parents at home. Others will have come to the UK later in life and will have varying levels of spoken and written English. Some will be professionally or vocationally qualified or experienced in their mother country, but do not have a good level of English, and it is possible that RPL could take some of this professional/vocational background into account. Others will have lacked the benefit of formal education and training, but are now in a setting where obtaining a vocational qualification is a possibility.

As assessors and teachers our job is to make sure that candidates are not denied access to vocational qualifications purely because they are not completely fluent in spoken or written English. An initial assessment should pick up any major areas of difficulty, and then planning will need to take into account any specific needs that arise from this. In a college setting, general or individual language support and the opportunity to attend classes in English for speakers of other languages (ESOL) may be available if needed. It may be that candidates are advised to improve their written and/or spoken English prior to starting their assessment process. Note that some awarding organizations have set fairly strict limitations on allowances made for performance when English is not the first language. It is important that you check the relevant rules on this.

8.4 Explain the value of reflective practice and continuing professional development in the assessment process

Reflective practice underpins professional development in many different occupational areas. It is based on the idea that by thinking systematically about specific experiences – what you and others have done and what has happened – you will be able to identify what went well, what could have been done better and how to improve next time. Reflective practice also helps people to examine not only their own practice, but their values and beliefs and how these might impact – positively or negatively on their practice. Stephen Brookfield (1995), who is one of the key writers on reflection, developed an influential reflective model, which suggests reflecting on experience using four 'critical lenses':

- your own view;
- learners' views;
- colleagues' views;
- perspectives/ideas from theory.

Using a variety of perspectives can move teachers/assessors from mere 'navel-gazing' to genuinely evaluating and developing their own practice.

Continuing professional development

A commitment to continuing professional development (CPD) is an important aspect of being a professional practitioner and effective vocational assessor. For example the Institute for Learning (IFL), the professional body for teachers, tutors and trainers in the LLS, has a requirement that all members need to record and reflect on their CPD. In order to retain membership, each member must complete at least 30 hours of CPD each year (or pro rata if they are part-time) to demonstrate that they are improving relevant knowledge and skills both in their subject area and teaching or training. A wide range of formal and informal activities could count as meaningful professional development. The IFL website identifies the following:

- reading relevant journal articles or reviewing books;
- training courses or formal development or study;
- peer review, mentoring or shadowing;
- online learning, including engagement in discussion forums and blogs;
- viewing and reviewing television programmes, documentaries and the internet.

However, it is important that members not only identify and reflect on their CPD, but evaluate the difference the CPD has made to their skills and knowledge of teaching, training and assessment. Part of this is the evidence of the impact on their own learners.

As assessors, you need to ensure your occupational competence is up to date. Apart from the activities identified in the list above, CPD could involve visiting workplaces, liaising with employers about their needs and requirements, and finding other ways of ensuring not only that your specialist expertise is of an appropriate standard but also that you are fully aware of current custom and practice in the workplace. It is sometimes possible to go on a short (one or two weeks) industrial placement where you could shadow someone working in your occupational area in order to keep your skills and knowledge updated.

Unit 2
Assess occupational competence in the work environment

LEARNING OUTCOMES FOR UNIT 2

1 Be able to plan the assessment of occupational competence
2 Be able to make assessment decisions about occupational competence
3 Be able to provide required information following the assessment of occupational competence
4 Be able to maintain legal and good practice requirements when assessing occupational competence

Your centre and awarding organization will have provided much of the assessment documentation you will use for this unit, together with guidance on how to use it. See Unit 1 for the background knowledge and understanding.

Your assessor should encourage a holistic approach, making best use of substantial evidence. For example an observation followed by questioning or discussion could show how you plan, manage, decide and record assessments, and so maximize the opportunity to provide evidence across whole units or a range of criteria.

Evidence requirements for this unit:

- Your evidence must cover all of the assessment methods listed below, with performance evidence for at least the following three methods: observation of performance in the work environment, examining products of work, questioning the learner.

- Your own performance evidence must be assessed by observation, the examination of products of work such as plans and records, and by questioning/discussion.

- You must carry out at least two assessments of learners' occupational competence (four assessments in all).

LEARNING OUTCOME 1:
BE ABLE TO PLAN THE ASSESSMENT OF OCCUPATIONAL COMPETENCE

ASSESSMENT CRITERIA

1.1 Plan assessment of occupational competence based on the following methods:
- observation of performance in the work environment;
- examining products of work;
- questioning the learner;
- discussing with the learner;
- use of others (witness testimony);
- looking at learner statements;
- recognizing prior learning.

1.2 Communicate the purpose, requirements and processes of assessing occupational competence to the learner.

1.3 Plan the assessment of occupational competence to address learner needs and current achievements.

1.4 Identify opportunities for holistic assessment.

1.1 Plan assessment of occupational competence based on the following methods

- observation of performance in the work environment; examining products of work; questioning the learner;
- discussing with the learner; use of others (witness testimony); looking at learner statements; recognizing prior learning.

Your evidence will be negotiated with your assessor, but one source could be an observation of your planning meetings with different candidates where you agree to observe, assess their products of work and question them following the observation – covering the three methods which you must use.

Your planning meetings could include discussing with your candidate:

- the units, criteria and required assessment methods;
- the activities they perform as a natural part of their work that would be suitable for observation;
- the criteria that can be evidenced through observation;
- whether one visit might involve observation of different tasks/processes;
- how more criteria could be covered by different assessment methods on the same visit;
- the amount of time needed for the process, for example how long the observation would need to be, and how long would be set aside for questioning if this took place after the observation;
- what the product(s) of work would be and what additional criteria they might cover;
- when and where discussion and feedback on performance can take place;
- any factors you would need to take into account relating to special requirements of the candidate;
- factors you would need to take into account when visiting, such as special procedures for you to sign in, specialist clothing, difficult layout of the workplace, activity taking place involving moving between different areas;
- date(s)/times.

Target your evidence to include copies of assessment plans. The awarding organization may provide templates for these or your organization may devise their own. It would be usual for the same planning documentation to be used across different awards in the same organization.

The assessment plan should indicate:

- what competences or outcomes and assessment criteria are being assessed;
- how and when they will be assessed;
- the methods that the assessor will use to make his or her decisions regarding the candidates' competence;
- the evidence that will be provided.

It may also indicate:

- others who will be involved, such as witnesses, workplace and, where relevant, independent assessors;
- any special circumstances that need to be taken into account;
- dates and times of assessment where possible.

If the assessment plan takes into account evidence from prior learning, this needs to be clearly identified in the methods section.

Other evidence will come from documents recording the planning process, such as assessment planning review forms, being asked questions about how you plan, and witness testimonies from candidates related to their experience of planning meetings. You may also write learner statements that explain how you approach the planning process. Some of these could also provide evidence for knowledge outcomes and criteria in Unit 2, Outcome 1.

1.2 Communicate the purpose, requirements and processes of assessing occupational competence to the learner

The candidate should be as involved as possible in the assessment process. You should be able to provide evidence of how you ensure candidates know:

- why they are being assessed using particular methods (purpose);
- what is being assessed and the criteria they are being assessed against (requirements);
- how the assessment process will take place (process).

Your evidence for competence in communicating with the learner-candidate is likely to be through being observed. In which case, you need to make sure during the assessment meeting that you communicate the 'Why, what and how' very clearly.

Do some preparation on this beforehand, for example working out in your own words how you would explain the purpose, requirements and processes of assessing occupational competence to different types of candidate. Depending on the candidate, you would need to adjust the level of language and amount of detail you include. Think for example about how you would alter your explanation to suit, first, a 16-year-old Level 1, and second, a 30-year-old Level 3 with previous experience in the workplace. All learner-candidates will need to be clear about the terminology used and what those terms mean for them in practice.

For example:

- Do they know what 'occupational competence' means?
- Do they understand what outcomes and criteria are, and how important these are in the assessment process?
- Do they understand how assessment decisions will be made?
- Do they understand the different types of evidence and what they need to do to provide these?
- Do they know the documentation they will need to use?

- Do they understand that assessment can be used to help them improve as well as measure achievement, and how this might work in practice?
- Do they understand your role and responsibilities and their role and responsibilities in the assessment process?
- Do they understand how the assessments will take place, and the journey to completing a unit or qualification?

You cannot assume learners/candidates know these things already, even if they are experienced workers. You will need to check them out by discussing them in a clear and constructive way that helps to set them at ease and involves them as much as possible.

1.3 Plan the assessment of occupational competence to address learner needs and current achievements

As an assessor/candidate, you will have to provide evidence on how you take into account learner needs. Your assessment plan should identify any specific needs your candidates may have, and agree the level and extent of their current knowledge and skills. Think of some examples you could provide if questioned, or that could be used in learner statements as supporting evidence.

Examples of statements on addressing specific needs

'One of my candidates is a working mother with three children. She works a late shift so that her husband can be home from work to take care of the children. I arranged to visit her workplace in the evening for the observation.'

'One of my candidates has been diagnosed with dyslexia. I have made sure that all course documents have been copied onto pale blue paper, as this makes it easier for him to read. We have also made sure that he has had extra support with his written work.'

The evidence for these statements would be enhanced by supporting witness statements from the candidates involved. (NB: your candidate witness statements might also evidence other criteria from Unit 2 or even other units, so make sure you maximize the possibilities when you ask them to produce the statements.)

In your evidence for establishing the candidate's current level of achievement, you may use results of initial assessments if appropriate, but you may also discuss their current work and invite them to identify where they are in relation to the relevant outcomes and assessment criteria for the unit. Some of your discussion might take into account RPL, either the previous experience they have had in this area of work, or previous certification. Notes from your assessment meeting, together with completed assessment plans would provide some of the evidence here.

1.4 Identify opportunities for holistic assessment

In your assessment planning meetings you should, wherever possible, aim to take a holistic approach. If someone is only taking one unit, identify how many outcomes and criteria might be met by three interconnected assessment methods, for example observation, examination of product of work and questioning. If they are taking the full award/certificate/diploma, identify through a mapping process the outcomes and criteria that could be covered across units by one observation visit or discussion. The mapping document could form part of your evidence. Descriptions of your approach could provide evidence through being questioned, discussion or a written statement.

As an assessor/candidate, work to holistic assessment principles for yourself – to maximize opportunity and save time and cost. If you have arranged to be observed assessing competence, examining products of work and questioning, discuss with your assessor whether you could also be observed carrying out an assessment planning meeting during the same visit. This might be a follow-on planning meeting with a candidate who has reached the next stage of his or her assessment, or an initial planning meeting with a different candidate. Your assessor might be there for a longer period of time, but you would have provided evidence against more criteria. If you are doing Units 1 and 2 concurrently, evidence from Unit 2 will cover criteria in Unit 1.

LEARNING OUTCOME 2:
BE ABLE TO MAKE ASSESSMENT DECISIONS ABOUT OCCUPATIONAL COMPETENCE

ASSESSMENT CRITERIA

2.1 Use valid, fair and reliable assessment methods including: observation of performance; examining products of work; questioning the learner; discussing with the learner; use of others (witness testimony); looking at learner statements; recognizing prior learning.

2.2 Make assessment decisions of occupational competence against specified criteria.

2.3 Follow standardization procedures.

2.4 Provide feedback to learners that affirms achievement and identifies any further implications for learning, assessment and progression.

2.1 Use valid, fair and reliable assessment methods including: observation of performance; examining products of work; questioning the learner; discussing with the learner; use of others (witness testimony); looking at learner statements; recognizing prior learning

As assessor/candidate you will need to provide evidence that shows your use of valid, fair and reliable methods. You will need to be observed observing, examining products and questioning. The assessment planning process and the assessment plans you negotiated with your candidate should show you discussed assessment methods and decided which will be fit for the purpose of assessing their competence. Your own assessor will be checking your understanding of the valid, fair and reliable assessment and how you apply these in your practice.

You might think that observing your candidates at work would automatically be a valid way of assessing whether they are competent, but make sure you can explain why, if questioned. When your assessor comes to observe you, s/he will be looking for evidence that:

- You are assessing the outcomes and criteria agreed in your assessment plan.

- The evidence you agreed with your candidate in the assessment plan is appropriate and enables him or her to address the agreed criteria.

- You carry out the observation without intruding on your candidate's capacity to perform naturally.

- You can deal effectively with a situation where the observation does not go to plan.

- If needed, you can adjust the assessment methods to give your candidate a chance to meet the agreed criteria, within the awarding organization regulations (eg picking up through questioning or discussion something that you have not been able to observe).

- Your feedback links your assessment judgement to the agreed criteria.

- Where appropriate, your feedback links back to national occupational standards.

Your assessor will also be looking at whether your assessment decisions are fair. You will need to show that you stick to the assessment criteria: for example, that you are not judging someone on their communication skills, if what is being assessed is their ability to make a healthy meal. When being observed, you will need to avoid leading questions or any suggestion of bias. Use of questions from a question bank might avoid this to some extent, but evidence should also include questions that have arisen from what you have observed. Your product evidence here might be completed questioning records. Some awarding organizations provide record sheets that identify by number the questions asked from the question bank, but then provide an additional sheet to record any extra questions you have included. Sometimes these record sheets are devised by the centre.

Before being assessed, it would be useful to prepare a written statement on how you avoid bias or discrimination, linking this to the awarding organization's policies and regulations. This statement can be used as evidence in your portfolio and prepare you for questions. It will also help you reflect on your own performance and become aware of any pitfalls that might occur when you were being observed.

Your assessment plan will have identified any specific learner needs. Arrangements to address these should be communicated to your assessor, perhaps when you are questioned, if they are not obvious when you are being observed. Discussion with your assessor following the observation of your performance might also cover specific learner needs that did not emerge in the planning process. For example, if when you arrived your candidates were stressed because they had to start late due to no fault of their own, you may take extra care to calm them and make them feel at ease before the observation. Drawing attention to this in the discussion with your assessor would provide evidence that you were making every attempt to be fair.

Your assessor will also be looking for evidence that your assessment is reliable:

- Performance evidence from your judgements on your candidate's performance, products and answers to questions will give an indication of whether your judgements are comparable to those of other assessors.
- Your assessment plans and records will show how many times you have/are planning to observe.
- Evidence from observation is supported by other relevant evidence that confirms that what has been observed is consistent with the candidate's normal standard of performance.
- Your candidates, to ensure that their performance is consistent over a period of time.
- Evidence of attendance at standardization meetings.

2.2 Make assessment decisions of occupational competence against specified criteria

Your evidence will be that you have:

- agreed the criteria to be assessed and recorded these in your assessment plan;
- stuck to the criteria when you assess; for example using these when carrying out an observation and recording your judgments on an observation sheet;
- provided oral/written feedback to the candidate that refers to the criteria.

TABLE 3.17 Competence in making assessment decisions

Evidence gathered through:	Competence can be confirmed when assessor/candidate evidence shows that s/he:
Observation of performance	• is clear what demonstrates competence against specified outcomes and criteria • has a means of recording whilst observing what outcomes and criteria have been met
Questioning	• uses pre-planned questions – question bank/self-devised • has determined the minimum level and detail required from candidate answers
Discussion	• ensures discussion remains relevant to the outcomes and assessment criteria being discussed • explores topics where candidate's evidence needs more clarification, and knows what is an acceptable level of clarification to prove competence • encourages candidate to be at ease so as to give him or her a fair opportunity to demonstrate occupational competence • keeps mindful of the level of response and discussion required • uses some extra probing questions to ask where candidate is not meeting the level required, so as to give him or her an opportunity to meet this level
Witness statements	• checks authenticity and currency • checks status of witness – what qualifies him or her to make a judgement? • Checks that statement links to criteria
Personal statements and explanations	• checks for coverage of specified criteria
Qualifications for RPL	• checks authenticity and currency • considers whether updating is needed to bring candidate up to current occupational competence

2.3 Follow standardization procedures

Your assessor will look for evidence that you know what procedures are in place and the audit trail that needs to be followed. You could include a learner statement itemising these procedures with a brief description of how you follow them, referring to supporting product evidence. Your IV/IQA should be able to supply records showing you follow standardization procedures. Examples include:

- records of attendance at standardization training sessions;
- records of attendance at standardization meetings with other assessors;
- sampling sheets where you comment on other assessors' judgements;
- sampling records you have provided for your IV/IQA;
- written feedback from the IV/IQA on how your practice compares with the rest of the team;
- written feedback from your IV/IQA, after observing you assess, that confirms the accuracy of your judgement;
- records showing monitoring of your assessments of different candidates doing the same units.

2.4 Provide feedback to learners that affirms achievement and identifies any further implications for learning, assessment and progression

Your evidence will be through your assessor observing you giving feedback to a candidate (performance evidence), or your records of written feedback (product evidence):

- affirming achievement against the criteria and summarizing where the candidate is now in achievement of the unit/qualification;
- identifying what further learning is needed – to enable success in this unit/future units;
- carrying out further assessment planning for the next assessment or, if the candidate has not achieved, for a reassessment; indicating what they need to do next to progress to future units, a higher level or future work opportunities;
- in graded programmes, identifying what candidates need to do to raise their performance to a higher grade.

Providing evidence of feedback after observation in the work environment

When your assessor observes you giving feedback, be aware of the following:

- Candidates are usually anxious to know what they have achieved and how well they have done. They also need to know how to improve further (even if all the agreed outcomes/criteria have been met). Just to tell candidates whether they are competent or not is not enough. Your role is also to let them know why you have made that decision.

- You should always set aside a proper time for feedback with the candidate so that you both have time to talk over the result and you are sure that the candidate fully understands the reasons for the assessment decision. For candidates who have not yet achieved competence, it is particularly important that they are given specific indications of where they need to improve, in a constructive way that will motivate them for the next time they are assessed.

- Feedback is best given orally, as soon after the observation as possible. It should be backed up with written notes, with a copy for the candidate. The candidate should be encouraged to discuss and ask questions.

- If face-to-face feedback is not possible following the observation, written notes can be left with the candidate to read through, and a date and time fixed as soon as possible to go through the notes.

- The written notes can be used as product evidence of your feedback.

(See Unit 4 Outcome 3 for examples of poor and good feedback on occupational competence.)

Giving written feedback

Candidates should be able to learn from their feedback. It needs to be written down for them, because normal human beings forget things, even things that are important. Candidates need to know:

- what they did well;
- how they performed against the specified criteria and standards;
- what needs to be worked on to bring it up to scratch and, where applicable (in QCF), to improve the grade;
- what they could think about to improve the breadth or depth of their understanding;
- whether the sources of information/references they selected are appropriate;
- what other resources they could use.

The summative assessment needs to summarize the full extent of what has been achieved and to detail what the candidate needs to do next. All records used in making the decision need to be available for both the candidate and the internal verifier.

LEARNING OUTCOME 3: BE ABLE TO PROVIDE REQUIRED INFORMATION FOLLOWING THE ASSESSMENT OF OCCUPATIONAL COMPETENCE

ASSESSMENT CRITERIA

3.1 Maintain records of the assessment of occupational competence, its outcomes and learner progress.

3.2 Make assessment information available to authorized colleagues.

3.3 Follow procedures to maintain the confidentiality of assessment information.

3.1 Maintain records of the assessment of occupational competence, its outcomes and learner progress

You will need to show that you keep accurate and up-to-date records of assessment that meet the requirements of the awarding organization and your own centre. The records themselves, and any descriptions of the systems put into place to make sure they are accurate and up to date, are your product evidence. Records should all be dated and signed by you and by whoever else is required to sign, for example the candidate or IV/IQA.

Evidence produced through questioning, discussion or written statements will show that you know about relevant legislation, policy and regulations involved and that you understand the reasons why clear and accurate records need to be maintained. You should show you know how these records fit into an audit trail that could be followed by internal or external quality-assurance staff if needed, in other words how your assessment records fit into the bigger picture of assessment recording and achievement within your centre. (See also Unit 1, Outcome 7, Units 4 and 5.)

You should show you use any electronic recording systems required by the awarding organization and the centre, for example through printouts of usage and/or observation in your work environment, or by inputting or accessing records (of a non-confidential nature). This could be arranged with your assessor to be included in an assessment visit to observe you with a candidate. A witness statement from your IQA/internal verifier could be used to confirm you maintain the accuracy and currency of data and that you have provided records as required for monitoring, tracking and quality-assurance purposes.

3.2 Make assessment information available to authorized colleagues

Authorized colleagues include:

- other assessors in your assessment team;
- IQAs, internal verifiers and lead verifiers who may need this for internal quality monitoring and enhancement;
- EQAs for monitoring the quality of assessment, internal quality assurance and overall performance at the centre;
- examinations officers for recording achievement and organizing certification;
- centre management, for auditing purposes and for providing statistics for external agencies such as BIS, SFA, YPFA, DfE, Ofsted.

If the information is paper-based, you will need to show how it is stored and who is responsible for retrieving it if required. If it is electronically accessed and stored, you need to show you know how to access it and how the system enables it to be shared with authorized colleagues. Witness statements from colleagues who can confirm that you have provided any assessment information they have requested, promptly and accurately, will provide supporting evidence.

3.3 Follow procedures to maintain the confidentiality of assessment information

Using a holistic approach, you could cross-reference some evidence from Unit 1, Outcomes 7 and 8 to show you know the centre's policy and procedures on confidentiality. Your internal verifier should be able to provide evidence from monitoring your practice that you keep assessment information confidential. It could be useful to prepare a learner statement that clearly states the procedures that affect you and how you follow these. You could include some examples of how you have carried these out in practice. This could include how you deal with sensitive issues in the workplace identified in discussion with the candidate and kept confidential, even if not strictly covered by legislation and how candidates work is kept safe and how they are reassured that their work is safe.

LEARNING OUTCOME 4:
BE ABLE TO MAINTAIN LEGAL AND GOOD PRACTICE REQUIREMENTS WHEN ASSESSING OCCUPATIONAL COMPETENCE

ASSESSMENT CRITERIA

4.1 Follow relevant policies, procedures and legislation for the assessment of occupational competence, including those for health, safety and welfare.

4.2 Apply requirements for equality and diversity and, where appropriate, bilingualism, when assessing occupational competence.

4.3 Evaluate own work in carrying out assessments of occupational competence.

4.4 Maintain the currency of own expertise and competence as relevant to own role in assessing occupational competence.

4.1 Follow relevant policies, procedures and legislation for the assessment of occupational competence, including those for health, safety and welfare

If your assessor observes you carrying out an observation, this may provide some direct evidence to show you are following relevant policies, procedures and legislation. For example you may be observed:

- providing evidence of identity and signing a visitors' book at reception (safeguarding);
- putting on special headgear, footwear or clothing (health and safety);
- washing hands before entering a sterile area (health and safety);
- giving feedback to a candidate about correct disposal of waste conforming to environmental legislation.

Questions about your knowledge and practices in following policies, procedures and legislation are likely to be included in your discussion with your assessor, perhaps following the observation of your performance.

You may also provide product evidence such as copies of risk assessments, IQA monitoring statements or guidance notes given to learners/candidates about your observation visits that ask for information about any specific health and safety requirements. Witness statements from a workplace where you observe could provide confirmation that you have carried out the correct health and safety procedures.

Details of key legislation affecting your work as an assessor can be found in Appendix 2.

4.2 Apply requirements for equality and diversity and, where appropriate, bilingualism, when assessing occupational competence

Again, your respect for equality and diversity may be apparent to an assessor observing your performance. For example:

- being accompanied by a note taker when observing someone who has a hearing disability;

- being sensitive and showing respect for particular cultural norms, for example being aware that some candidates would not be comfortable being given feedback alone with an assessor of the opposite sex (diversity);

- using the appropriate coloured paper for written feedback for a dyslexic candidate (equality);

- enabling a Welsh candidate to be observed and questioned using the Welsh language (bilingualism).

Questions about your knowledge and practices in respecting equality and diversity are likely to be included in your discussion with your assessor, perhaps following the observation of your performance. Product evidence could show documents of your actions ensuring equal and fair treatment to candidates, such as copies of:

- assessment planning forms where you have discussed and taken into account candidates' special requirements;

- applications to awarding organizations for reasonable adjustment to assessment or special considerations for assessment (these have to be made by the centre manager, but you could include copies of your communications to the centre manager that led up to the forms being sent);

- e-mails or other forms of communications making arrangements that take candidates' special requirements into account.

4.3 Evaluate own work in carrying out assessments of occupational competence

Your evidence for self-evaluation might be a product of work, such as a reflective journal, or it might emerge as a result of a discussion with your assessor following an observation of your performance. Here you might be encouraged to evaluate your own performance. You might ask yourself questions after each assessment such as:

- How effectively did I carry out that assessment and feedback?
- Was there anything I didn't anticipate?
- How did I deal with this?
- What went well?
- What could I improve?
- If I had to change anything, what would I do differently next time?

Try to get into the habit of using a reflective journal to note down your experiences, thoughts and feelings relating to your development as an assessor over a period of time. This will provide useful practice in self-evaluation, for example if an assessor asks you to self-assess prior to giving their feedback, as well as providing evidence against criteria across a number of units.

You might also include statements that give examples of how you use evidence from formal observations of your practice, for example feedback from IQAs and from candidates to improve your practice.

4.4 Maintain the currency of own expertise and competence as relevant to own role in assessing occupational competence

There are four main aspects to keeping your knowledge and skills up to date in order to be a credible and effective assessor of occupational competence in the workplace. Your evidence here needs to show how you:

- maintain your own subject specialist expertise in the vocational area you are assessing through continuing professional development;
- keep up to date with relevant government legislation, awarding organization regulations, policies, specifications and guidance, sector skills council developments and national standards developments, as well as organizational procedures related to assessment and quality assurance;
- keep up to date with employer requirements and new/revised work practices in your specialist occupational area;

- keep up to date with new developments in vocational education and training, including approaches to teaching, learning and assessment and use of new technologies.

Your evidence for keeping up to date could be in the form of a statement placing your evidence in context and supported by a careful selection of product evidence (only a sample, not a whole boxful!). These could be seen during a visit from your assessor and include:

- evidence of membership of organizations related to your own occupational area;
- evidence of membership of organizations related to the qualifications you assess;
- programmes/notes from input/training sessions and conferences on your occupational area;
- programmes/notes from input/training sessions from the awarding organization/your accredited centre;
- notes from reading relevant publications, such as specialist news-sheets, magazines and journals;
- printouts from online specialist discussion groups, wikis, blogs, Facebook groups and information sites, including VLEs.

Your assessor could then record what s/he has seen and how this meets the agreed criteria.

If you are teaching or training in an educational/training environment, you will need to be a full or associate member of the Institute for Learning (IFL). Evidence of CPD is a condition of continued membership of IFL, so whatever you produce for this could also provide evidence for your assessor qualification.

Unit 3
Assess vocational skills, knowledge and understanding

LEARNING OUTCOMES FOR UNIT 3

1 Be able to prepare assessments of vocational skills, knowledge and understanding
2 Be able to carry out assessments of vocational skills, knowledge and understanding
3 Be able to provide required information following the assessment of vocational skills, knowledge and understanding
4 Be able to maintain legal and good practice requirements when assessing vocational skills, knowledge and understanding

Evidence requirements for this unit:

- Your evidence must cover all of the assessment methods listed below, and there should be performance evidence for at least three of the methods.
- Your own performance evidence must be assessed by observation, by examining your products of work such as plans and records, and by questioning/discussions.
- As a candidate-assessor you must show evidence of carrying out at least two assessments of two learners' skills, knowledge and understanding (four assessments in total).

LEARNING OUTCOME 1:
BE ABLE TO PREPARE ASSESSMENTS OF VOCATIONAL SKILLS, KNOWLEDGE AND UNDERSTANDING

ASSESSMENT CRITERIA

1.1 Select methods to assess vocational skills, knowledge and understanding that address learner needs and meet assessment requirements, including: assessments of the learner in simulated environments, skills tests, oral and written questions, assignments, projects, case studies and recognizing prior learning.

1.2 Prepare resources and conditions for the assessment of vocational skills, knowledge and understanding.

1.3 Communicate the purpose, requirements and processes of assessment of vocational skills, knowledge and understanding to learners.

1.1 Select methods to assess vocational skills, knowledge and understanding which address learner needs and meet assessment requirements, including: assessments of the learner in simulated environments, skills tests, oral and written questions, assignments, projects, case studies and recognizing prior learning

Unit 1, Outcome 2 evaluated different assessment methods. Your evidence must cover the assessment methods listed above for Unit 3. However your awarding organization may allow the use of other appropriate methods, for example reflective journals, which could be a valid method of assessing how well learners understand what they are doing and can evaluate their own and others' performance.

Your evidence should show why you chose certain methods. Table 3.18 suggests some possible reasons that you could explain in more detail in discussion with your assessor.

TABLE 3.18 Possible reasons for choice of assessment method

Reason for choice of method
It is specified by the awarding organization
It fits the purpose and type of assessment, for example initial, formative, summative
It is a recognized means of assessing certain knowledge
It enables learners to achieve the specified outcomes and assessment criteria
If grading is used, it gives learners the chance to achieve criteria at pass, merit or distinction level
It relates to a real-life work or work-related situation
It takes into account the specific needs of an individual learner/group of learners
It is holistic and time/cost-effective
It helps to motivate and engage the learners
It uses new technology that enhances the learners' experience of assessment

Your assessment briefs are products of work that will provide evidence for all three assessment criteria in this section. They will identify the methods used for a particular task. To make sure you cover all the required methods, you will probably need more than one assessment brief as evidence.

Briefs should:

- give clear guidance on the task;
- map the task against the assessment criteria and, if used, grading criteria;
- identify what learners need to provide as evidence;
- if graded, show clearly what learners have to do to achieve grades at pass, merit or distinction level for that assessment task;
- give the timings, locations and conditions of assessments;
- identify the resources/materials/equipment needed to carry out the task;
- indicate how late submissions are dealt with.

Other products of your work as assessor might be:

- the approval document for the awarding organization confirming that your IV/IQA has agreed the assessment brief (which would include approving the methods used);
- your scheme of work and sessions plans that show how you cover the range of assessment methods;
- the assessment schedule agreed with the assessment team, which ensures coverage of all assessment criteria and grading criteria, where applicable.

1.2 Prepare resources and conditions for the assessment of vocational skills, knowledge and understanding

Your evidence should show how you make sure all necessary resources are available and the assessment is carried out under the conditions specified by the centre/awarding organization (Table 3.19). Your assessment brief will have identified the resources/materials/equipment needed for the assessment activity. You will need to have enough copies of the brief for all your learners (including copies that take into account special requirements, for example with large print for sight-impaired, or a coloured background for dyslexic students). If learners need to access the brief electronically, you need to show they understand how and when to do this.

Your evidence might be provided through an observation where you carry out an assessment, providing, organizing and monitoring the necessary resources. Your product evidence might include:

- copies of assessment briefs detailing the resources needed;
- lists of materials/equipment that the learners must use to complete an assessment;
- copies of the resources you produce or supply;
- reading lists;
- lists of websites;
- communications with technicians/other assessors, booking or organizing the use of resources/equipment/communications with learners/candidates or with other assessors if the 'resources' are people, for example, acting as clients in a simulated-environment.

TABLE 3.19 Ensuring correct resources and conditions

Method	Resources and conditions
Assessments of the learner in simulated environments	There are sufficient materials, equipment and space for all learner-candidates
	All equipment is available, and has been checked to see that it works and is safe and in the right place
	Any special clothing required is available
	Any ingredients/materials etc that are necessary for the tasks to be completed are available
	Learners are clear about the date and timings of the assessment
	Any others involved, eg other assessors; 'customers'/'clients' are aware of what is happening and the time(s) when they are required
Skills tests	*Vocational skills tests*: materials/equipment/clothing available as above
	Functional skills tests: paper-based: enough copies, quiet space to complete, clear instructions given, safeguards against copying from others
	Functional skills tests: on-line: no technical problems, quiet space, clear instructions, safeguards against copying
Oral and written questions	*Oral questions*: bank of oral questions for use with learners accessed/designed
	Appropriate time and space arranged for questioning in quiet private environment where possible
	Written questions: sufficient copies available Checked/piloted beforehand to make sure they are understandable and valid
	Time and space allocated for learners to concentrate and complete

TABLE 3.19 *continued*

Method	Resources and conditions
Assignments	Approved by internal quality assurer/verifier
	Sufficient copies for all learners
	If involving group work, clear strategy for how groups are to be chosen and how individual contributions will be recognized
	If involving outside visits, ensure places are open on the dates needed, where relevant any outside personnel aware that visit will be made, appropriate risk assessments completed
	Any necessary materials, information sources etc available
Projects	As assignments
Case studies	Sufficient copies, accuracy and currency of case study information and scenario checked
	If taken from a real-life case, ensure that confidentiality of the source is maintained; this could mean ensuring anonymity, by changing any specific features of the case which might identify those involved
Recognizing prior learning	Ensuring the candidate is clear about and provides all relevant evidence for RPL
	Making sure that details of unit/outcomes/criteria against which RPL is being claimed are available, together with any relevant regulations, documents or advice sheets on the process

You will also need to explain how you make sure that the assessment takes place in the right conditions. These will include:

- regulatory conditions set out by the awarding organization that specify the location/timings/amount of supervision/arrangements for assessment;
- regulatory conditions such as health and safety requirements;
- 'common-sense' conditions such as adequate space/lighting/tables/ workbenches for each learner to carry out the assessment task comfortably.

1.3 Communicate the purpose, requirements and processes of assessment of vocational skills, knowledge and understanding to learners

The learners/candidates should be as involved as possible in the assessment process. You should be able to provide evidence of how you ensure they understand what they need about the assessment and the assessment criteria they are being assessed against. Product evidence for this would be the clear, well-written assessment brief you provide for them, which has gone through formal approval processes. When being questioned by your assessor, you will explain how you ensure all learners/candidates are clear about the terminology used and what those terms mean for them in practice. For example, you might show how you:

- give them an overview of the vocational skills, knowledge and understanding needed to work in their chosen vocational area;
- help them understand the unit specifications, outcomes and criteria;
- if appropriate, help them understand the grading process and how they can improve their grades;
- ensure they use the correct documentation;
- explain your role and responsibilities and their role and responsibilities in the assessment process;
- check they know what 'authentic' evidence means and the importance of signing to confirm the work has been produced by them;
- explain how and when the assessments will take place and the stages to completing the unit or qualification.

LEARNING OUTCOME 2:
BE ABLE TO CARRY OUT ASSESSMENTS OF VOCATIONAL SKILLS, KNOWLEDGE AND UNDERSTANDING

ASSESSMENT CRITERIA

2.1 Manage assessments of vocational skills, knowledge and understanding to meet assessment requirements.

2.2 Provide support to learners within agreed limitations.

2.3 Analyse evidence of learner achievement.

2.4 Make assessment decisions relating to vocational skills, knowledge and understanding against specified criteria.

2.5 Follow standardization procedures.

2.6 Provide feedback to the learner that affirms achievement and identifies any further implications for learning, assessment and progression.

2.1 Manage assessments of vocational skills, knowledge and understanding to meet assessment requirements

Here you will need to show how you organize assessments, taking into account:

- centre and awarding organization regulations, procedures, documentation and timescales for feedback and reporting of results;
- special learner requirements;
- the context and environment of the assessment – health and safety; minimizing potential interruptions; providing necessary equipment, materials, paper-based/electronic resources; ensuring anyone else involved, for example technical staff in a workshop, is well-briefed.

Performance evidence where you are observed carrying out an assessment with an individual learner or group of learners/candidates can demonstrate how you ensure:

- The space is organized in the best way; for example:
  - *classroom tests*: enough room between each learner/candidate so they can't copy;
  - *workshop-based practical skills tests*: sufficient personal work area so the activity can be carried out with space for the observer to be able to see what is being done.
- Each learner is given the same opportunity for assessment.
- You manage your time so that you can assess each learner.
- You have back up plans for any unexpected occurrences, for example if a learner is off sick or the room is not vacant when you arrive and you have to wait to get in.
- You have all the documentation to hand and have a system for recording results.
- You allow enough time for feedback, if appropriate.

2.2 Provide support to learners within agreed limitations

Teachers/assessors will be supporting their learners in many different ways and your evidence needs to show how you diagnose, arrange, offer and review support needs. This could include an observation report of assessment planning or review meetings for two learners on two occasions, where individual support needs are identified, special requirements are taken into account and action plans are agreed and reviewed to provide the necessary support.

Documentary evidence could include:

- records of these meetings;
- records of initial assessments;
- individual learning plans;
- records of formative assessments and feedback;
- special consideration forms and correspondence;
- correspondence about support arrangements, for example for learners with visual, auditory, physical impairments, bilingual learners;
- written reflections on learners (maintaining confidentiality) that evaluate the nature and quality of support you have given them, linking this to relevant legislation and issues related to equality and diversity.

You also need to show that you are aware of the amount of support that is acceptable under centre and awarding organization regulations, for example providing an amanuensis, additional time for diagnosed dyslexia or allowing a specified number of drafts. This includes knowledge of the conditions for assessment, such as the amount of support allowed and the level of supervision required. For example:

- Credit would not be awarded for coursework that the candidate has not produced independently, and access to assessment arrangements should not interfere with this principle.

- Even though the candidate may usually be eligible to have a longer time period to complete a task (eg because of emotional or learning difficulties), special arrangements cannot be made if the timing is crucial to the assessment – for example hair colouring has strict timings that are essential to the task.

Evidence here could be a statement summarizing key documentation from awarding organizations.

Note: There may be some differences in the amount of support allowed by awarding organizations, such as allowances for learners/candidates whose first language is not English. There may be a limitation that requires a history of need and provision to be established from the learner's country of origin before support such as a reader is made available. You will need to check your awarding organization's access policy.

2.3 Analyse evidence of learner achievement

Over the duration of a course, your learners/candidates will produce a range of evidence that you as teacher/assessor will need to analyse. In the summative assessment for each learner, you will check whether the evidence overall is valid, current, authentic and sufficient to meet the assessment criteria. Where applicable, you will also analyse the learners' grades and identify what they will need to do to achieve higher grades in their future work.

As a candidate-assessor your analysis might be evidenced through observation of feedback to individual learners or through discussion of learners' evidence with your assessor. Documentary evidence could include supporting documentation such as results-recording forms with learners' profiles of evidence, marks and grades. Another form of documentary evidence could be written feedback sheets.

Sometimes candidate-assessors find it hard to know what 'analysis' looks like. The written feedback below for a learner on a diploma in art and design, and covering a number of units, shows how a teacher/assessor might analyse a learner's achievement and make suggestions for improvement in future. This teacher has taken care to use friendly and motivational language, has been specific about what has been achieved and what could be done to improve, including improving grades from pass (P) to merit (M). She also shows a good grasp of the learner's work.

Example of teacher/assessor analysing learner achievement

You worked incredibly hard to produce a series of expressive and sensitive life-drawings, showing clear development and progression of your observational drawing skills – Well done. (Units 1+2)

After a slow start and a period of being a bit 'stuck', your chosen theme exploring high and low culture through juxtaposing ballet shoes with your location of Camden town was really interesting, resulting in an attractive and effective outcome that met the requirements of the brief – great (Units 78, 82). You also demonstrated an independent approach to sourcing your own materials, which is great and should continue.

Your sketchbook for this project was quite thin, however, and would have benefited from a deeper and more diverse approach to researching your theme (M1, Unit 78). Collecting imagery and taking independent research trips could have been helpful in pushing your ideas further, as could exploring a wider range of materials to help you communicate your concept – could you have referred back to previous projects more, revisiting mark-making, painting or printing techniques? (All units). Further evidence showing ideas-development, plus purposeful experimentation using a wide range of 2D and 3D materials in a refined way, would enable you to achieve a merit in Units 78 and 82.

Would exploring textiles have been useful too, in order to further explore the surface of your ballet shoes? Your use of materials overall, plus your written evaluation, enabled you to achieve M2 of Unit 2 – considered exploration of materials in forthcoming projects could enable you to achieve M1.

Your artist research is thorough, which is great, but you are still not adding your own comments and analysis to your own or others' work enough (M1, Unit 2)! This is what we are most interested in and is necessary in order to achieve high grades.

Ongoing analysis of your own working process, plus thorough, diverse research at the start of each project is necessary in order to hit the ground running.

A really interesting outcome... with some strong life-drawing – please see below for your action plan to maximize achievement.

Note: using a holistic approach, this type of written feedback would also be appropriate evidence towards Criteria 2.4. and 2.6 (see below).

2.4 Make assessment decisions relating to vocational skills, knowledge and understanding against specified criteria

Your assessor will need to see examples of your assessment decisions, together with the basis for making those decisions. You will need to be able to justify your judgements through evaluating the evidence (as the teacher did in the example given in Outcome 2.3 of this unit) and linking it back to the criteria identified in the assessment plan and assessment brief. See also Unit 1 Outcome 5 for the factors to take into account when making and justifying an assessment decision.

Your evidence might include:

- Copies of written feedback and action plans to learners as above. This should be accompanied by copies of their work, where appropriate, so your assessor can see the evidence you are using. If your written feedback relates to an observation of performance, then include copies of completed centre-devised checklist(s), evidence-recording forms and/or written notes that have helped you make the decision.

- Being observed giving oral feedback to different learners, using assessment criteria and, where applicable, grading criteria to structure your feedback – referring to the assignment plan and assessment brief.

- Copies of individual task marking sheets and unit mark sheets (which summarize separate task grades into an overall unit grade).

- Copies of completed assessment-recording documentation that will be presented at standardization meetings.

- Statements or explanations of what you take into account, including validity, sufficiency, currency, authenticity and how you ensure the evidence is reliable and reflects learner performance that can be repeated or transferred to other situations.

- Witness statements, for example from an internal verifier, confirming the accuracy of your judgements and that your decisions comply with any centre/awarding organization's regulations/conditions.

2.5 Follow standardization procedures

Your evidence here should show how you meet requirements for ensuring that your assessment judgements are accurate and consistent with the judgements of other assessors. Product evidence will include completed standardization forms (where you are named as one of the participants) and could include a witness statement from your internal verifier, confirming you have participated effectively and have shown you understand and follow the processes (this could be part of the verifier's witness statement covering 2.4).

2.6 Provide feedback to the learner that affirms achievement and identifies any further implications for learning, assessment and progression

See sample of feedback Outcome 2.3 and suggestions for evidence (2.4) and principles of good feedback, Unit 1, Table 3.16.

LEARNING OUTCOME 3: BE ABLE TO PROVIDE REQUIRED INFORMATION FOLLOWING THE ASSESSMENT OF VOCATIONAL SKILLS, KNOWLEDGE AND UNDERSTANDING

ASSESSMENT CRITERIA

3.1 Maintain records of the assessment of vocational skills, knowledge and understanding, its outcomes and learner progress.

3.2 Make assessment information available to authorized colleagues as required.

3.3 Follow procedures to maintain the confidentiality of assessment information.

3.1 Maintain records of the assessment of vocational skills, knowledge and understanding, its outcomes and learner progress

Your evidence here will be mainly products of work – primarily the completed records that have to be maintained and made available where required. Your awarding organization will supply much of the documentation, but your centre may provide additional documents. They may also name the documents differently. Key records will include all or some of the following:

- interview information, including details of original certificates seen;
- initial assessment information – results of skills tests, diagnostic tests, learning preferences, special learner requirements or support needs;
- individual learning plans;
- assessment plans and reviews;
- assessment briefs (mapped against criteria);

- assessment grading criteria (used to mark each candidate's evidence and indicating characteristics of evidence needed against each grade);
- formative feedback and action planning;
- summative feedback and action planning;
- assessment decision form;
- observation-recording forms;
- progress/monitoring reports;
- tutorial records;
- individual and group tracking documents;
- unit mark record sheets;
- records of standardization marking (carried out by someone else for your learners);
- records of standardization marking (carried out by you for another assessor);
- enrolment, retention, progression and achievement data for each class.

You should be able to explain how you maintain and use these documents and also how you ensure that they are kept secure. Make sure you know about your organizational systems for receiving work – for example receipts when work is handed in – and systems for storing work, and that you have back-up systems for your records – for example remote server storage or back-up copies if stored electronically, and make sure that authorized people know where they are, in case you have to be absent without warning.

3.2 Make assessment information available to authorized colleagues as required

You should be able to explain who the authorized colleagues would be – for example, course leader, other assessors, IQAs, verifiers, examinations officers, centre managers – and give some examples of when you would need to make this information available. A witness statement from your IQA (an extended version of the one used as supporting evidence for other criteria in this unit, could confirm that you do this – and confirm 3.3 (see below)). Other evidence could be records of e-mails/memos with attachments, showing that information was sent in response to a request.

3.3 Follow procedures to maintain the confidentiality of assessment information

Your evidence will link to 3.2. You need to show you are aware of the required procedures – include a summary of your centre's procedures for confidentiality. You could explain how you follow these in a learner statement and refer to meeting the requirements of the Data Protection Act. A witness statement from your IQA could confirm that you do this (see 3.2).

In discussion, you can explain to your assessor how your centre ensures that student work is stored securely, and how long records need to be stored before they are destroyed.

LEARNING OUTCOME 4:
BE ABLE TO MAINTAIN LEGAL AND GOOD PRACTICE REQUIREMENTS WHEN ASSESSING VOCATIONAL SKILLS, KNOWLEDGE AND UNDERSTANDING

ASSESSMENT CRITERIA

4.1 Follow relevant policies, procedures and legislation relating to the assessment of vocational skills, knowledge and understanding, including those for health, safety and welfare.

4.2 Apply requirements for equality and diversity and, where appropriate, bilingualism.

4.3 Evaluate own work in carrying out assessments of vocational skills, knowledge and understanding.

4.4 Take part in continuing professional development to ensure current expertise and competence in assessing vocational skills, knowledge and understanding.

4.1 Follow relevant policies, procedures and legislation relating to the assessment of vocational skills, knowledge and understanding, including those for health, safety and welfare

Your evidence will need to show you know and follow the relevant legislation (see Unit 1.4, page 000) and are familiar with awarding organization and centre policies and procedures. Observation by your assessor can confirm that you follow these requirements. Supporting evidence might be:

- assessment-recording documents (see Outcome 3);
- any risk assessments you carry out;
- records of participation in standardization meetings;
- other evidence from Outcomes 3.2 and 3.3;
- other evidence from 3.2 and 3.3.

- an appropriate witness statement (eg internal verifier/IQA/course leader/centre health and safety officer);
- evidence of communication about health and safety or welfare issues (observing confidentiality where appropriate);
- documentation that shows you have followed procedures related to plagiarism or special consideration/requirements for candidates.

4.2 Apply requirements for equality and diversity and, where appropriate, bilingualism

Many awarding organizations, such as OCR, and many local and national organizations in the education and training field, produce very useful guidance notes on good practice in equality and diversity. These can all be found by searching the internet. Your evidence needs to show how you follow legal, organizational and awarding organization requirements for addressing equality and diversity as identified in the centre policy that is produced as part of obtaining awarding organization approval. You should be aware that awarding organizations are clear that even if the learner's circumstances require special arrangements, these must not give them an advantage over other learners taking the same assessment. Nor should the arrangements affect the validity or reliability of assessment, which must be comparable in level of difficulty with the assessments undertaken by other learners.

Your evidence should demonstrate how you show respect for equality and diversity in your assessment practice (see Unit 1, Outcome 8). For example give examples on how you make sure:

- Assessment methods and processes are geared to the specific needs of individuals or groups.
- None of the resources used for assessment contain discriminatory language or images.
- The resources used are produced or customized to address the needs of learners with disabilities.
- Resources have been produced that address the needs of bilingual learners, ie those whose first language is not English.
- Within reason, that the assessments are timetabled to accommodate the different circumstances of learners.
- A learner is not disadvantaged by missing an assessment for reasons beyond their control, such as accident, illness, bereavement.

You might show samples of communications about special requirements, or examples of resources you have produced to address particular learners' needs. You might have witness statements from learners/candidates describing how you had helped them access assessment by arranging, for example, a signer for a candidate with a severe hearing disability.

4.3 Evaluate own work in carrying out assessments of vocational skills, knowledge and understanding

Your college or training centre will have comprehensive systems for evaluating the quality of courses and evaluating teacher performance. This will include observations of teaching and assessment undertaken for internal quality-assurance purposes. EQAs check to ensure that such systems are in place and working effectively.

Your evidence might show how you participate in internal and external quality-assurance systems and how you evaluate your work with help from others, for example through learner/candidate feedback, discussions with the IQA and through appraisal meetings with your line manager.

Your evidence should also demonstrate how you evaluate your own work to improve your assessment practice. This might be through discussion with your assessor, but it might also be evidence from a reflective journal or from your lesson plans where they have a section where you evaluate a session. Here you might ask yourself questions such as:

- Did learners understand what they needed to do to meet the criteria?
- Was the quality of work better/worse than last year? What might be the reasons for this?
- Did I mark and return assessments within the required timescale?
- Was I clear enough in my feedback?
- Were there any student complaints about the assessment? Were any of them justified?
- Would I approach the assessment differently next time?

4.4 Take part in continuing professional development to ensure current expertise and competence in assessing vocational skills, knowledge and understanding

There are four main aspects to keeping your knowledge and skills up to date in order to be a credible and effective teacher/assessor of vocational skills. These are:

1 Maintaining your own subject specialist expertise in the vocational area you are assessing through continuing professional development.

2 Keeping up to date with relevant government legislation, awarding-body regulations, policies, specifications and guidance, sector skills, council developments and national standards developments, as well as organizational procedures related to assessment and quality assurance. This may involve Points 3 and 4.

3 Keeping up to date with employer requirements and new/revised work practices in your specialist occupational area.

4 Keeping up to date with new developments in vocational education and training, including approaches to teaching, learning and assessment and use of new technologies.

You need to be able to show how you are covering the four aspects above. This is likely to involve you in:

- attending local, regional, national briefing meetings/training seminars;
- attending conferences;
- attending courses to acquire higher level certification in your specialism;
- keeping in contact with other specialists through specialist forums or discussion groups online;
- work-shadowing;
- peer observation;
- attending employer forums;
- visiting different workplaces;
- reading relevant publications;
- regular visits to relevant websites.

A log of your attendance and participation in such events and activities will be a useful record to maintain and use as a basis for evidence. You need to be ready to explain how, for example, attendance at a conference has impacted on your practice.

CPD and IFL

If you are teaching or training in an educational/training environment, you will need to be a full or associate member of the Institute for Learning (IFL). The IFL has specific requirements for CPD in order to retain IFL membership, which are discussed in the section on 'Continuing professional development' at the end of Unit 1. You can use CPD required by your employer for the IFL, but you can also choose to undertake other CPD that falls outside your employer requirements. Look on the IFL website for further information. As part of continued IFL membership you are required to reflect on your professional skills and CPD. The IFL has an electronic resource, 'REFLECT', to help you with this.

Unit 4
Understanding the principles and practices of internally assuring the quality of assessment

LEARNING OUTCOMES FOR UNIT 4

1 Understand the context and principles of internal quality assurance
2 Understand how to plan the internal quality assurance of assessment
3 Understand techniques and criteria for monitoring the quality of assessment internally
4 Understand how to internally maintain and improve the quality of assessment
5 Understand how to manage information relevant to the internal quality assurance of assessment
6 Understand the legal and good practice requirements for the internal quality assurance of assessment

U nit 4 is about the knowledge and understanding that underpin effective internal quality assurance.

Some of you will be reading or taking this unit purely for interest, as you do not have to be a practising internal verifier or internal quality assurer (IV/IQA) to complete the unit. If you are already, or planning to be, an IV/IQA you will check the assessments of the assessors for whom you are responsible, which means you come to the role with a good understanding of the quality assurance of assessment (see Units 1, 2 and 3). Unit 4 gives information and ideas about checking the quality of both work-based and vocational assessments. The information and ideas should help you in the work you do to achieve this unit, but also inform the related practical units – Unit 5 and, if you are a team leader, Unit 8.

Different awarding organizations will suggest different ways in which you can show you have met the outcomes for the unit. Assessment methods particularly suited to checking your knowledge and understanding will be used: for example, written assignments, projects, recorded statements, being questioned or taking part in discussions with your assessor. Your own experiences as a candidate will not only help you to understand the assessment process even more, but help you to help your own learners and candidates.

If you are a manager responsible for staff acting as IQA/IVs, this chapter should give you some idea of the time requirements needed for effective and developmental internal quality assurance.

LEARNING OUTCOME 1: UNDERSTAND THE CONTEXT AND PRINCIPLES OF INTERNAL QUALITY ASSURANCE

ASSESSMENT CRITERIA

1.1 Explain the functions of internal quality assurance in learning and development.

1.2 Explain the key concepts and principles of the internal quality assurance in learning and development.

1.3 Explain the roles of practitioners involved in the internal and external quality-assurance process.

1.4 Explain the regulations and requirements for internal quality assurance in own area of practice.

1.1 Explain the functions of internal quality assurance in learning and development

Internal quality assurance has critical importance. It has the functions of directly influencing:

- *The performance of delivery and assessment teams.* For example, good IQAs can spot areas for improvements long before they become a problem. If, for instance, a particular candidate or group seems to be progressing slowly, this can indicate that candidate learning is hindered, perhaps because delivery teams do not realize the need to present information in challenging and exciting ways, or because they ignore the learning style preferences of candidates. If the assessments seem inconsistent, this can indicate that assessors lack confidence with making judgements, or that there need to be more standardization events held with assessors.

- *Learners' progress.* For example the IQA can monitor the action plans agreed by assessors and candidates, and help assessors review agreed targets. This might lead in turn to candidate assessments progressing more rapidly, or in a more holistic way.

- *Candidates and employers views on training.* If employers have confidence that the qualification their employees are taking is well planned and efficient in its use of employees' time, that the assessment is to national industry standard, that all parties involved in the delivery and assessment are conversant with current industry skills and thinking, and that those with the qualification are working more effectively, they will be supportive of training, rather than seeing it as an expensive cost with no reward. It is also good if employers are involved in award ceremonies or are willing to provide 'good news' copy for the local press.

- *Centre policy.* The IQA compliance with legislation on health and safety, accessibility, continuing professional development, record keeping, risk and data collection.

- *The reputation of the qualification.* The IQA maintains national standards through rigorous monitoring of assessment practice, and ensures compliance with awarding organization requirements.

It is important to remember that, when awarding organizations give grades to centres, the grade can never be higher than that awarded to the internal verification process. Even if assessment practice, resources and support for candidates are outstanding or satisfactory, but internal quality-assurance practice falls short of the awarding organization's requirements, the overall grade given to the centre will show that the centre is not complying adequately with those requirements. However, if a centre consistently performs well at internal verification, then the awarding organization will implement a 'lighter touch' verification process, for example through remote sampling.

1.2 Explain the key concepts and principles of the internal quality assurance in learning and development

The overall concept or idea behind the internal quality assurance of assessment is that of equitable assessment. All holders of any particular qualification should have been judged to be at an acceptable, agreed level of knowledge and skill. To do this, IQAs follow two sets of standards: first, their own national occupational vocational standards, such as health and social care, construction or learning and development, and second, the standards for internal quality assurance. IQA decisions are subject to rigorous scrutiny from external quality assurers.

Related concepts are those of standardization – the process by which IQAs compare the practice and processes of those involved in the delivery and assessment of qualifications – and of quality improvement whereby assessors and others are helped to develop and update their practice so that national and organizational standards are maintained.

The principles that good IQAs uphold are those of consistency, reliability, fairness and validity of assessment (see Unit 1), together with the principle of support for candidates and assessors, and open communication to relevant persons. Internal quality assurance helps to minimize risk to the assessment process.

Table 3.20 summarizes some measures by which quality may be assessed.

TABLE 3.20 Measures of quality

Quantitative measures	Qualitative measures
Numbers of enrolled, 'in progress', withdrawn and completed candidates	Availability of resources
	Policies and procedures
National benchmarking data for the qualification	Feedback from assessors and other centre staff
Time taken from enrolment to completion	External verifier reports on process
	IQA/internal verifier or other internal quality reports
Audit trails checking compliance	
Data from satisfaction surveys	Reports from other examiners or inspectors
Records of complaints	
Equal opportunities monitoring data	Staff CPD records

1.3 Explain the roles of practitioners involved in the internal and external quality-assurance process

The external quality-assurer/external verifier role

EQAs/EVs are experienced senior practitioners in the broad area of the standards they verify. Their role is to approve centres that wish to offer qualifications, approve the schemes that approved centres wish to implement, and monitor the quality of assessment and internal verification procedures – in other words, that they are being carried out to the approved national standards for assessment and quality assurance and for the vocational area (such as construction). The EQA/EV is the main link between the centre and the awarding organization, and should also be the person who can give answers to queries from centres, for example on the acceptability of certain evidence or on the interpretation of certain performance criteria. This means that external verifiers must keep themselves up to date with the frequent changes in systems, structures and practice, so that they can respond accurately and swiftly to centre queries as well as making accurate decisions. Usually, EQAs/EVs are line-managed by their awarding organization administrative managers and are supported by their regional lead EQA/EV for their occupational area(s).

Awarding organizations are moving towards 'remote sampling' of centres, whereas a few years ago it was common for an external verifier to make a couple of visits a year to a centre. Remote sampling inevitably means that data has to be transferred between centres, and this is normally done online, using secure systems.

The IQA/internal verifier coordinator role

Many centres will have an IQA/internal verifier coordinator (IQAC), who allocates the workloads of all the IQAs/internal verifiers and manages the team of IQAs/IVs and assessors at a senior level (see Unit 8). This person is the point of contact with the awarding organization and the organization's quality manager (if that is a different person from themselves). An IQAC will usually act as the team leader for the IQAs/internal verifiers, ensuring that information and procedures are fully consistent within the internal verification team (see Units 5 and 8).

Within all but the smallest organizations there will probably be more than one person acting in the IQAC role. Where this is the case, the IQAC will coordinate the activities of all the IQAs/internal verifiers and assessors for whom he or she is responsible. IQACs may need to manage across a number of related vocational awards areas. They are responsible for planning and implementing an overall internal verification strategy. This must be in compliance with the appropriate assessment strategy for the qualification being taken by candidates. IQACs take responsibility for ensuring that both candidates and assessors show evidence of consistent occupational competence and that assessments and internal quality assurance conform to national standards. In addition, they must ensure that the centre keeps to relevant legislation and codes of practice, including the NVQ Code of Conduct and the JAB Guidance if their assessors are assessing NVQs. It is the IQAC role to see that this happens by ensuring that:

- There is regular contact with the awarding organization.
- Assessors have sufficient occupational competence and have records of recent occupational and assessment updating.
- Assessors are given all the necessary help and information they need to be able to assess effectively and efficiently.
- The quality of assessments is monitored and standardized on a regular basis.
- The IQA/internal verifier is available to answer queries if assessors experience difficulties.

The Internal Quality Assurer/internal verifier role

The role of the IQA/internal verifier (see Unit 5) is to monitor the work of the assessors for whom they are responsible, through observation, meetings and checking of data and records. They will use internal verification plans to ensure they keep track of all assessors, candidates, workplaces and qualifications for which they are responsible. Much record keeping will be on secure online systems, using documentation provided by the awarding organizations. IQAs/internal verifiers should participate in appropriate training and standardization events to keep up to date and be sure they are making sound judgements. This role is crucial to the quality assurance of QCF and NVQ qualifications, and for the reputation of the centres offering the qualifications. The role is at Level 4, showing that IQAs/IVs have a managerial rather than a supervisory role.

The work-based assessor role

The work-based assessor (see Unit 3) uses observation and questioning to check a candidate's competence against occupational standards, completes records of observation, and gives written and oral feedback to candidates in a way that helps their practice to develop. Assessments can also be made of candidate products, such as a cupboard made by a joiner or a website produced by a media candidate. The assessor will then, through questioning and discussion, find out how well the candidate understands the consequences and context of that activity.

The vocational assessor role

The vocational assessor (see Unit 3) uses a wider range of activities and evidence to make judgements than does the work-based assessor, and generally works in an education and training context such as an FE College or a training centre. This is because candidates may be asked to demonstrate their knowledge and understanding of a topic in varying degrees of depth, and this requires different techniques. Vocational assessors record their results and give feedback to candidates, both orally and in writing. Depending on the qualification, they may be required to grade work. The types of evidence that assessors may judge could include:

- reflective journals;
- essays and assignments;
- project work;
- the candidate's oral or written answers to questions;
- observation of the candidate's practice;

- products from the candidate, such as a log book or an item he or she has made, an endorsed video or photographic evidence;
- a report from the candidate or from the candidate's peers;
- judgements from others, including work-based assessors and witnesses;
- evidence from the candidate's prior experience;
- simulated work experiences.

The independent assessor role

Some NVQs and vocational qualifications require independent assessment. The independent assessor must be fully qualified as an assessor and is often a specialist in the candidate's vocational area. The involvement of an independent assessor can bring some internal quality control into the internal assessment process. Independent assessment is not the same as 'double marking' or standardization, where two assessors assess the same piece of work. The independent assessment is the only one for the prescribed piece of work or activity. It has been introduced in some cases to replace previous external testing, where work was sent away to be marked by external assessors. The independent assessor does not necessarily meet the candidate (though many do), but does assess an agreed substantial part of the candidate's work, often a complete unit or a complete assignment. Sometimes an independent assessor may carry out a specialist observation if there is a very specific area of expertise within a vocational area that needs to be assessed.

The expert witness

Whilst this role is less widely used than in the past, it can be useful to check candidate progress or products with an occupationally competent person who is familiar with the candidate's work practice. If expert witness information is used to make a judgement, then full details of the witness and his or her experience should be available to the internal verifier before the evidence is used.

The internal moderator role

Internal moderators perform a similar role to IQAs/internal verifiers. The term is more often used in organizations with less emphasis on training and more on 'education', such as further education colleges, the Open College Network and the Open University. The process of moderation is much like aspects of standardization, where a group of assessors share their assessments and check that similar standards are being applied to grading and assessment.

Centre administration staff

Centre staff usually maintain candidate registration and certification records, administer the taking of fees, and may devise and print publicity and centre information for candidates.

Regulatory adviser role

Regulatory advisers understand the issues connected with different occupational areas, and can advise on legislative or code of practice matters.

Different combinations of roles

Within the roles identified there are clearly opportunities for different combinations and variations depending on the nature and size of the organization. For example, an assessor may be a work-based assessor for one candidate, a vocational assessor for a second and an independent assessor for a third. Assessors might also be qualified as, or be working towards being, IQA/internal verifiers and have their own allocation of assessors to support and mentor. One combination of roles that must never occur is that of assessor and IQA/internal verifier with the same candidate. That does not prevent someone from acting as an assessor with one candidate and then as an IQA/internal verifier with a candidate who has been assessed by another assessor. Centres need to ensure they have enough staff to avoid compromising quality through IQAs/internal verifiers having too little time to carry out their role.

Example 1

A candidate working in a large engineering firm is advised and assessed for her NVQ qualification by her immediate supervisor, in the role of work-based assessor. The supervisor from another section, a qualified A1 assessor, acts as the independent assessor, assessing one of the candidate's NVQ units. The senior manager of the section is the IQA/internal verifier, monitoring the process and procedures of the assessment and arranging for external verification.

Example 2

A candidate with considerable management experience, working within a local authority, wishes to claim credit towards a QCF Management qualification for learning achieved in the past. One of the local authority training officers, acting in the role of adviser, discusses with her what evidence would be appropriate. Another training officer acts in the assessor's role and makes an assessment judgement on the evidence. The line manager from another section, who has achieved D34 and has demonstrated to the EQA that he has upgraded his skills to the new IQA units, acts as internal verifier.

Example 3

A candidate is trained by her line manager (a trained vocational assessor) in retail. The organization is small and has joined with two other small organizations to form a consortium, which has registered as an approved centre. Her vocational and work-based assessors are from the other two organizations within the consortium, as is the internal assessor. The external work-based assessor does one observation, but her line manager acts as the observational assessor for all other work-based assessments. This arrangement allows these small centres to run their own awards in a cost-effective and efficient way, without compromising quality or integrity. The activities of all these four staff are managed by a fifth, who takes on the role of internal verifier coordinator.

1.4 Explain the regulations and requirements for internal quality assurance in own area of practice

See Appendix 2 for details of legislation.

You need to show you are keeping to regulations and requirements issued by:

- *Your workplace*: for example times and frequency for meetings of assessors, completion of internal quality documentation.
- *The awarding organization*: for example the completion of specific documents required before the visit of an external verifier, maintenance of a CPD file for self and assessors.
- *Regulatory bodies*: eg Ofsted.

- *The vocational area for the qualification(s) for which you are responsible*: eg the assessment strategy set down by a relevant sector skills council.
- *Relevant government legislation*: for example ensuring that the Data Protection Act is observed for relevant government legislation.
- *Adhering to conditions identified through an Ofsted visit.*

In some cases, regulations and requirements for one area need to be checked against those from another to ensure compliance. For example, there needs to be a clear procedure for recording complaints and their outcome, and how the organization or individual would action a complaint that needed referral. The procedure for complaints and appeals must meet the requirements of the awarding organization and must be followed where necessary. The organization's own complaints and appeals procedure needs to be checked against that for the relevant awarding organization, to see whether any adjustments need to be made.

LEARNING OUTCOME 2: UNDERSTAND HOW TO PLAN THE INTERNAL QUALITY ASSURANCE OF ASSESSMENT

ASSESSMENT CRITERIA

2.1 Evaluate the importance of planning and preparing internal quality-assurance activities.

2.2 Explain what an internal quality-assurance plan should contain.

2.3 Summarize the preparations that need to be made for internal quality assurance, including: information collection, communications, administrative arrangements, resources.

2.1 Evaluate the importance of planning and preparing internal quality-assurance activities

Planning ensures that internal quality assurance takes place in a structured way, allowing time for problems to be identified and for improvements to be made whilst candidates are taking their qualification. If IQA activities are left until the last minute, typically swinging into place when the external verifier announces that monitoring is due, then the implication is that IQA is seen as a 'tick box' activity, rather than as a mechanism for reflection and improvement. Some organizations are able to give more time and flexibility to internal quality assurance than others. Advance planning and preparation help to minimize risk to the centre's decisions by ensuring that problems (if any) are identified and resolved well before a candidate has completed a qualification. Worst case scenarios are that a 'block' can be put on certification, meaning that candidates have to wait until fixed points before the centre can apply for certification, or worse, that candidates have to be told that they must be reassessed because of internal QA failings.

IQAs need to plan their audit trails and monitoring, particularly where there are limited resources, to make best use of their time. Planning:

- makes sure that the correct time and resources are allocated to IQA over particular timescales;

- provides the opportunity to gather and analyse existing data, allowing the IQA to identify where their time and attention should be focused;
- cuts down the actual time spent in the recording of workplace monitoring or the sampling of assessment judgements, through pre-preparing necessary documents with basic information (eg candidate and assessor names, registration numbers);
- helps everyone to know, well before deadline dates, what will be expected from them, and what information needs to be submitted, when, to whom and in what format;
- should ensure that IQA is carried out on a regular basis, and covering all stages of the assessment cycle.

Another way of looking at the importance of planning for IQA is to consider the risk to accuracy, validity, fairness and consistency if the planning is ineffective or absent.

Risk to quality and progress of candidates' achievement will be minimized by regular monitoring of the assessor tracking documents for groups and individuals. These should show when assessments are planned and how and which performance criteria are met as a result of each assessment. Sampling strategies will address minimizing different categories of risk that, if not included in the plan could result in, for example:

- unresolved variance of understanding of assessment between assessors;
- candidates at different centres being treated inconsistently;
- the assessment of some units never being monitored;
- some assessment methods being favoured for sampling over others (perhaps because of time or cost implications);
- limited sampling over time, for example infrequent interim sampling;
- a focus on a particular type of candidate over others, for example those appearing to be from ethnic minority backgrounds (selected by name) being sampled more often.

Having said that, occasionally taking a candidate sample based on a random approach, such as 'six male and six female candidates all named Chris, or all born in 1984' can identify areas of concern that have not been found with other more logical approaches.

Monitoring the rate at which assessors are conducting assessments (not reviews) with their candidates, and checking on a regular basis that there are clear signs of candidate progression, should show up whether individual assessors are experiencing any difficulties and alert you to the need for help. Problems could include a learner cancelling a number of planned assessments, or perhaps the assessor not being available at times when a candidate is available for workplace assessment.

EQAs will let centres know what information they require well in advance of a visit, and there may be specific forms to be completed, probably provided by the awarding organization. However, internal quality assurance should not be totally dependent on external quality assurance, but should be an integrated process to meet the needs of, occurring throughout the lifetime of each qualification.

Note: also see Unit 8, which gives complementary information on planning.

2.2 Explain what an internal quality-assurance plan should contain

Your working plan (previously known as the internal verification plan) will be amended and updated regularly as a result of IQA monitoring activities. Most awarding organizations will have specific documentation to be completed that will inform this plan. In any event, the IQA plan needs to cover the following elements:

- The assessors for whom the IQA is responsible, the registered candidates for whom each assessor is responsible and the candidate workplace(s).
- The standards and units that each candidate is taking, along with the methods of assessment used for assessing achievement. A representative sample of assessor judgements recorded against assessed work can then be identified from various stages of the assessment cycle. The sample will cover all assessors, all types of records, all candidates, all units of assessment, all assessment methods, all types of evidence and all assessment locations.
- A verification schedule that gives the dates for monitoring the practice and quality. These include dates when assessors will be carrying out standardization of grading (where applicable), dates for sampling assessor records, dates for meeting with assessors to discuss their assessments, the monitoring of assessment in practice and, if different, dates for providing feedback.
- Standardization dates, where assessors will undertake a variety of exercises designed to help them make the same judgements on the same or similar evidence. Plan for these or additional meetings to, for example, discuss information from awarding organizations, practise completing documentation, or check understanding of particular units or criteria.

Computerized records make it easy to update plans, and add comments.

The IQAC (see Unit 8) may liaise with IQAs/IVs regarding the timing of sampling, monitoring and standardizing of decisions, and team standardization exercises and sampling. Each centre will need to decide how much time is going to be allocated to internal quality assurance and be able to justify that the time allocation is sufficient to prevent risk.

2.3 Summarize the preparations that need to be made for internal quality assurance, including: information collection, communications, administrative arrangements, resources

Information collection

Your assessor team will need to understand what information you will need to collect, how it is to be recorded, on what system or documents, and at what points in the process such information is likely to be required. You may be lucky and get information sent to you by return, but it is likely that there will be at least one assessor who has fallen behind with data. That is a reason for regular monitoring, actually looking at data held by assessors and checking they are up to date. If copies of assignments are needed for standardization, photocopying will need to be arranged. Candidate portfolios may need to be gathered in, sometimes from candidates who do not regularly attend a centre, and assessors will need to have duplicate copies of judgements and comments they have given to candidates.

Many assessors will be using e-assessment software, which can be interrogated remotely by the IQA/IV and enables them to sample assessor and candidate work online.

Where paper-based methods are concerned, the IQA/IV will need to determine what assessments they wish to see, and communicate this requirement to the assessor. This will require the assessor to submit a copy of their assessment tracking documentation, so that the IQA/IV can select an appropriate sample. Information about previous past practice (eg from the previous EQA or from previous IQA/IV activity) can also be used to inform the sample. With any luck, the IQA/IV will be able to receive copies of assessment reports from the assessor, rather than candidate portfolios. It will then be up to the IQA/IV to determine whether the candidate evidence needs to be looked at as well. This approach can help minimize the risk of the IQA/IV re-assessing candidate work, rather than monitoring the quality and accuracy of the assessment judgements.

Communications

IQAs/IVs will need the details of how to contact all assessors, candidates and employers. The IQA/IV should have in place an effective method of communication with his or her assessors. This is likely to involve e-mail, but might well include other methods, such as mobile texts or even Skype. The effectiveness of that communication will be shown by the response time from the assessor, and the receipt of the required documentation or information.

Assessors will need to be informed well in advance of key dates – when, for example, standardization meetings will be held. If workplace observations are to be made, these need setting up in negotiation with the candidate, the employer and the assessor, so plenty of time needs to be given for arranging such visits.

Administrative arrangements

Time will need to be given to completing as much awarding organization and centre documentation in advance as possible (eg lists of candidate names and registration numbers). Liaison may be needed between different departments, such as those teaching and assessing, and administration or finance. Requests for reports to be generated need to be given well in advance of when they are needed. An administrator may find it easier to run regular reports for quality assurance say, on a monthly basis, rather than having to drop everything to meet an IQAC or EQA request for data. Requests to schedule in photocopying may also need to be made well in advance of monitoring or standardization events, even if the documentation is not yet available.

Resources

Requests may need to be made from line managers to cover for assessors attending standardization events, or even to release staff so that they can make external workplace visits. Expenses may be required by some staff. Rooms and refreshments may need to be booked, and it is likely that computers will need to be available to check data or to access candidate evidence. As an IQA/IV, you need to be aware of the budget allocated to internal quality assurance and assessment activities, and regularly monitor spending on this. An assessor who, thorough inefficient planning, is making unscheduled visits to candidates can soon spend the travel expenses budget, or get into difficulties with having enough time for other assessment activities such as writing feedback reports.

LEARNING OUTCOME 3: UNDERSTAND TECHNIQUES AND CRITERIA FOR MONITORING THE QUALITY OF ASSESSMENT INTERNALLY

ASSESSMENT CRITERIA

3.1 Evaluate different techniques for sampling evidence of assessment, including the use of technology.

3.2 Explain the appropriate criteria to use for judging the quality of the assessment process.

3.1 Evaluate different techniques for sampling evidence of assessment, including the use of technology

Monitoring technique	Methods	Comments
Sampling assessment records	Tracking documents, planning documents, records of assessments against criteria/standards (and the evidence, where appropriate), written feedback	At time and place to suit IQA; shows timescale of how individuals are progressing; shows whether assessor is regularly engaging with the candidate, and how they are making judgements; identifies those assessors who base their judgements on 'is the evidence present?' without necessarily judging its quality; shows quality of written feedback; online assessor documentation, especially if able to be interrogated remotely by the IQA, can be very timesaving and effective

Monitoring technique	Methods	Comments
Sampling assessors' practice	Observation of workplace assessment, professional discussion, oral questions, written records	Expensive on time so needs careful planning; can check out affective side of assessment practice, as well as accuracy of judgements and quality of face-to-face techniques; can check assessor understanding then and there, and give feedback and support immediately
Sampling candidate and assessor products	Observation, discussion, video evidence	If the product is immovable and at a distance, video evidence accompanying the assessor report can save time and money Physically large candidate portfolios need storage space and careful handling to avoid injury – ask for assessor's comments first with samples of the evidence before requesting full candidate portfolio evidence
Expert witness testimony	Questions, discussion, written records	Gives a more independent view; can identify gaps in current vocational knowledge (of assessor and candidate); can be more difficult to offer constructive criticism or support depending on role of witness vis-a-vis candidate or assessor; need to check witness experience and details
Feedback from candidates	Questions, learner satisfaction surveys, complaints	Can identify overall satisfaction with assessment process; might be compromised if candidates are anxious at talking to IQA, or have axe to grind
Vertical, horizontal and theme-based sampling	Sampling plans	Gives variety and structure to sampling plans

3.2 Explain the appropriate criteria to use for judging the quality of the assessment process

See Unit 1 for a full explanation of the terms in the examples below.

The sampling strategies devised by the IQA need to cover the criteria below. However, instead of using the criteria to judge the candidate evidence (which is the job of the assessor), the IQA is judging the quality of the assessment process. Therefore, it is the assessor's evidence that is used to make the judgements.

Examples

Criteria	Assessor evidence	Method of assessment by IQA
Authenticity	Assessors have signed and dated their own assessments; they have noted checks they have made to assure themselves of the authenticity of their candidates' work	Sampling assessor records
Validity	Assessor copies of assessment plans agreed with candidates, showing methods of assessment against criteria	Sampling assessment records
Sufficiency	Assessed candidate evidence	Sampling plan to show monitoring against all criteria at initial, formative and summative stages of candidate progress
Currency of evidence	Assessor records show dates of candidate evidence presented to them, particularly RPL evidence	Sampling assessor records

Criteria	Assessor evidence	Method of assessment by IQA
Accuracy of assessment decisions	Assessor records showing how evidence meets the unit assessment criteria	Standardization exercises; sampling assessor records; observation of workplace assessment; video evidence
Consistency of assessor decisions	Assessor records showing how evidence meets the unit assessment criteria	IQA samples same assessor decisions against same units for a sample of candidates, and standardizes for a number of different assessors assessing the same unit
Assessor record keeping	All records completed accurately and up to date on correct documentation, and stored correctly	Spot checks; return rate when asking for information

LEARNING OUTCOME 4: UNDERSTAND HOW TO INTERNALLY MAINTAIN AND IMPROVE THE QUALITY OF ASSESSMENT

ASSESSMENT CRITERIA

4.1 Summarize the types of feedback, support and advice that assessors may need to maintain and improve the quality of assessment.

4.2 Explain standardization requirements in relation to assessment.

4.3 Explain relevant procedures regarding disputes about the quality of assessment.

4.1 Summarize the types of feedback, support and advice that assessors may need to maintain and improve the quality of assessment

See Unit 1 for detailed information that will be useful to assessors. In addition, the majority of awarding organizations now provide a wide range of information and training events covering many aspects of the assessment and quality assurance process.

Some examples

Types of feedback

- verbal, following observation of assessor by IQA/IV;
- written, following IQA/IV sampling of assessor judgements;
- group feedback during standardization exercises;
- briefings following EQA/EV – team comments, individual actions for assessors.

Support

- inexperienced assessor shadows an experienced assessor to improve confidence in own practice;
- standardization exercises to build confidence in making accurate judgements;

- attendance at training events – eg updating on awarding organization guidance and advice;
- access to websites and documents with information relating to assessment, awarding organizations, relevant vocational areas.

Advice

- organizing workplace visits, maintaining documentation, sharing records;
- legislation, policies and procedures that need to be followed;
- giving oral or written feedback;
- how to avoid candidate complaints.

Assessors should be trained to write up their assessment reports, both formative and summative, so that the way they have made their judgement is clear to the candidate. Not only do they need to give a grade or make a judgement on competence, but that judgement needs to be backed up by a written report. This may take the form of assignment feedback for vocational candidates or a report against the assessment plan that a workplace candidate is following.

IQA/IV feedback to assessors needs to be for their eyes, and not for their learners. Our 'Points for feedback' (Table 3.16) apply as much to IQAs/IVs giving feedback to assessors as they do to assessors giving feedback to candidates. The overall purpose of giving feedback to assessors is that, by improving the individuals' performance, the overall quality of assessment improves. See Unit 1 for more detailed information on feedback.

Below are some comments commonly given by assessors to their candidates that would need to be challenged if (hopefully, when) picked up through IQA sampling.

Vocational assessment

1 'Well done.'
2 'Excellent work, but you still need to add a bibliography and give another example. Pass.'
3 'You have written your assignment within the word count, used three sources and answered the four points in the assignment brief. Good pass.'

In the first example, the candidate has no idea of what has been well done and could easily draw the wrong conclusions, which could have bad consequences later. The assessor could be praising effort rather than achievement, for example. Often, an assessor wants to encourage a candidate, particularly if it is the candidate's first assignment. In this case, distinguishing between effort and achievement is vital, particularly if the candidate needs to develop his or her writing or research techniques. The candidate also needs to know why the assessor thinks aspects of the work have been well done so he or she can build on this for future assignments.

The second example cannot be a true statement. If work is excellent, the highest accolade possible, then there should be no outstanding items for inclusion. The academic work itself could be 'excellently written, with appropriate references'. However, a pass grade should not have been awarded if there are essential components outstanding. A clear assessment plan can be used by candidates as a checklist before handing in assignments.

The third example is representative of those assessor comments that seem to give the candidate some feedback but, in reality, just state back to him or her the required criteria. It tells the candidate nothing about why the work was good – was it because of the examples chosen, the sources, the fact that it was within the word count or all three? If the assessor cited the actual examples and sources and explained why they were good, this would also provide some evidence if the assignment were to be lost or if the assessor's comments were included in a standardization exercise.

Should IQA/IQAs/internal verifiers find examples of written feedback such as the above (or, worse still, none!), a standardization meeting can be a useful environment for improving practice.

Competence-based assessment

1 'This work meets the criteria.'
2 'I have assessed all your evidence for (x qualification) as a pass. Please make sure you cross-reference all the evidence before I pass your file to the IV.'
3 'You have collected all the required evidence into your portfolio. Before I can pass it to the IV to be signed off, you need to put in your CV and make sure that you and your candidate have signed all the necessary documents.'

In the first case, there is no way that the IQA can judge how the assessment has been made. The assessment needs to be returned to the assessor. The assessor will need to indicate as a minimum what criteria have been met, what evidence was seen in order for this judgement to be made and its location, where the assessment took place and when, what was done well, and any areas where things could be done differently or better (even if criteria have been met).

In the second case, candidates taking competence-based qualifications are normally judged 'competent' or 'not yet competent' rather than 'pass' or 'fail'. The IV may not want to look at the portfolio, but will need to look at the assessor's comments against the evidence. The assessor should have kept copies of the assessments and written feedback made to the candidate.

The assessor in the third example seems to misunderstand his or her own role and that of the IQA/internal verifier. The evidence that an IQA/

internal verifier may wish to see should be that which the assessor has already assessed against the national standards. The IQA/internal verifier is more likely to need to see the assessor's assessment records. These records should detail the documents that have been shown by the candidate to the assessor and how they are relevant to the qualification. A curriculum vitae is unlikely to give any evidence of the candidate's current competence, but might be referred to in the assessment report following a professional discussion or as part of the information seen by an assessor or adviser at induction for the qualification.

It is possible that the IQA/internal verifier might request a whole portfolio for sampling purposes, but it is more likely that he or she will request evidence that shows how an assessor has assessed a particular unit or element.

4.2 Explain standardization requirements in relation to assessment

Each awarding organization should have a policy and/or procedures on how standardization is expected to be used. This must be followed by the centre, but it is possible that the centre will have its own quality-assurance timetable. This could result in additional standardization exercises, or in cross-centre exercises.

Centres often use standardization (or moderation) as a way of building teacher, assessor and team confidence in making judgements, as well as for general team development.

Standardization is a process whereby all assessors are given tasks which help them to check that they are making similar judgements given the same candidate assessment to judge, whether this is a workplace observation or a written task or assignment.

The IQA/IV (or IQAC if there is one) will identify assignments, Units or activities that will be used by all team members to help them agree judgements. Video is sometimes used as a focus for making judgements on workplace or classroom observations. Written work will be photocopied so that all participants in the standardization exercise have a copy. All references to the actual name of candidates, and their assessors, need to be removed to avoid bias and to preserve confidentiality. Participants each have a set of the assessment criteria, and are given a set time to assess the examples of work. Then there is a discussion around the results of the assessments; it is important that each assessor understands exactly where and why they need to change their assessment should they not be within the consensus of opinion.

4.3 Explain relevant procedures regarding disputes about the quality of assessment

One of the roles of the IQA is to ensure everyone knows the procedures relating to disputes; candidates should all have a complaints policy detailing the way that problems are resolved. The centre procedure normally needs to be used first, and typically would advise the candidate and assessor in resolving the problem. The IQA would become involved if this did not work, and failing resolution at this stage, the IQAC (in a larger centre). Only if all else fails would the EQA get involved.

Clear assessment plans that ensure candidates and assessors have all the supporting documents they should have (and have both read and understood them), and monitoring assessments on a regular basis, are the best ways of preventing disputes. Record keeping is essential if disputes are to be resolved easily.

The understanding of centre appeal procedures and awarding organization appeal procedures, and of how to avoid complaints, should be a regular part of assessor and IQA team development.

LEARNING OUTCOME 5: UNDERSTAND HOW TO MANAGE INFORMATION RELEVANT TO THE INTERNAL QUALITY ASSURANCE OF ASSESSMENT

ASSESSMENT CRITERION

5.1 Evaluate requirements for information management, data protection and confidentiality in relation to the internal quality assurance of assessment.

5.1 Evaluate requirements for information management, data protection and confidentiality in relation to the internal quality assurance of assessment

The awarding organization and the centre both need to have access to information gathered through internal quality assurance of assessment. Each awarding organization will need to approve the systems used by different centres, and their external verifiers will need access to, and possibly training in how to use, the system when they visit.

As with information related to assessment practice the management of this information by IQAs/IVs is subject to the requirements of the Data Protection Act (see Unit 1, Outcome 7). All staff should be aware of who can and cannot access records, according to the requirements of the Data Protection Act, which has eight key principles (see Appendix 2). Some of these are especially relevant to internal quality assurance record-keeping, in particular for information that is kept electronically, or intended for transfer to electronic records at a later date. For example, the principle that 'Personal data shall be accurate and, where necessary, kept up to date' is fairly self-explanatory – it is common-sense to expect data to be accurate! However, sometimes, as IQA/IV you will need to make decisions on how to interpret a key principle. A good example of this is the requirement that 'Personal data shall be adequate, relevant and not excessive in relation to the purpose or purposes for which they are processed'. Each of the terms used is subject to interpretation:

- What amount of data can be considered 'adequate'?
- How do you decide what is relevant data?
- How do you decide how much data needs to be obtained and retained?

Within your organization there should be policies and procedures related to record-keeping, but you will need to ensure that the data kept are fit for the purpose required. In a larger organization the centre manager or IQAC may be the main person to negotiate any necessary additions or amendments to the standard organizational record systems; in smaller organizations, it will be the IQA's responsibility to ensure that the data kept are sufficient to meet awarding organization requirements as well as the requirements of their own organization.

Types of information

IQAs/IVs will need to maintain the following information and have systems for sharing and processing this appropriately with their centre and with the external verifier:

- centre information;
- awarding organization information;
- their sampling strategy;
- course/qualification start and finish dates;
- lists of each cohort of candidates, with the assessors linked to each cohort;
- schemes of work and timetables for taught programmes.
- records of standardization of assessment activity;
- records of sampled assessment;
- data from internal quality assurance activities;
- actions resulting from internal quality assurance;
- actions resulting from external quality assurance;
- a list of current assessors and their candidates;
- CPD plans for each assessor for whom they are responsible (unless this is the role of the IQAC).

Centres need to know not just that they are meeting legal and funding requirements, but that they are operating efficiently and effectively. Analysis of easily available data can help with this. Such data and records can be:

- awarding organization enrolment numbers for each candidate;
- candidates enrolled, withdrawn and continuing at various census points;

- candidates who have completed, with start and finish dates;
- average time of completion of a qualification or a particular unit;
- candidate comments – praise or problems;
- class size;
- class attendance;
- percentage of candidates getting particular grades (on non-NVQ qualifications);
- retention rate (those who remained on the programme as a percentage of those who were initially enrolled);
- achievement rate (those who achieved the qualification as a percentage of those registered for it).

Reports to centre managers and external verifiers that include these data are very useful and also give teachers and assessors feedback on their perform-ance and where changes might need to be made. For example, if there is a low retention rate, some of the reasons could be:

- poor pre-course guidance or induction;
- poor teaching;
- poor learner support;
- inconvenient times or location for the course;
- a lack of feedback to candidates;
- slow progress with workplace assessments, causing candidates to lose motivation;
- an unusually high number of candidates with external issues that are nothing at all to do with the course (redundancy, for example).

Confidentiality and Information Management

The majority of records will now be kept electronically. One of the great benefits of electronic records for quality assurance is that IQAs/IVs can access assessor records whenever and wherever they choose. These records are likely to be uniform in style, which means comparisons are easier. There needs to be an agreed secure system for those eligible to access the informa-tion, and a procedure for backup and retrieval, and which also needs to take account of how records can be accessed should key staff become unavail-able, eg through extended illness.

Even if all the documents, records and data are available in electronic format, many people still prefer to keep their records, or some of them, in paper format. Guidance documents and copies of standards are normally available via the web, but a paper copy is often preferable for quick refer-ence. Assessor records which are photocopied or carbonized, are easier to keep in that format. However, the latter do need to be kept securely, along with any candidate portfolios or assignments that are required for internal or external quality assurance. If a lockable cupboard cannot be found for storing portfolios or assignments, they do at least need to be in a locked room (not left on a table in an open corridor, as we have witnessed). All staff should consider what the implications are of taking candidate work or records away from a centre; damage or loss to candidate work can be a very difficult issue to resolve, especially if there are no backup copies of the work or records.

When candidates and assessors are having verbal feedback sessions, standardization or any activity which could be deemed sensitive to either party, these should take place in areas as private as possible.

LEARNING OUTCOME 6: UNDERSTAND THE LEGAL AND GOOD PRACTICE REQUIREMENTS FOR THE INTERNAL QUALITY ASSURANCE OF ASSESSMENT

ASSESSMENT CRITERIA

6.1 Evaluate legal issues, policies and procedures relevant to the internal quality assurance of assessment, including those for health, safety and welfare.

6.2 Evaluate different ways in which technology can contribute to the internal quality assurance of assessment.

6.3 Explain the value of reflective practice and continuing professional development in relation to internal quality assurance.

6.4 Evaluate requirements for equality and diversity and, where appropriate, bilingualism, in relation to the internal quality assurance of assessment.

6.1 Evaluate legal issues, policies and procedures relevant to the internal quality assurance of assessment, including those for health, safety and welfare

A centre will normally have a collection of policies and procedures which have been checked by the awarding organization as part of the centre approval process. The IQA/IV needs to know how these policies and procedures need to be used as part of the internal quality assurance process, and which are likely to be the areas of most risk. Previous external quality assurance reports will give information on issues which need to be dealt with more carefully, as well as those where the centre was thought to be working well, and IQA/IVs need to be informed of the results, so that appropriate action can be taken.

As IQA/IV you need to be aware of relevant legislation and regulations and be clear about how, where and when they will impact on internal quality assurance. You will need to ensure that your assessors adhere to health and safety legislation, safeguarding requirements and equal opportunities policies when they carry out their assessments.

You also need to ensure that you consider legislation and policies related to the welfare of your assessors, such as planning their assessor allocation so they are able to manage their workloads without undue stress. There needs to be good communication between team members to avoid team members working in isolation. Even if there is an Internal Quality Assurance Coordinator taking overall responsibility for the coordination of the quality assurance team, each IQA/IV needs to report back their findings on a regular basis.

6.2 Evaluate different ways in which technology can contribute to the internal quality assurance of assessment

Technology now impacts on every aspect of life to an extent that was almost impossible to imagine even a decade ago. It is quite likely that a very significant proportion of candidates and assessment and IQA staff will have mobile phones or personal organizers with internet access and the means to take videos, record sound and take photos. Some will be able to use Skype features. All candidates, assessors and IQA staff will have computer access, mostly owning their hardware or having them provided in the workplace, but also being able to book time in college learning centres, training centres or libraries. The potential of technology to contribute to the IQA process is therefore significant, though not without its drawbacks.

Recording and sharing information

- The centre may have signed up to an awarding organization's preferred system of recording and transferring documentation, or may have implemented its own.
- E-mail and related applications can be used to plan team meetings, seeking availability quickly and securely transferring data between people.

Monitoring assessments

E-portfolios can allow IQAs to look at all aspects of the assessment process between candidate and assessor, as they give the facility to scan documents, include video and photographic evidence, and record plans and judgements.

- E-portfolios can be used for sampling, and are also invaluable if the centre has remote EQA as, by agreement, the EQA can be given access to the system.
- Skype can be used to hold meetings between members of the assessment team or IQAs, which is invaluable if the team is scattered over a wide area.

- If the equipment is available, virtual meetings can be set up to discuss the results of sampling or double-marking exercises.

Information

- Websites make it easy to access awarding organization and national information that affects IQA.
- Team staff development exercises using web material can help with updating.

6.3 Explain the value of reflective practice and continuing professional development in relation to internal quality assurance

Perhaps the best way of helping learners learn, and of being clear on the requirements of assessing to quality standards, is to put oneself in the position of the learner. 'It's never too late to learn' applies just as much to IQA staff as it does to their candidates. Of course, if you are reading this book as a registered candidate, you can already appreciate this fact. Otherwise, even a day course on 'Making Christmas cards' or 'How to take better digital photos' (as long as there is an element of constructive criticism from the tutor) will help develop empathy, which can be used to maximize effective interactions with assessors.

Awarding organizations have minimum requirements for annual continuing professional development, as do professional organizations (such as the Institute for Learning and the Chartered Institute of Personnel and Development). The value of this requirement related to IQA is that it gives staff an opportunity to plan a varied programme of interesting and useful events for themselves that will:

- help keep them factually updated with current standards and legal, awarding organization and centre requirements;
- enable them to meet and discuss with others involved in aspects of quality assurance;
- enable them to reflect on their practice, applying lessons learnt from, for example, standardization;
- maintain expertise in a changing environment and with changing technology.

6.4 Evaluate requirements for equality and diversity and, where appropriate, bilingualism, in relation to the internal quality assurance of assessment

Centres will often have targets to meet, set in response to government initiatives. Here is an example:

> **Example**
>
> A centre wants to increase the percentage of female or ethnic minority candidates on particular courses to mirror the percentage of those groups in the local population. The internal quality assurance process will need to take such targets into account. Data on registrations could be fed back to those responsible for marketing and publicity, and data on progression needs to be shared with assessors and other IVs, as well as teaching or training teams, if these comprise different staff.

Other examples might be:

- the allocation of assessors of a particular gender – for example, in some health and social care situations;
- arrangements that take in to the personal needs of candidates and assessors;
- sensitivity to religious and cultural backgrounds, eg planning assessments and internal quality assurance to avoid holidays and religious festivals;
- ensuring requests for support in cases of dyslexia, bilingualism or a need for translators are within requirements.

Also see Unit 1, Outcome 8.

Unit 5
Internally assure the quality of assessment

LEARNING OUTCOMES FOR UNIT 5

1 Be able to plan the internal quality assurance of assessment
2 Be able to internally evaluate the quality of assessment
3 Be able to internally maintain and improve the quality of assessment
4 Be able to manage information relevant to the internal quality assurance of assessment
5 Be able to maintain legal and good practice requirements when internally monitoring and maintaining the quality of assessment

If you are a candidate taking this unit as part of a qualification, you must: monitor the assessments of at least two assessors, who each have a minimum of two candidates. Between them, these assessors should be assessing across the range of units for a qualification. No simulation can be used for this unit. You will be assessed through observation of your performance, the documents you produce (work products) and being questioned. Evidence for Unit 5 will apply to much of Unit 4, and evidence from Unit 8 (the workplan) will probably count as, for example, the internal verification strategy and sampling plan needed as evidence for Unit 5.

LEARNING OUTCOME 1: BE ABLE TO PLAN THE INTERNAL QUALITY ASSURANCE OF ASSESSMENT

ASSESSMENT CRITERIA

1.1 Plan monitoring activities according to the requirements of own role.

1.2 Make arrangements for internal monitoring activities to assure quality.

1.1 Plan monitoring activities according to the requirements of own role

Some IQA/IVs have wider roles than others, including managerial activities or links with awarding organizations (see Unit 8), while others are responsible solely for the assessment practice of several assessors, and report to a manager.

Your quality-assurance strategy should ensure that candidate assessment is fair and carried out to the standards of the awarding organization and centre, so that there is no risk to the quality of the qualifications awarded. The strategy should incorporate staff development as part of continuous improvement. The evidence for this will be a strategy document, probably on not more than a side of A4, which outlines the range of actions you will be taking to minimize risk and ensure compliance. If you are monitoring NVQ qualifications, you will follow the principles outlined in the Joint Awarding Body guidelines.

Your monitoring of assessors needs to be planned over time, so that you are confident that standards are maintained and do not decline. Previous EV reports should show how well the centre is doing and whether there are any current action points that the IQA/internal verifier should be following through that need special attention. Your monitoring should aim to cover at least the following areas:

- details of all assessor qualifications, skills and planned CPD;
- qualification, registration and certification details of candidates;
- all units being assessed, and all methods of assessment;

- all education and training environments (vocational candidates) and employer premises (work-based learning candidates);
- witnesses and mentors;
- candidate assessment plans, and expected completion dates of individual units and complete qualifications for each candidate;
- dates of standardization activities planned for assessors;
- observation of assessor practice at different stages (initial, formative, summative), including their written and oral feedback to candidates, and records showing judgements against criteria;
- areas of risk, such as new qualifications, staff absences, new admin processes and inexperienced assessors.

Your evidence will be your internal quality-assurance plan. It is likely to be a grid where you can list all the monitoring activities against the weeks of the year. Then the initials of assessors can be entered against the activities and planned dates. As monitoring takes place, the actual dates can be entered, along with notes as to the outcomes.

1.2 Make arrangements for internal monitoring activities to assure quality

This will involve liaison and preparation:

- checking out the dates for observations and reviews with assessors;
- ensuring candidates understand you are monitoring their assessors' performance, and not their own;
- making arrangements for workplace visits, and establishing whether anything like protective footwear is required;
- booking rooms for standardization exercises and checking out equipment required;
- checking with the awarding organization about any qualification updates, and making sure that everyone is using the required documentation;
- knowing how to use paperwork, software or hardware related to the assessment and IQA process;
- planning questions to ask assessors and others relating to their practice, including their understanding of the application of policies and legal issues;
- incorporating any information from internal and external quality reviews into the monitoring plan as necessary.

A timetable of dates for sampling with no strategy is inadequate, as it is not linked into any programme of continuous improvement.

LEARNING OUTCOME 2:
BE ABLE TO INTERNALLY EVALUATE THE QUALITY OF ASSESSMENT

This is where you implement your sampling strategy and internal verification plan. Using the plan you have made, amended in the light of your preparations, you will undertake various planned monitoring activities, keeping records of what you do. Your assessor will arrange to observe you carrying out this part of your role. The records you make as you carry out the activities will form part of your evidence.

ASSESSMENT CRITERIA

2.1 Carry out internal monitoring activities to quality requirements.

2.2 Evaluate assessor expertise and competence in relation to the requirements of their role.

2.3 Evaluate the planning and preparation of assessment processes.

2.4 Determine whether assessment methods are safe, fair, valid and reliable.

2.5 Determine whether assessment decisions are made using the specified criteria.

2.6 Compare assessors' decisions to ensure they are consistent.

2.1 Carry out internal monitoring activities to quality requirements

When sampling written assessment judgements, IV/IQAs look for written records that are signed and dated. It will be important to see whether learner-candidates have acted on assessors' advice and also whether the assessors are following through actions that they have asked their candidates to undertake. Effective working relationships between candidate and assessor will be shown through the assessment planning and review documentation, and any written feedback between candidate and assessor. If there is no evidence of written feedback, you will need to check whether oral feedback is going unrecorded, and plan with the assessor how to formalize its recording. Records of assessment need to be in duplicate. The learner-candidate needs a copy, and the assessor needs a copy. Assessors' copies should be kept in such a way that they and others are unable to alter the documentation.

Dating and signing all entries helps this process. These dates and signatures provide an audit trail that an auditor (ie an IQA or EQA) can use to track any aspect of the assessment process against the appropriate standards. Online systems should be able to prevent any changes to a candidate's evidence or an assessment decision once data has been entered. It is interesting to look at the information available about candidate progress if assessors do not use the convention dd/mm/yyyy for dates. In our experience, assessors have sometimes just put the month and year rather than the actual date. This causes problems!

Example of problem with unclear recording of dates

If you label the start of an assessment process merely as June 2011 and its completion merely as August 2011 the candidate record could indicate anything between one and three months as the completion period.

Completion times possible when names of months only are given (June 2011 to August 2011):

01.06.2011	01.06.2011	30.06.2011
31.08.2011	01.08.2011	01.08.2011
3 months	2 months	1 month

Detail and accuracy is important where any records (paper-based or electronic) or data entries are made, and as the example above shows, can give much more information as to a candidate's progress.

Your own monitoring should cover, for example, the assessment planning process with a newly registered candidate, as well as the monitoring of independent assessments, of observational assessors and of final unit assessment and feedback to candidates. Sampling of finally assessed units is just one of the many parts of this process.

More detail can be gained by contacting a sample of candidates, looking at any centre quality feedback forms, checking complaints, and reviewing assessment plans and feedback forms, particularly those on which the candidate responds to the assessor's feedback. A measure of a good working relationship is the number of sound completions within the original estimated time that individual assessors achieve with their candidates. Slippage from this may indicate a misplaced reluctance on the part of the assessor to motivate candidates or keep them to deadlines, or poor communications between candidate and assessor.

Ensuring that individual assessors are planning and preparing effectively can be done by viewing copies of assessment plans and by talking to assessors, candidates and workplace supervisors. Depending on your role, you might need to check that the assessor has considered the effectiveness in terms of both cost and estimated completion time of conducting the assessments. The separation out of training, assessment and administration costs such as photocopying and postage might need to be considered. You will need to be sure that assessors are making best use of workplace visits by well-planned assessments that cover a wide range of performance indicators, and that professional discussion is similarly effectively planned. You may also need to look at the use of observational and independent assessors, witness statements, postage costs and the times taken by individual assessors to support candidates through to completion.

2.2 Evaluate assessor expertise and competence in relation to the requirements of their role

As the activities relating to IQA are carried out, you can start to analyse the results so that you can see whether any assessors need additional support, or perhaps whether any might be ready to take on the challenges of internal quality assurance themselves, or whether you need to adjust assessor/candidate allocations.

All awarding organizations require proof of relevant qualifications so a central IQA file containing evidence of each assessor's qualifications, and their CV and CPD records, is very useful. (If assessors do not wish their original certificates to be lodged with the centre, a photocopy endorsed by a qualified EV/EQA and the quality manager for the centre will be an acceptable substitute.) All assessors should have the opportunity to attend updating sessions, whether provided by the awarding organization or cascaded through the IQA/internal verifier. You need to check that they have understood their training and are able to follow the systems. Records of your monitoring and of assessor attendance at training sessions are both evidence to show your assessor.

Assessors can make self-assessments of their perceived needs that can be compared with the skills they need to perform their role. These can be checked against the requirements that you have identified as being mandatory and advisable to the centre's good-quality practice, and action plans for each assessor drawn up on this basis. Most organizations have annual appraisals where individuals negotiate yearly action plans with their line managers. These may not cover the detail required here related to assessment, so you may need to conduct your own needs identification.

Relevant and recent work-based experience is important for all assessors (and trainers), so work experience placements in industry, as well as teaching and training candidates in their vocational subjects and occupational areas, can help to keep assessors updated. This is particularly important for assessors who are based in colleges or training companies, who may spend much of the week away from the real work environments of their candidates. Assessors of fast-moving vocational subjects such as engineering, IT or media will need to be familiar with technical developments in those areas.

Assessors should be competent in information and communications technology (ICT) skills, so that they can take communicate electronically, use electronic recording systems and download information from the internet, for example from SSCs and awarding organizations. The ability to word-process, photocopy and scan material is now a key workplace skill, as is the ability to keep updated filing systems. The introduction of professional discussion, which must be recorded, means that assessors need the skills and equipment to make effective recordings, maybe using mobile devices or discreet video/audio equipment.

2.3 Evaluate the planning and preparation of assessment processes

You will be monitoring the effectiveness of assessors' negotiation planning with learner-candidates through looking at samples of individual learning plans and assessment plans, and evidence of negotiation and liaison with other staff or supervisors contributing to training for the assessments. Activities where assessors are able to compare different planning records are useful. You will be checking how these plans were followed in reality and why any deviations occurred.

Some questions you will ask yourself are:

- How well are assessors setting clear, holistic tasks for assessment, covering as wide a range of criteria as possible?
- How do I know that candidates are set realistic timescales for achievement?
- How can I tell from the assessors' documentation how the planning and preparation processes have been negotiated with the candidate? How can I tell whether candidates have all the appropriate planning documentation, including assessment briefs and/or assessment criteria?
- Are assessment plans being updated regularly following assessments in the workplace? How do I know?
- How clear are the processes, with dates where applicable, for the return of assignments with assessor comments, for written feedback following workplace observations, for oral feedback and for practice or draft assessments where these are part of the programme?
- What evidence is there that assessors have acted on the results of previous monitoring and standardization events?

2.4 Determine whether assessment methods are safe, fair, valid and reliable

Assessment plans made with candidates should give the information required. You will be looking for:

- *Safe decisions*: confident, accurate judgements that meet the standards for assessment and are well justified.
- *Fairness*: using the same procedures and standards for all, whilst allowing for recognized individual differences.
- *Validity*: the chosen methods of assessment are suitable for the situation; look at how individual assessors test the validity of recognized prior achievement.
- *Reliability*: that the candidate, on a different occasion, would reach the same standard.

2.5 Determine whether assessment decisions are made using the specified criteria

The specified criteria are those listed in the unit, and identified in assessment plans.

You will need to check that assessors are assessing against the standards, rather than their perception of what is acceptable, and that their recording against criteria is done accurately and cumulatively. Assessors need to be supported to justify their decisions against the standards. Simple tick statements such as 'The evidence clearly meets the requirements' are not enough. The IV needs to be clear as to why the assessor believes this is so, and should be able to check the assessor's decision-making process and see exactly how the assessor has come to his or her decisions.

2.6 Compare assessors' decisions to ensure they are consistent

Once sufficient data has been gathered to make comparisons against at least two assessors, the process of comparing for consistency can begin. It is through comparing decisions made in the workplace and from assessment of written work that you will begin to notice differences. Some of these may not be significant, for example, the style of written feedback. Other differences may be great enough to need addressing via an urgent face-to-face meeting with the assessor. You will begin to build up a bank of information that will be the basis for exploration by your assessors in a standardization event.

You need to plan to assess consistency of assessment:

- *Over time*: for example, does an assessor become more lax or more strict?
- *Over the same unit or evidence*: for example, are there differences in an assessor's judgement of the same unit presented by different candidates?
- *Between assessors*: best done through standardization exercises following initial monitoring.

● *Over different levels of qualification.*
● *Over methods*: for example, do assessors give more feedback on some methods (say observation) than on a written assignment?

Keep records that show who, how, what and when you have monitored concerning the assessment practice of your assessors, and what you consider has been found about assessment practice, and why.

TABLE 3.21 Processes to ensure consistency of assessment

Process	Description
Double marking	One assessor marks a piece of work. Another assessor then marks the same piece of work. The mark is then compared and adjusted, if needed. Usually used where grades or numerical marks are involved.
Internal moderation/internal verification	An agreed sample of marked student work is presented for internal moderation by internal moderators. Internal moderators are designated moderators within the organization or course team, whose role is to look at work, based on an agreed sample, and to agree or disagree with the decisions. In some courses, the internal moderator may have the right to recommend that assessment decisions, marks or grades are changed, but in all cases s/he will have the role of identifying any general issues of quality that have arisen from the moderation.
External examination/external moderation	An external moderator is someone outside the organization who has the professional ability to look at an agreed sample of marked work, give informed advice on the quality of the assessment processes, and confirm or query the assessment decisions made by the assessors. Generally the external moderator produces a formal report.
	In QCF qualifications external quality assurers have a broader role than an external moderator, although they carry out the same functions.
	The term 'external examiner' is used in some programmes, especially in Higher Education. An external examiner generally carries out the same work as an external moderator. Generally the external examiner produces a formal report.

LEARNING OUTCOME 3:
BE ABLE TO INTERNALLY MAINTAIN AND IMPROVE THE QUALITY OF ASSESSMENT

ASSESSMENT CRITERIA

3.1 Provide assessors with feedback, advice and support, including professional development opportunities, that help them to maintain and improve the quality of assessment.

3.2 Apply procedures to standardize assessment practices and outcomes.

3.1 Provide assessors with feedback, advice and support, including professional development opportunities, that help them to maintain and improve the quality of assessment

The IQA/IV has the rewarding role of helping assessors improve and share their good practice. See Unit 1, Outcome 7 for detail on feedback.

All feedback should be constructive and enable the assessor to see what he or she is doing well and to act on any identified points for improvement that have been identified. Your EQA/EV may observe you giving feedback in person, and will look at your records.

Some methods of supporting assessors are:

- a library of documents, awarding organization publications, sector skill publications, training videos, books on assessment and quality assurance, and supporting information on QCF qualifications offered;
- lists of training courses offered internally and externally;
- mentors for newly qualified assessors;
- a programme of meetings for the year, including general information, standardization and monitoring;
- a 'buddy' system for qualified staff;
- a monthly information sheet, containing updates on assessment practice;
- training needs analysis and continuing personal development plans for staff;

- written feedback on assessment decisions and observation monitoring.

You will need to give feedback to individual assessors who have had their decisions sampled through EQA monitoring, so that they know whether their judgements have been verified as correct or whether they need to reassess any assessment decisions already made.

Giving assessors opportunities to develop their assessment experience will require matching experienced assessors with those new to assessing itself or new to assessing in a particular vocational area. Support may be required for all assessors as they work with the new standards, until you are satisfied that they have successfully updated their practice.

3.2 Apply procedures to standardize assessment practices and outcomes

Carrying out assessment standardization arrangements will include holding meetings with assessors at which: i) they all assess the same evidence; and ii) they assess evidence from each others' candidates. Records need to be kept of attendees, the units sampled and the evidence used. The findings of the exercise should be analysed and reported, with action points where necessary.

There should be a planned timetable for assessors to get together to standardize their assessment decisions. It might be helpful to plan the timetable so that there is always some standardization activity between EV visits, indicating who will be required to attend, so that assessors understand their commitments. Standardizing observation practice can be done using video evidence of candidates performing tasks, which can be viewed by individual assessors or as part of a peer exercise, and by having assessors complete assessment observation forms and then reviewing them. Different types of candidate evidence can be copied for assessing by a number of assessors, and a range of completed units can be assessed by different assessors, allowing a review of differences and similarities in assessment practice, ways of giving written and oral feedback, and recording. It is also instructive to ask assessors to consider the minimum knowledge they require for the successful assessment of knowledge, by using a range of the questions in the standards and asking for written responses.

Your standardization plan, attendance sheets and standardization reports from each session need to be available for quality assurance and EQA/EV scrutiny.

LEARNING OUTCOME 4:
BE ABLE TO MANAGE INFORMATION RELEVANT TO THE INTERNAL QUALITY ASSURANCE OF ASSESSMENT

ASSESSMENT CRITERIA

4.1 Apply procedures for recording, storing and reporting information relating to internal quality assurance.

4.2 Follow procedures to maintain confidentiality of internal quality-assurance information.

4.1 Apply procedures for recording, storing and reporting information relating to internal quality assurance

You should be able to access relevant information records on assessment practice and internal quality swiftly and easily. This information will include candidate/assessor allocation, sampling plans, tracking documents and records of standardization activities, records of registered, certificated and 'in progress' candidates, and the correct codes for courses. In some centres, the IQA or internal verifier may be responsible for reviewing organizational policies relevant to internal quality assurance to see whether they need updating with respect to assessment and verification.

Basically, information needs to be:

- Recorded on the documentation approved by the centre and the awarding organization, whether this is done online or on paper.
- Updated regularly and stored in approved formats (a requirement of the Data Protection Act).
- Manageable: duplicate copies of assessor comments to candidates need to be kept, along with internal verifier/IQA reports and reviews, but candidate portfolios may not need to be kept in centres at all unless they are requested for an external quality sample. Large portfolios of candidate work are not only a health hazard to backs and shoulders, but can get lost or damaged, and require lots of storage space.

Reporting mechanisms will vary according to the centre, but usually information held by an individual IV/IQA will need to be in a format that can be added to that of other IVs working for a centre coordinator. The information will be needed to complete documentation prior to EV/EQA sampling, much of which will be remote, and probably for internal organization quality checks.

It's advisable to keep all the information relating to a particular awarding organization and its qualifications visits together, whether this is online, paper-based or a combination of the two.

4.2 Follow procedures to maintain confidentiality of internal quality-assurance information

Centre quality-assurance records, whether maintained by assessors, internal verifiers/IQAs or managers, need to be kept in approved secure locations, protected by passwords or locks to cabinets or doors. However, it is important that a trusted person knows the location of keys and passwords should access be needed to the information in the absence (for example, through extended illness) of the main information holder.

Candidate work and assessor and IQA records should not be left lying around where they can be read by others, particularly other candidates. It can be difficult to remember to maintain confidentiality in phone calls in open plan offices.

LEARNING OUTCOME 5:
BE ABLE TO MAINTAIN LEGAL AND GOOD PRACTICE REQUIREMENTS WHEN INTERNALLY MONITORING AND MAINTAINING THE QUALITY OF ASSESSMENT

ASSESSMENT CRITERIA

5.1 Apply relevant policies, procedures and legislation in relation to internal quality assurance, including those for health, safety and welfare.

5.2 Apply requirements for equality and diversity and, where appropriate, bilingualism, in relation to internal quality assurance.

5.3 Critically reflect on own practice in internally assuring the quality of assessment.

5.4 Maintain the currency of own expertise and competence in internally assuring the quality of assessment.

5.1 Apply relevant policies, procedures and legislation in relation to internal quality assurance, including those for health, safety and welfare

You need to be aware of, and uphold, the requirements of the:

- Data Protection Act;
- copyright acts;
- HSAW Act;
- centre privacy and confidentiality arrangements;
- centre policies to protect staff, such as anti-stress policies, which might need to be considered when allocating assessor loads to IVs;
- awarding organization and centre complaints policies;

- insurance arrangements for staff using their cars for business purposes, and for making visits on others' premises.

Having a list of such policies, procedures and legislation is useful as a reminder, but the important thing is to have evidence that you are applying the requirements in practice. Such evidence may come from minutes of meetings held with assessors or other centre staff, information briefings to assessors, records of complaints and health and safety incidents (hopefully very few, and all resolved quickly) and staff records.

You also need to be aware of policy from organizations connected with educational policy, standards and quality, such as Ofqual, the Alliance of Sector skills Councils, LSIS and BIS (See Appendices 1, 2 and 3).

5.2 Apply requirements for equality and diversity and, where appropriate, bilingualism, in relation to internal quality assurance

See Unit 1 for details on this relating to assessment. The same principles apply with internal quality assurance.

5.3 Critically reflect on own practice in internally assuring the quality of assessment

The data you get from monitoring and standardization exercises will give you feedback on how well you and your team have achieved the targets that were set in the internal quality-assurance plan. This data will have come in over time, allowing opportunities to adjust performance without waiting until a particular time in the assessment cycle.

Colleagues and mangers are additional sources of information, as well as candidates. Your organization may have systems whereby candidates and learners comment on their experience through 'end of programme feedback' or via websites, or via a 'learner voice' committee. Check these sources for information that might refer to perceptions and experiences of the assessment and internal quality-assurance process.

It would be sensible to do a detailed reflection using as broad a base of data as possible shortly before the EQA monitoring request is due for the qualifications for which you are responsible. This will enable you to clarify the areas where your IQA has gone well and, more importantly, set targets for improvement (and we all know that however good we are, we can always do better!). This will put you and the centre in a position of awareness of planned future development and show that you and your team are well prepared.

5.4 Maintain the currency of own expertise and competence in internally assuring the quality of assessment

Moderating your decisions on an assessor with those of other IVs can help to reassure you that your decisions are sound, as can the feedback from your external verifier or taking part in standardization exercises yourself. Most awarding organizations provide events for IQA staff to attend, and there are various events and written materials available from private providers. Continuing to act as an assessor is a good way of maintaining currency, because understanding the assessment process is key to effective internal quality assurance. You will also need to fulfil the requirements of professional organizations (eg IfL or the awarding organization) regarding a minimum number of days of continuing professional development.

PART FOUR
Coordinating internal quality assurance

Unit 8
Plan, allocate and monitor work in own area of responsibility

LEARNING OUTCOMES FOR UNIT 8

1 Be able to produce a work plan for own area of responsibility
2 Be able to allocate and agree responsibilities with team members
3 Be able to monitor the progress and quality of work in own area of responsibility and provide feedback
4 Be able to review and amend plans of work for own area of responsibility and communicate changes

In this unit, it is assumed that the context for planning, allocating and monitoring work is related to internal quality assurance (IQA). In this context, you are probably the person liaising with an awarding organization, and likely to be either the centre manager or the internal quality assurance coordinator (IQAC).

As a potential or current IQAC candidate for the unit, you will be assessed using workplace evidence. This will comprise your work plan (internal quality-assurance strategy and plans), evidence of communication between you and team members, observation and witness testimony. Examples given will be related to tasks and issues that are related to managing of internal quality assurance. Please refer to Units 1 and 4 for additional background on the knowledge and skills related to the planning and monitoring process, and to Unit 5 for the practice of internal quality assurance.

LEARNING OUTCOME 1:
BE ABLE TO PRODUCE A WORK PLAN
FOR OWN AREA OF RESPONSIBILITY

ASSESSMENT CRITERIA

1.1 Explain the context in which work is to be undertaken.

1.2 Identify the skills base and the resources available.

1.3 Examine priorities and success criteria needed for the team.

1.4 Produce a work plan for own area of responsibility.

1.1 Explain the context in which work is to be undertaken

Your work plan will cover the internal quality-assurance activities you need to undertake for the awarding organization and your centre. You will be managing and implementing quality-assurance activities for the internal verifiers and the assessors for whom you hold responsibility. You will have a sound assessment and quality-assurance background, and be familiar with the occupational and vocational standards and qualifications that the centre uses, as well as relevant legislation.

You will refer to the documentation received from the awarding organization, together with previous EQA/EV reports, as these will provide guidance on what is required, from a general regulatory position, but also specifically relating to your centre practice and development needs. Your work plan will need to include activities related to your part in external quality assurance. The awarding organization's requirements will influence your work plan because you will need to ensure that the required information has been gathered and evaluated and reported correctly. It's often a good idea to find out whether the EQA/EV will be planning any workplace visits, or whether the monitoring will be remote, carried out through examination of the documentation sent to them.

The overall context of your work plan could be described within a 'broad title', which you might amplify in discussion with your assessor. Here are some examples that would give readers of the plan a good 'fix' on your work context.

Example 1

John Smith College: Department of Service Industries: Plan for managing C&G IQA for hospitality and catering qualifications, January 2012–July 2012; Covering 12 assessors, five IQA staff, seven qualifications at four levels, reporting to M.Y. Manager (contact 07712345); workplace assessment in seven locations within a 12-mile radius.

Example 2

Wonderful Hair Salon: Work plan for managing three assessors and eight apprentices, start Sept 2011. Qualification: VTCT Level 3 Diploma in hairdressing (QCF) qualification. assessment in salon. Manager and IQA: Andrew Locksmith.

1.2 Identify the skills base and the resources available

You need to know what you can expect from your staff and the physical resources at your disposal. You might make a list of all relevant assessors, their vocational qualification(s), their assessor (and quality assurance, if appropriate) experience and their qualifications. If you can identify this information in an online document that also allows you to update their CPD and agreed target areas for improvement, then you will be simplifying your paperwork. You will also discover or already know the individual needs, strengths, weaknesses and preferences of your staff. The means of obtaining this information could be through appraisal, interviews, standardization exercises and targeted staff development events.

Your staff resources may need fine tuning. You may have staff who are well qualified, but lack experience. You may have experienced staff who are restricted in the days they can work. You also need to look carefully at the allocation of staff to ensure that quality is not compromised. Table 4.1 gives an example based on the allocation of IQA staff to assessors.

After reviewing and judging the planned assessment evidence against criteria, the assessor ensures that the results of assessments are properly fed back to, and recorded for, the candidate. Assessors sign off units and/or individual assignments for candidates once they have been assessed as meeting all assessment criteria. They ensure that all materials and methods used follow good equal opportunities and health and safety practices. They also

TABLE 4.1 IQA allocations to assessors

Example 1	*Two assessors, A & B, and one IQA/IV, C.*
	Good, because the IV is able to standardize and is separate from the assessment process.
Example 2	*Three assessors, A, B and C.*
	Assessors B and C are both qualified IQAs/IVs.
	B quality-assures the work of A and C. C quality-assures the work of B.
	Medium risk, as B and C could get complacent and are also standardizing with each other. There is no standardization between the results of A, B and C unless this is specifically arranged.
Example 3	*10 assessors, one IQA/IV.*
	Low risk, because the IV can standardize across the 10 assessors
	High risk if anything happens to the IQA/IV.
	A second IV is needed or support with decision making, and to minimize risk.
Example 4	*Eight assessors, all qualified as IQAs/IVs, who work in pairs verifying each other's assessments.*
	High risk: too many variables of assessment practice and too little independence. Better to select one to manage the IQA (assuming no one else does this), leaving the rest to assess, and build-in regular standardization events between the assessors and the IQA/IVs. The role of the IQAC could rotate amongst the team.

contribute to, and participate in, the organization's quality-assurance systems. Assessors might be working towards their assessor qualification themselves, in which case an already qualified assessor must countersign all of their decisions.

You also need to review and identify all the physical resources on which your plan will depend, such as allocation of rooms, training and assessment time, time for travelling to assessment appointments, required records and paper-based or software resources, as well as any financial considerations. Resources previously allocated may have been cut, or you may need to think of additional ways to fund assessment/IQA activity.

Much of this information will be kept in your centre's quality-assurance file in the form of, for example, sampling plans, assessor records and reports of data analysis.

These days, most awarding organizations have a cache of relevant documentation available for download on their websites. Some is supportive information, such as:

- internal verifier checklists;
- exemplar internal verifier sampling strategies and plans;
- instructions for conducting examinations.

Other documents are to be used to record and return data, such as:

- centre update form;
- registration, results and dated entry submission forms (if you are lucky, admin staff will complete forms like this);
- internal monitoring forms.

Your centre admin team or your EQA/EV (or the awarding organization admin team) will be able to advise you on their documentation requirements, and the formats in which they wish to receive them. This may mean that you or your IQA/IV and assessors need training in the relevant software and hardware.

1.3 Examine priorities and success criteria needed for the team

As team leader, you will be reviewing priorities set at previous quality-assurance visits, priorities set by your organization, and more 'personal' ones identified by you and your team. The success criteria may be explicit within these priorities.

Examples of success criteria:

- All candidates have achieved their qualification within one year.
- Employer satisfaction is 90 per cent or higher.
- All assessors meet the new QCF qualification requirements within six months.

Information you might use to check achievement of success criteria might be:

- data showing achievement rates that indicate where assessors are being particularly effective, or need support in moving c andidates on;
- using the results of standardizations to tackle, for example the assessment of particular units that have more variation of assessor decisions;

- analysis of internal achievement data, tracking sheets etc that identify whether, for example, observations are often cancelled;
- the results of discussions with assessors relating to the above and their individual targets for improvement; for example, assessor A needs to improve written feedback, assessor B is trialling a new online tracking format;
- feedback from a development session for staff where they were asked to demonstrate their ability to use the awarding organization's website for a variety of purposes;
- benchmarking data matching IQA/IV assessor and candidate activity against data from another centre or a previous run of a qualification.

1.4 Produce a work plan for own area of responsibility

This is the actual document from which you will work, and that will provide substantial evidence for you as a candidate. Its format may be dictated by your organization, you may have documentation to use or adapt given to you by an awarding organization or you may have complete freedom. You may have your plan in hard copy though, for efficiency purposes, online documents are much more quickly updated and shared. Table 4.2 outlines the process of preparing a work plan.

TABLE 4.2 Preparing your work plan

Questions that the planner needs to ask	Examples of information the plan needs to give
What do we expect to happen over the time of the plan?	List specific outcomes, eg assessment targets, Set SMART team targets, organization targets etc
How will we allocate responsibilities for monitoring work activities?	Skills and experience of team members, availability, timetables etc
How will progress be monitored?	Meetings with staff, standardization activities, workplace monitoring etc
What resources are needed?	Staff time, hardware/software, centre and awarding organization information, standards information, candidate information, budget sufficient to cover training needs etc
What specific activities need to be done to support the achievement of the outcomes?	Matching staff resource to candidate need, checking records of candidates, assessors, IQA/IV, liaison with eg employers, creating sampling and monitoring checklists, planning IQAC activity to meet key dates, communication arrangements etc

Note the verification date of the next planned contact with the EQA/EV. You are likely to have to supply a range of material to the EQA/EV at least 15 working days before his or her external verification, whether this is a visit in person or a remote sampling. If the EQA/EV has not contacted you 30 days before the planned visit, it is advisable to contact him or her to confirm dates, times and what is wanted. Evidence of action to be taken by the centre following the last external quality assurance will definitely be required, as will details of any changes in the centre that affect assessment, such as new staff or assessment schedules. You will need to check that all the likely requirements are covered in your work plan.

LEARNING OUTCOME 2:
BE ABLE TO ALLOCATE AND AGREE
RESPONSIBILITIES WITH TEAM MEMBERS

ASSESSMENT CRITERIA

2.1 Identify team members' responsibilities for identified work activities.

2.2 Agree responsibilities and SMART (specific, measurable, achievable, realistic and time-bound) objectives with team members.

2.1 Identify team members' responsibilities for identified work activities

The range of work activities will depend on the size and function of your organization. They could cover teaching, learner support, giving advice, workplace assessment visits, reviewing and evaluating data, assessing candidates on and off site, attending meetings, marketing and publicity, talking to employers, attending awards ceremonies and carrying out quality-assurance activities. The evidence that you have done this effectively will ultimately be found in the achievement of the objectives you set.

As a team leader, you will no doubt take the 'bones' of your plan and work with your team to get agreement for its finalization and implementation. You will need to plan time to meet with IQA/IV staff to check that the workloads given to them and the assessors are manageable, that they are clear on how to keep records and when and how they will report back to you. It is usual for IQAs/IVs to work with their delegated assessors to ensure that, in turn, the assessors can meet the workload. In any case, as the IQAC, you will be monitoring the workload of assessors. Assessment of particular units may be allocated to specific assessors with vocational expertise in that subject, such as Afro and Asian hair, or brickwork, in which case there will need to be clarity on timings of assessments if a candidate needs to complete the study for a number of related units before the assessment of a specific unit. Some assessors may be allocated to do externally based assessments, or it might be that all assessors assess in a variety of locations.

You may work with a team that has worked together to further identify personal preferences – for example, there may be a team member who enjoys indexing taped assessor discussions, or who is particularly good at running standardization exercises or who is really good at working with candidates with particular learning difficulties.

Where staff are new, or perhaps have been in the organization a long time but are unused to working as part of your team, you may wish to set up peer support, work shadowing or mentoring arrangements using experienced staff.

This book does not cover management concepts and principles in detail. You may find it useful to refer to research on negotiation, working in teams or leading teams. There is a vast literature available on these subjects.

2.2 Agree responsibilities and SMART (specific, measurable, achievable, realistic and time-bound) objectives with team members

Having identified the responsibilities and clarified the priorities and success criteria, you are likely to have a meeting or discussions at which personal and organizational objectives are agreed with the team and individuals. Contingency plans can be drawn up for identified problems and concerns. You will need to have these written down, with each team member having a copy.

Objectives that are set need to be achievable. Through negotiation, you will be able to work with your team and confirm the work plan objectives (see Table 4.3).

TABLE 4.3 Questions you could ask when setting SMART objectives

1. Does the wording of this objective explain clearly what is expected? (*Specific*)
   For example, all workplace assessment visits will be completed and monitored within the next four months.

2. What data will we need to collect to show that we are able to meet the target? (*Measurable*)
   For example, numbers of candidates needing workplace visits, assessor availability, candidate assessment plans agreed, employers in agreement.

3. Do we need to adjust the objective to be sure of meeting our target? (*Achievable*)
   For example, does the timescale need to be put back, should the centre recruit another assessor or IQA/IV, do candidates need more training to ensure they are ready for assessment?

4. Are we aware of internal and external demands of which we need to take account? (*Realistic*)
   For example, have we accounted for the date of the next EV monitoring or Ofsted visit, does staff training need to take place, will snow prevent visits in February?

5. How long have we got to do this? Have we got the resources to meet the requirements? (*Time-bound*)
   For example, when will monitoring be scheduled in to feedback progress, has contingency been built in, have we agreed reporting dates with stakeholders, does everyone have the timetable and information they need to hit targets within the agreed timescale?

LEARNING OUTCOME 3:
BE ABLE TO MONITOR THE PROGRESS AND QUALITY OF WORK IN OWN AREA OF RESPONSIBILITY AND PROVIDE FEEDBACK

ASSESSMENT CRITERIA

3.1 Identify ways to monitor progress and quality of work,

3.2 Monitor and evaluate progress against agreed standards and provide feedback to team members.

3.1 Identify ways to monitor progress and quality of work

This should be formal and regular, for example through appraisals or regular individual or team reviews, but may also occur informally through informal discussions, one-to-one chats and self-assessment activities, the results of which are shared. Your own assessor may wish to observe you actively monitoring team members and giving them feedback.

You are likely to have regular review of IQA/IV and assessor records, including the rate and quality of candidate achievement, by observing assessment practice, arranging and participating in standardization exercises, and by having discussions with staff and candidates. A tracking document is likely to be one of the ways in which you keep a record of your monitoring activities, and you will use the results to refer to your plan and see how the team is progressing with its targets.

Monitoring will definitely include standardization of assessment decisions, observation of assessment practice and examination of assessor records – and needs to be on a regular basis. You need to set aside sufficient time to do this. Your monitoring will be against the priorities and success criteria you have set. It is no good doing this task only when you realize the external quality assessment is due.

3.2 Monitor and evaluate progress against agreed standards and provide feedback to team members

Your feedback will be the proof of the effectiveness of your monitoring and evaluation. When you give oral feedback to your team, ensure this is backed up by written key points that provide the evidence on which you are basing that feedback – this might be your notes taken after examining tracking documents where you are checking IQA comments on how effectively work-based candidates are achieving passes against the criteria agreed in the assessment plan, or your comments against the IQA monitoring of written feedback completed by vocational assessors following the project assessment of a cohort of learners.

This might include reports of standardization exercises. You could present data given to you by IQA/IV staff relating to the numbers of active and completed candidates for whom your team is responsible, and analyse the data, looking for trends such as candidates who are slow to achieve. This may well lead you to take action in the form of arranging development to support certain assessors to be more effective.

Each monitoring activity you do, whether in the workplace observing IQA in action or reviewing IQA documentation, needs to be carried out in pre-agreed ways using the QCF standards as your guide.

Once you have obtained the data at various monitoring points, it needs to be analyzed and compared against expectations of the agreed targets and outcomes. It is then that you can make a judgement as to whether your team as a whole, or some individuals within it, need to change their practice, or whether you need to amend the targets in your work plan. Changes may be based on candidates entering or leaving the qualification, staff changes, or altered internal or external factors from your own organization or awarding organization. Some might be simple, such as having to move the date of a planned standardization because of staff sickness; others may be more complicated, such as having to increase the number of assessments you sample because you can see differences of assessors' interpretation in their assessment of a particular unit, or planning for more sessions on discussing how holistic assessment can be applied to a qualification.

The feedback you give to your team and to stakeholders needs to be constructive and supportive, showing how you have assessed evidence from monitoring against expectations and how issues have been identified, and what plans are in place to overcome them. Any changes that have taken place (eg team and candidate changes, budget constraints, changes in qualification specifications) since the plan was agreed and implemented will need to be addressed in the evaluation, so that it remains up to date.

LEARNING OUTCOME 4:
BE ABLE TO REVIEW AND AMEND PLANS OF WORK FOR OWN AREA OF RESPONSIBILITY AND COMMUNICATE CHANGES

ASSESSMENT CRITERIA

4.1 Review and amend work plan where changes are needed.

4.2 Communicate changes to team members.

4.1 Review and amend work plan where changes are needed

The results of monitoring and feedback and updating records will have given you the data to judge the results of your observations against the individual and team objectives that were agreed. You may well have your own preferred ways of showing where you need to make changes in your plan, and showing when changes have been made, whether this be dated amendments to a handwritten plan, coloured or italicised text inserted into your online plans, differently numbered and dated versions of your plan, post-it notes (problematic if they drop off, though) or some other technique.

A team meeting will give the opportunity to renegotiate the plan, getting agreement for its implementation but also providing an opportunity for sharing good practice, identifying key areas of concern and reviewing roles and responsibilities. If the changes identified need to be made during the timescale of the original plan you made, then it's a question of integrating any new objectives or actions and continuing with your internal monitoring. If you have come to the end of a particular planning cycle, particularly if part of the review data is overall results achieved by candidates, then you and your team are in an excellent position to review the suggested changes together, and launch merrily into your next agreed work plan together.

4.2 Communicate changes to team members

Having surveyed the data, both qualitative and quantitative, that is available to you, and drawn your conclusions as to changes that need to be made (preferably in written and/or numerical/graphical format), negotiated with staff, you will produce a revised work plan. It is often helpful to present this information alongside a succinct, detailed written report, attaching any appropriate data or source material in the form of appendices. This can then form part of the evidence that might be required by external quality assurance, or by other managers in your centre.

The members of your team with whom you communicate will be those identified on your work plan. They will normally be the assessors and IV/IQA staff for whom you have responsibility, and possibly other managers or awarding organization staff such as EQAs/EVs. Every organization has its own methods of communication, with more and more information being passed electronically.

As the IQAC you will monitor how information is getting to all members of you team, and whether there are any weak links in the chain. It is easy to see who have not cleared their pigeonholes – not as easy to know who have not opened e-mails, read attachments or omitted to read the latest newsletter from the awarding organization. Meetings on a team or individual basis are probably the only really certain way of checking that individuals have read, and more importantly, understood the information they are being asked to consider and the responsibilities they have agreed to undertake.

Hopefully, you can now look forward to the time when you are able to communicate the news of successful internal and external quality-assurance monitoring.

A FINAL WORD

Productive and enjoyable work is an important part of people's lives. In this time of austerity, both younger and mature people still have the opportunity to be fully and continuously employed. Developing the knowledge and skills that will help them to be successful applicants for jobs and good employees is a vital component of the UK education and training system.

Well developed, rigorous and supportive assessment, carried out by highly trained and knowledgeable assessors can not only help to ensure good working practices, but also help to train and motivate those starting out on their working lives.

This is why we began writing this book many years ago. We continue to believe that it and subsequent editions have a purpose for those involved in vocational assessment and quality assurance of assessment. We hope our readers have found them a useful resource in their important work in helping to develop the workforce of today and tomorrow.

APPENDIX 1
Major changes affecting vocational education and its assessment over the last 30 years

1981 'New Training Initiative', Manpower Services Commission (MSC) identifies need to increase skills of workforce to cope with new patterns of working, developments in new technology and increased competition from overseas. First mention of need for 'Standards of a new kind'.

1986 'Review of Vocational Qualifications: A report by the working group', MSC and Department of Education and Science (DES) concludes that there is a low take-up of vocational qualifications. Perceived by employers as relying too much on theory as opposed to practice. Confusion and overlap on the provision available, with difficulties in access, progression and transfer of credits. Problems with methods of assessment and little recognition of learning outside formal programmes.

1986 Government White Paper 'Working Together: Education and Training', DES. Proposes the development of new qualifications based on national standards defined by industry and operating within a coherent qualifications structure.

1986 National Council for Vocational Qualifications (NCVQ) established to carry out proposals from the White Paper, including the accreditation of standards, development of a new qualifications framework, development of NVQs, liaison with awarding bodies and monitoring of quality-assurance procedures. NCVQ set up as an independent body, with initial government funding covering England, Wales and Northern Ireland. It has no legal powers but must promote the new vocational initiative through cooperation with relevant bodies. The Scottish Council for Vocational Education Training (SCOTVEC) has the same remit in Scotland.

1986   New Occupational Standards Branch created at MSC. Given responsibility for setting up industry lead bodies to develop occupational standards. Where possible, the lead bodies build on existing organizations – for example industrial training boards such as the Construction Industry Training Board (CITB).

1988   Government White Paper 'Employment for the 1990s' (DES) reaffirmed the need for standards and qualifications based on competence and recognized by employers. Proposes establishment of local Training and Enterprise Councils (TECs) to be responsible at local level for the planning and delivery of vocational training and enterprise programmes.

1990   Training Agency (formerly MSC) becomes absorbed in the Training, Enterprise and Education Directorate (TEED) at the Department of Employment.

1991   Government White Paper 'Education and Training for the 21st Century' (DES) proposes that General National Vocational Qualifications (GNVQs) designed to provide broad-based vocational preparation should be introduced into the national qualification framework (NQF).

1992   National targets for education and training announced. These set targets for young people, adults and employers. National standards for training and development issues by Training and Development Lead Body (TDLB).

1994   Government White Paper 'Competitiveness: Helping businesses to win', Department of Trade and Industry (DTI). £300 million to be spent on strengthening education and training. Review of NVQs announced to ensure they 'stayed up to date and continued to observe strict standards'. Five hundred NVQs covering 150 occupations representing 80 per cent of all jobs now approved.

1994   Revised national standards for training and development issued by Training and Development Lead Body (TDLB).

1995   (July) Department for Education and Employment (DfEE) created from merger of Department for Education and the Department of Employment.

1996   (January) A report on a review of 100 NVQs and SVQs (Chair: Gordon Beaumont) supported NVQ/SVQ concept. Indicated widespread concern over rigour and consistency of assessment and complexity of language of standards. Eighty per cent of employers considered competence-based standards were right for vocational qualifications.

1996 (March) Review of qualifications for 16 to 19-Year-Olds report (Chair: Sir Ron Dearing) makes a large number of recommendations for improving current provision. Endorsed Beaumont review. Changes the term 'Core skills' to 'Key skills' and suggests Key Skills requirements should be considered when designing NVQs. Recommended the merger of NCVQ and Schools Curriculum and Assessment Authority (SCAA) to support a cohesive academic/vocational qualifications framework.

1996 Education Act. Department for Education and Employment (DfEE) created.

1996 Government White Paper 'Competitiveness: Creating the enterprise centre of Europe' (DTI) emphasizes need for providers of training and qualifications to undergo rigorous quality-assurance procedures.

1997 Qualifications and Curriculum Authority (QCA) set up, whose aim is to set up a coherent and comprehensive system of vocational qualifications.

1997 Employment National Training Organisation (ENTO) formed from a merger of the Employment Occupational Standards Council (EOSC) and Occupational Health and Safety (OHS) Lead Body. The first NTO to represent different groups found throughout all sectors of industry. Publication of 'External Verification of NVQs' by QCA.

1998 (March) QCA publishes 'Internal Verification of NVQs', 'Assessing NVQs' and 'Revised Common Accord'. Responsibility for National Occupational Standards devolved to regulatory bodies.

1999 QCA publishes 'Developing Assessment Strategies for NVQs'.

1999 Further Education National Training Organization (FENTO) 'Standards for Teaching and Supporting Learning in the FE sector' published.

2000 'Learning and Skills Act', Department for Education and Employment (DFEE) establishes Learning and Skills Council (LSC) and establishes arrangements for inspection of FE.

2000 QCA publishes 'The NVQ Code of Practice'. Clearly sets out ways in which organizations should be accredited to run and assess NVQs. It includes a tariff of sanctions to be applied by external verifiers where centres are not in compliance with the code.

2001 'Special Educational Needs and Disability Act', Department for Education and Skills (DfES); Aim is to improve access to education and training.

2001 Learning and Skills Council (LSC) publishes the national 'Equality and Diversity Strategy'. Addresses widening participation and promotes inclusion.

2001 By this date, 3.2 million NVQ certificates issued, 60 per cent at Level 2, and 19 per cent at Level 3. 762 NVQ titles, down from a maximum point of 976.

2002 Sector Skills Development Agency (SSDA) set up by government to fund and support the new Sector Skills Councils. Joint remit for vocational qualification system given to QCA, LSC and SSDA.

2002 Joint Awarding Body (JAB) 'Guidance on Internal Verification of NVQs'. Document backed by awarding bodies, which states how internal verification will be approached by them all.

2002 ENTO publishes the Learning and Development standards to replace the TDLB standards Review of National Qualifications Framework.

2002 (November) DfES strategy document 'Success for All: Transforming post-16 learning and skills in England'.

2003 EmpNTO rebadges as ENTO. White paper '21st Century Skills – Realising our potential: individuals, employers, nation', DfES. Sets out a national skills strategy.

2004 DfES Standards Unit produce 'Equipping our Teachers for the Future'. Reforms initial teacher training for the learning and skills sector.

2004 (October) The DfES-commissioned working group report on 14–19 reform, the Tomlinson Report.

2005 Lifelong Learning UK (LLUK) takes over the role of former NTOs related to education and training, including FENTO.

2005 'Disability Discrimination Act' DfES. Puts a positive duty on the public sector to address disability and equality.

2005 (February) White paper '14–19 Skills', DfES.

2005 (November) Foster review of further education, 'Professionalising the Workforce'.

2006 NVQ Code of Practice revised and replaces 2001 version.

2006 (March) White paper 'Further Education: Raising skills, improving life chances' (DfES). Skills task force set up. Commitment to produce well-qualified professional teachers for FE and the LLS as a whole. 'Train to Gain' set up to encourage employers to develop the qualifications and skills of their workforce.

2006 (December) Leitch review, 'Prosperity for All in the Global Economy: World class skills', sets ambitious targets for 2020; identifies vocational skills gap.

2007   (February) Secretary of State for Education announces school-leaving age will be raised to 18 years by 2013 in England; training for apprenticeships and work-based training will be included.

2007   'FE and Training' Act.

2007   All GNVQs now withdrawn.

2007   LLUK new 'Professional Standards for Teachers, Tutors and Trainers in the Lifelong Learning Sector' are approved. Standards Verification UK (SVUK) responsible for endorsement.

2007   Change of Prime Minister from Tony Blair to Gordon Brown. DfES replaced by Department for Children, Schools and Families (DCSF) and the Department for Innovation, Universities and Skills (DIUS).

2007   (December) Children's Plan 'Building Brighter Futures' (DCSF); among many other laudable aims, by 2010 employers should be satisfied with young people's readiness for work, as child poverty, illiteracy and anti-social behaviour would be reduced.

2008   (February) 'Education for All'(14–19) (DCSF).

2008   (May) The Office of the Qualifications and 14–19 Examinations regulator (Ofqual) is set up to regulate (amongst others) NVQs and vocational qualifications, and to regulate awarding bodies and the organizations that deliver their qualifications. Work starts on matching qualifications to the Qualification and Credit Framework. The Quality Assurance Agency (QAA) regulates university degrees.

2008   (August) Beginning of global recession, 'efficiency' savings throughout government until present (2011) and beyond.

2008   (November) 'Education and Skills Act', jointly sponsored by DIUS and DCSF; young people required to participate in education or training until their 18th birthday; introduction of (initially 5) Diplomas with the intention of closing the vocational/academic divide and eventually replacing A levels and GCSEs; there is a significant centralizing process against a growing desire for local autonomy.

2009   'Apprenticeships, Skills, Children and Learning Act'; Skills Funding Agency (SFA) created.

2009   (June) DIUS abolished, with responsibilities subsumed into new Department of Business Innovation and Skills (BIS).

2009   QCA is abolished and its functions subsumed by the new Qualifications and Curriculum Development Agency (QCDA).

2009   (November) 'A New Framework for Higher Education'. Universities to cater more for student needs, publication of more information about success/drop-out rates, closer links with industry in course design and funding, continued attempts to widen participation in HE. Signalled major review of funding for Higher Education (HE).

2010   'Children, Schools and Families Act', DCSF.

2010   (March) Revised National Occupational Standards for Learning and Development are developed by LLUK sector skills council. The revised qualifications for assessment and quality assurance (AQA) are part of this development.

2010   (May) a Conservative and Liberal-Democrat coalition government takes over from Labour; DCSF becomes Department for Education (DfE), and there are drastic budget cuts to schools; programme of reform of quangos and qualifications quickens pace. QCA abolished and remit taken over by QCDA and Ofqual.

2010   (June) Academic Diplomas introduced in 2008 are abandoned to save estimated £22.2m; support is reduced for existing vocational diplomas.

2010   (October) Browne Review looks into future of funding for HE. Proposal to remove the cap on HE tuition fees.

2010   (November) 'Skills for Sustainable Growth; (BIS) places apprenticeships at the heart of developing work-related skills and knowledge.

2010   (December) LLUK unsuccessful in retaining licence to operate as a sector skills council.

2011   (March) The Wolf Report – 'Review of Vocational Education for 14–19' – suggests 'ways of improving vocational education for 14–19 and promoting successful progression into the labour market and into higher level education and training routes'.

2011   (April) transfer of LLUK footprint responsibilities to Learning and Skills Improvement Service (LSIS)

2011   (July) Ofqual sets up Innovation Advisory Group, to initially look at drivers and (regulatory) barriers to innovation in qualifications.

2012   Universities will charge up to £9,000 a year for HE tuition fees.

APPENDIX 2
Relevant legislation

Health and safety legislation

Health and Safety at Work Act, 1974.

Food and Environment Protection Act (FEPA), 1985.

Reporting of Injuries, Diseases and Dangerous Occurances (RIDDOR), 1995.

Provision and Use of Work Equipment Regulations (PUWER), 1998.

Control of Substances Hazardous to Health (COSHH), 2002.

Equality and diversity legislation

The Equality Act 2010

The Equality Act brings together, and strengthens, a number of previous existing pieces of legislation, including race and disability. One of the key changes is that it extends the protected characteristics to encompass:

- age;
- disability;
- gender reassignment;
- marriage and civil partnership;
- pregnancy and maternity;
- race;
- religion or belief;
- sex;
- sexual orientation.

The act also makes explicit the concept of 'dual discrimination', where someone may be discriminated against or treated unfairly on the basis of a combination of two or the protected characteristics.

Public Sector Equality Duty (PSED) 2011

General duty on public bodies and those discharging public functions to eliminate discrimination, harassment and victimization, advance equality of opportunity and foster good relations. Specific duty to publish data, assess impact, set equality objectives, annual reporting of progress.

Safeguarding children, young people and vulnerable adults

The area of safeguarding has assumed increasing importance in regulations and procedures related to vocational education and training, with Criminal Records Bureau (CRB) checks mandatory for those wishing to gain employment in this area.

Children's Act (2004)

Statutory duty of key people and bodies to safeguard and promote welfare of children.

Education Act (2002)

Schools and FE colleges have same statutory duty.

For guidance on how safeguarding issues impact on education and training organizations see, for example, the government produced *Guidance Handbook for FE colleges, Adult and Community Learning, Work-based Training Providers* (Nightingale, 2007). The main focus is for organizations to:

- create a safe learning environment to promote well-being and security;
- minimize abuse and raise awareness of abuse.

The Data Protection Act (1998)

This has eight guiding principles:
  Personal data:

1 Shall be processed fairly and lawfully.
2 Shall be obtained only for one or more specified and lawful purposes, and shall not be further processed in any manner incompatible with that purpose or those purposes.

3 Shall be adequate, relevant and not excessive in relation to the purpose or purposes for which they are processed.

4 Shall be accurate and, where necessary, kept up to date.

5 Processed for any purpose or purposes shall not be kept for longer than is necessary for that purpose or those purposes.

6 Shall be processed in accordance with the rights of data subjects under this Act.

7 Appropriate technical and organizational measures shall be taken against unauthorized or unlawful processing of personal data and against accidental loss or destruction of, or damage to, personal data.

8 Shall not be transferred to a country or territory outside the European Economic Area unless that country or territory ensures an adequate level of protection for the rights and freedoms of data subjects in relation to the processing of personal data.

APPENDIX 3
Official bodies concerned with quality assurance

Official bodies	Responsibility
Office of Qualifications and Assessment Regulations (Ofqual)	• Regulating general and vocational qualifications, examinations and assessments in England, and vocational qualifications in Northern Ireland. • Giving formal recognition to bodies that deliver qualifications and assessments. • Accrediting awards and monitoring activities of awarding organizations.
Quality Assurance Agency for Higher Education (QAA)	• Guiding and monitoring the quality of teaching, learning and assessment in UK universities and colleges offering higher education courses.
Sector Skills Councils (SSCs)	• Building a skills system led by employer demand. • Developing and maintaining national occupational standards used as basis for QCF vocational qualifications.
Institute for Learning (IFL) Professional body for teachers, tutors, trainers and student teachers in the further education (FE) and skills sector	• Registering teachers and trainers in FE and skills sector. • Keeping an overview of continuing professional development. • Conferring the professional status of qualified teacher learning and skills (QTLS) through the professional formation process.
Awarding organizations	Each awarding organization is responsible for: • maintaining the standard and integrity of its qualifications; • development and implementation of specifications for qualifications; • quality assurance of assessment – verification/moderation procedures; • conduct of examinations and external tests; • procedures for recording and tracking decisions; • processing and publishing results; • providing support and training to staff working on its qualifications.

ABBREVIATIONS FOR DEPARTMENTS AND ORGANIZATIONS

See Appendix 1 for abbreviations in use prior to 2007.

AQA	Assessment and Qualifications Alliance
ASSC	Alliance of Sector Skills Councils
BIS	Department for Business, Education and Skills
BTEC	Business and Technology Education Council
CBI	Confederation of British Industry
C&G	City and Guilds
DCSF	Department for Children, Schools and Families
DfE	Department for Education
DIUS	Department for Industry, University and Skills
DWP	Department of Work and Pensions
FAB	Federation of Awarding Bodies
FE	Further Education
FES	Further Education and Skills Sector
Habia	Hair and Beauty Sector Skills Body
HE	Higher Education
HEA	Higher Education Academy
IFL	Institute for Learning
JAB	Joint Awarding Body
LLS	Lifelong-learning sector
LSS	Learning and Skills Sector
LSIS	Learning and Skills Improvement Service
NTO	National Training Organization

OCR	Oxford, Cambridge and RSA Examinations
Ofqual	Office of Qualifications and Examination Regulation
Ofsted	Office for Standards in Education, Children's Services and Skills
QAA	Quality Assurance Agency
QCDA	Qualifications and Curriculum Development Agency
SASE	Specification of Apprenticeship Standards for England
SFA	Skills Funding Agency
SQA	Scottish Qualifications Authority
SSC	Sector Skills Council
SVUK	Standards Verification United Kingdom
UKCES UK	Commission for Employment and skills
YPLA	Young People's Learming Agency

Terms and abbreviations connected with Assessment and Quality Assurance qualifications

AQA	Assessment and quality assurance
Award	A QCF qualification of between 1 and 12 credits (10–120 hours)
Certificate	A QCF qualification of between 13 and 36 credits (130–360 hours)
CPD	Continuing professional development
credit	The value of around 10 hours of learning
CTLLS	Certificate in Teaching in the Lifelong-learning Sector
DTLLS	Diploma in Teaching in the Lifelong-learning Sector
Diploma	A QCF qualification of 37 credits or more (370 hours +)
EV	External verifier
ICT	Information and communications technology
ILPs	Individual learning plans

IQA	Internal quality assurer (previously internal verifier)
IV	Internal verifier
IVC	Internal verifier coordinator
L1, L2	Level 1 to Level 8 in the QCF; The level equates to the difficulty of a course or qualification; some level equivalencies are L2 = GCSE, L3 = A level, L4 = Higher Apprenticeship/Foundation degree; L8 = PhD
NEETS	(Those) not in education, employment or training
NOS	National occupational standards
NVQ	National Vocational Qualification
PTLLS	Preparing to teach in the Lifelong-learning Sector
QCF	Qualifications and Curriculum Framework
RPL	Recognition of prior learning
VQ	vocational qualification (work-related)

SUPPORTING MATERIALS

Anderson, LW and Krathwohl, DR (eds) (2001) *A Taxonomy for Learning, Teaching, and Assessing: A revision of Bloom's taxonomy of educational objectives*, Longman, New York

Bloom, BS (ed) (1956) *Taxonomy of Educational Objectives, the Classification of Educational Goals – Handbook I: Cognitive domain*, McKay, New York

Brookfield, S (1995) *Becoming a Critically Reflective Teacher*, Jossey-Bass, San Francisco

Dearing, R (1995) *Review of Qualifications for 16–19 Year Olds*, SCAA, London

Department of Business, Innovation and Skills (2010) *Skills for Sustainable Growth; Strategy document*, Department of Business, Innovation and Skills, URN 10/1274, Full Report 2010

Roth RA (1989) Preparing the reflective practitioner: transforming the apprentice through the dialectic, *Journal of Teacher Education*, 40 (2), pp 31–35

Reports

Leitch Report (2006) 'Prosperity for All in the Global Economy: World class skills', online: **http://webarchive.nationalarchives.gov.uk/+/http://www.hm-treasury.gov.uk/d/leitch_finalreport051206.pdf**

Tomlinson Report (2004) *14–19 Curriculum and Qualifications Reform: Summary of final report*, online: **https://www.education.gov.uk/publications/standard/publicationDetail/Page1/DfE-0976–2004**

UK Commission for Employment and Skills (2008) *Skills for the Workplace: Employer perspectives: evidence report*, online: **http://www.ukces.org.uk/publications/er1–skills-for-workplace-employer-perspectives**

Wolf Report (2011) *Review of Vocational Education*, online: **https://www.education.gov.uk/publications/standard/publicationDetail/Page1/DFE-00031–2011**

Goskills (2010/11) *Sector Skills Assessments in England: Summary reports*, online: **http://www.goskills.org/index.php/research_publications/36**

Useful websites (England)

All public services in one place: **www.direct.gov.uk/en/ EducationAndLearning/QualificationsExplained**

Alliance of Sector Skills Councils: **http://www.sscalliance.org/**

Assessment and Qualifications Alliance: **www.aqa.org.uk**

Apprenticeships: **http://www.apprenticeships.org.uk/**

City and Guilds: **www.city-and-guilds.co.uk**

Department for Education **www.education.gov.uk**

Department for Work and Pensions: **www.dwp.gov.uk**

Edexcel: **www.edexcel.org.uk/qualifications**

EDI plc: **www.ediplc.com**

Excellence gateway: **http://ww.excellencegateway.org.uk**

Federation of Awarding Bodies: **www.awarding.org.uk**

Higher Education Academy:

Institute for Learning: **www.ifl.ac.uk**

Learning and Skills Improvement Service (LSIS): **www.lsis.org.uk**

Ofqual: **www.ofqual.gov.uk**

Ofsted: **www.ofsted.gov.uk/**

Open university: **www8.open.ac.uk** › Vocational qualifications

QCF: **http://www.ofqual.gov.uk/qualifications-assessments/89–articles/ 145–explaining-the-qualifications-and-credit-framework**

Skills Funding Agency: **www.skillsfundingagency.bis.gov.uk**

UK Commission for Employment and Skills: **http://www.ukces.org.uk/**

Young People's Learning Agency: **http://www.ypla.gov.uk**

Websites (Wales, Scotland, Northern Ireland)

CCEA (Northern Ireland): **http://www.rewardinglearning.org.uk/**

DELLS (Wales): **http://wales.gov.uk/topics/educationandskills/?lang=en**

SQA (Scotland): **http://www.sqa.org.uk/sqa/CCC_FirstPage.jsp**

Useful websites for supporting information

Bloom's learning taxonomy: **http://www.learningandteaching.info/learning/ bloomtax.htm**

Changes to NVQs and training structures

http://www.businessballs.com/nvqs_national_vocational_qualifications.htm

Models of reflection: http://www.brainboxx.co.uk/a3_aspects/pages/ReflectionModels.htm

Equality and diversity: http://www.sfbn-equality-diversity.org.uk/

INDEX

NB: page numbers in *italic* indicate figures or tables